My Work with Borderline Patients

My Work with Borderline Patients

Harold F. Searles, M.D.

Jason Aronson Inc.
Northvale, New Jersey
London

THE MASTER WORK SERIES

First softcover edition 1994

Copyright © 1986 by Harold F. Searles

All rights reserved. Printed in the United States of America. No part of this book may be used or reproduced in any manner whatsoever without written permission from Jason Aronson Inc. except in the case of brief quotations in reviews for inclusion in a magazine, newspaper, or broadcast.

Library of Congress Cataloging-in-Publication Data

Searles, Harold F. (Harold Frederic), 1918–
  My work with borderline patients.

  Includes bibliographies and index.
  1. Borderline personality disorders — Treatment.
2. Psychoanalysis. 3. Psychotherapist and patient.
I. Title. [DNLM: 1. Countertransference (Psychology)
2. Personality Disorders. 3. Psychoanalytic Therapy.
4. Transference (Psychology) WM 460.6 S439m]
RC569.5.B67S43 1986   616.89   86-20639
ISBN 0-87668-930-6 (hardcover)
ISBN 1-56821-401-4 (softcover)

Manufactured in the United States of America. Jason Aronson Inc. offers books and cassettes. For information and catalog write to Jason Aronson Inc., 230 Livingston Street, Northvale, New Jersey 07647.

To Sylvia

Contents

Preface

Psychoanalytic therapy with borderline patients has been of great interest to me for many years. The earliest clinical incident described in this book occurred in 1947, about two years before I began my nearly 15 years of work at Chestnut Lodge. Although most of my work there was with various of the chronically schizophrenic patients who composed, then, the bulk of the patient population, some of my patients were borderline; and over the years I heard many staff presentations of the latter kind of patients and participated in innumerable discussions, formal and informal, with colleagues who were treating such individuals in their Lodge caseloads.

Moreover, my private practice, begun prior to my going to Chestnut Lodge, continued throughout my "full-time" work on the Lodge staff (as was freely done by my colleagues there, with our employer's knowledge and consent). A quite appreciable number of my private patients, ever since I began in private practice in 1948 (the year before I went to the Lodge), have been borderline persons.

I have analyzed, for varying lengths of time, some thirty psychiatrists and a considerable number of psychologists, psychiatric social workers, and fellow-professionals in various related disciplines. Although I have not felt free to use clinical vignettes from my work with these colleagues, I have found that there is no lack of borderline psychopathology among these highly qualified and effective persons. Another way of putting it is that I know that I am far from alone, among mental health professionals, in carrying around my own share of proclivity for the use of borderline defenses.

In short, I became convinced, long ago, that borderline phenomena will be encountered in any deep-reaching course of psychoanalysis or intensive psychoanalytic therapy, for these phenomena are part of the general human condition.

Over more than thirty years, I have presented papers and done teaching-interviews with patients at dozens of teaching institutions and professional meetings. Until I left Chestnut Lodge early in 1964, these involved, more often than not, my work with schizophrenic individuals, and it was not uncommon for me to sense, on the part of the audience, a kind of awe in listening to me present a paper concerning my work with chronically schizophrenic patients, much as though the listeners were hearing a report from an explorer returned from Mars. But when I left the Lodge and entered full-time private practice, I began to write, more and more, of work with borderline individuals and to interview such persons in my teaching-interviews. Now, it felt to me, there was relatively little awe on the part of the audience, for—as became evident in my discussions with them—they themselves were working every day with such patients and, I sensed, were no strangers to such processes within themselves.

This book contains by no means all of my writing relevant to this topic. I have limited myself to including here only two papers that have appeared in an earlier book of mine (*Countertransference and Related Subjects*). A third, highly relevant paper is "Transitional Phenomena and Therapeutic Symbiosis," which appeared in that same book. I myself regard my experience with chronically schizophrenic patients, and my writings concerning that experience, to be closely relevant to the topic of this volume.

Acknowledgments

I am grateful to Dr. Jason Aronson for his having taken the initiative which led to this book's publication, and for his sustained interest in this project; to Joan Langs, Editorial Director of Jason Aronson Inc., for her consistently gracious and helpful, as well as creative, work with me over the three years of our collaborations; to Production Editors Carolyn D. Emmett and Lori Williams for their skillful and kindly collaboration with me; to Barbara Sonnenschein, Director of Editorial Production, for her superbly experienced care of the manuscript during the final editing, production, and design of the book; to Norman A. Senior, my attorney, for the drawing up of the book contract; and to Josephine W.

Parker, C.P.S., for her expert typing, originally, of most of these papers.

My debt of gratitude to the many patients I have treated, during the past nearly forty years, is evident on most of the pages of this book.

HAROLD F. SEARLES, M.D.

My Work with Borderline Patients

Part I

Basic
Principles

Chapter 1

Techniques
of Therapy

The Analyst's Interpretations Are Less Important
than Is His Non-Verbal Participation

Early in the development of psychoanalytic theory and technique, traumatic events in the patient's early years were regarded as having a central role in the etiology of emotional illness. In recent decades, as we have learned more about the psychodynamics of family life, non-verbal communication, and the causation and treatment of psychotic and borderline states which have their origin largely in the pre-

This chapter was originally published in 1978 as a paper: Psychoanalytic therapy with the borderline adult: Some principles concerning technique," in *New Perspectives on Psychotherapy of the Borderline Adult*, pp. 41–65, edited by J. F. Masterson; New York: Brunner/Mazel.

verbal, or very early verbal, eras of infancy and childhood, we attach generally less significance to isolated traumatic events in the patient's developmental years, than to ongoing attitudes on the parts of various childhood-family-members toward the patient (and on his part toward them), and upon the prevailing emotional atmosphere, day after day, which pervaded the early home.

In pace with this shift in focus, so it seems to me, the emphasis in our psychoanalytic technique has shifted such that interpretations are now accorded about the same order of importance, in the armamentarium which we employ during the over-all course of a psychoanalytic treatment, as traumatic events are now allotted in our understanding of the causation of the patient's illness. Interpretations are important, to be sure; but of far greater importance is the emotional atmosphere or climate of the sessions, day after day and year after year.

As regards the treatment of the borderline patient, any discussion of interpretations has to be linked with the patient's predominant level of ego-functioning, which in turn is largely a factor of the evolution and eventual resolution of the patient's transference-borderline-psychosis. Since appreciable regression can, and at times necessarily does, occur on the part of analyst as well as patient, the analyst's varying levels of ego-functioning are also a highly significant variable.

My discussion here is integrally related with that which I presented in three papers (Searles 1970, 1971, 1973) concerning autism, symbiosis, and individuation. Those three modes of ego-functioning I described as being of importance not only in patients suffering from schizophrenia of whatever degree of severity, but also in predominantly neurotic individuals in whom subtly-present areas of autism come to light in their analyses.

In work with the borderline patient, the analyst finds that his countertransference-burden consists, perhaps for year after year, largely in his unfreedom to make effective transference-interpretations, in marked contrast to a later, ambivalently-symbiotic, phase in the patient-analyst relationship, during which he can make such interpretations with a far higher degree of freedom and effectiveness.

In the second (i.e., second-written, although first published in 1970) of those three papers, entitled "Autism and the Phase of Transition to Therapeutic Symbiosis," I described as characteristic of that phase of transition that the analyst now begins to find it feasible effectively to make transference-interpretations. This transition phase likewise stands in contrast, as regards the timeliness of transference-interpretations, to the subsequent phase of therapeutic symbiosis, in which such interpretations are almost limitlessly in order.

This chapter is confined largely to a discussion of the problems presented by the borderline patient whose ego-functioning is predominantly autistic in nature. I hope to focus in a future paper upon that variety of borderline patients whose ego-functioning is more mature than this—is predominantly ambivalently-symbiotic in nature. But a portion of my remarks here will pertain clearly to those latter patients.

The State of the Patient's Ego-Integration and Ego-Differentiation

The state of his ego-integration and -differentiation is incomplete in characteristic ways which impair greatly his ability to utilize verbal interpretations. He is unable to differentiate, at an unconscious level, between fantasy and reality, or between verbalization and physical activity (with the result that verbal aggression, from the analyst, may have fully the impact of physical aggression). He has not yet established a durable internalized image of himself, or of his analyst, or both. He cannot function reliably in terms of both his own and the analyst's having—each of them—his own individuality and subjective reality, and with a sense of relatedness between these two persons and their respective realities. Instead, for him, either his is the only reality there is, or the analyst's reality is the only one.

The Analyst Feels Drawn to Impose His Own Reality upon the Patient

One of the major technical difficulties in working with him has to do with his flawed sense of reality—not only outer but also inner reality, including that of his own identity—and his consequent need for the analyst to help him to resolve this flaw in his experience of reality. A major aspect of this difficulty, for the analyst, is his finding himself under great pressure to impose his own reality upon the patient, rather than struggling through, mutually with him, to help him to achieve a sense of reality valid for the individual patient himself. Helene Deutsch (1942), in her classic paper concerning the "as-if" type of emotionality and spurious reality-relatedness so prevalent among borderline patients, helped to alert us to the danger that such a patient will emerge from analysis with only his usual shallowly-adaptive sense of reality, patterned now upon the personality-functioning of the analyst, just as it had been patterned upon that of a series of parent-figures prior to the analysis.

The studies concerning infantile psychosis by Mahler (1968) and her co-workers are of central importance here.

She reported that

> It is the specific unconscious need of the mother that activates, out of the infant's infinite potentialities, those in particular that create for each mother "the child" who reflects her own *unique* and individual needs. . . .
>
> Mutual cuing during the symbiotic phase creates that indelibly imprinted configuration—that complex pattern—that becomes *the leitmotif for "the infant's becoming the child of his particular mother"* (Lichtenstein 1961, p. 207).
>
> *What we seem to see here is the birth of the child as an individual (cf. Lichtenstein 1964)* (pp. 18–19).

Lichtenstein (1961) states that

> While the mother satisfies the infant's needs, in fact creates certain specific needs, which she delights in satisfying, the infant is transformed into an organ or an instrument for the satisfaction of the mother's unconscious needs. . . . *Out of the infinite potentialities within the human infant, the specific stimulus combination emanating from the individual mother "releases" one, and only one, concrete way of being this organ, this instrument.* This "released" identity will be irreversible, and thus it will compel the child to find ways and means to realize this specific identity which the mother has imprinted upon it (pp. 207–208).

A number of authors have described their finding that the early, poorly-integrated life-experiences on the part of borderline and schizoid (as well as schizophrenic) individuals can become integrated in awareness, and thus contribute to a firmer sense of reality and of personal identity, through the medium of the unfolding transference and the interpretation of that transference. Khan's (1974) writings portray, in a particularly beautiful way, the process wherein those previously-unintegrated, dissociated affective experiences from the patient's early childhood are first experienced by the analyst, in the course of the psychoanalytic therapy.

The repetition compulsion is, in my view, an unconscious attempt not merely to "relive" an earlier experience, but to *live* it for the *first* time—to live it, that is, with full emotional participation.

The potential power which such a patient's transference gives to the analyst, power which when wrongly used can impose still another pseudo-reality and pseudo-identity upon the patient, is clearly enormous. In a paper entitled, "The Function of the Patient's Realistic Perceptions of the Analyst in Delusional Transference," I (Searles 1972) reported a relevant finding from my work, then more than 18 years in duration, with a chronically schizophrenic woman who long had manifested an appallingly severe ego-fragmentation and identity-confusion. That is, I reported my gradually discovering to what a significant degree her delusional-transference experiences were reactions to (and often identifications with) various attributes, heretofore largely unconscious to me, of my own personality-functioning during our sessions.

I cannot believe that any analyst can help a patient to make contact with, and to integrate, the latter's heretofore-dissociated early-life experiences without some contamination by the analyst's own dissociated early-life experiences, which the analyst succeeds (so to speak) in projecting upon, and leaving projected upon, the patient's childhood-self. But surely we should strive to keep such contaminants to a minimum.

Unconscious Denial as an Expression of the Striving for Autonomy

Concerning more localized, but still massive, instances of the unconscious defense-mechanism of denial, for something like two decades now I have felt convinced that this defense is so formidable for the reason that it is maintained with the power that is, in essence, the individual's striving for autonomy. Spitz' (1957) volume, *No and Yes—On the Genesis of Human Communication,* provided substantiation for this impression that I had gained from work with adult patients. Spitz reported, for example, from his observations of the nursing infant, that "The refusal [to nurse] through head-rotating avoidance emerges at the stage at which the earliest ego organization has just come into being. This form of volitional refusal behavior in the feeding situation continues during the progressive unfolding of the ego in the months which follow" (p. 94).

The practical relevancy of this, in my work with borderline patients whose defenses include massive denial, is that when I encounter a particularly striking instance of the patient's omission of any mention of a highly significant recent event, or of what I know to be a centrally important aspect of his current life situation, I am cautious about pointing out to him this striking omission. The reason is that he is so quick to foster his intendedly free-associational role's becoming, instead, the familiar one of his being the object of intended brain-programming by the analyst. That is, it often feels impossible for me to point out to him that he has said nothing about such-and-such a subject, without my conveying at the same time the implication that he has not been free-associating "correctly"—that he should have been reporting thoughts and feelings about that particular subject instead.

This state of patient-analyst interaction should, theoretically, be susceptible of interpretation to the patient—including interpretation of his largely unconscious wishes to be brainwashed rather than to become a full-fledged partner with the analyst in their mutual endeavor, an endeavor which involves both their brains and their two individual selves. Equally important would be any interpretations of the patient's projection upon the analyst, here, of the patient's own unconscious aim of brain-washing the analyst in a single-mindedly authoritarian fashion. Stierlin's (1959) paper, "The Adaptation to the 'Stronger' Person's Reality— Some Aspects of the Symbiotic Relationship of the Schizophrenic," is relevant to this subject.

But in actual practice, I rarely, if ever, find that these so-resistant patients are accessible to such interpretations. As a result, I come more and more, as the years go on, to leave it to them largely to arrive at their own interpreting of their conflicts and their characterologic defenses against those conflicts. I have come to count it a rare instance of job-satisfaction when I find a patient coming bit by bit to discover, on his own and largely unhindered by me, some important aspect of his ego-functioning which has been obvious to me, and has seemed to me tantalizingly close to being interpretable by me, for many months and, in many instances, for several years.

Parenthetically but in a similar vein, I have come a long way from my beginning-analyst's burdened sense of conviction that if a patient has succeeded in remembering a detailed dream, and beyond that in reporting relatively voluminous associations to the dream, it is unthinkable for me to fail to offer an interpretation. A very considerable share of my time, since those early days in my analytic career, has been spent in working with borderline patients whose voluminous dream-reports, and free-associational reporting, clearly have been in the service of their unconsciously giving

me to feel the sense of uselessness, uncreativeness, and deadness which has been one of their own most centrally-impor-
tant dissociated ego-aspects. I came long ago to believe,
moreover, that this more fundamental state of things in the
transference will not be interpretable, as such, for probably
many months or even some years, and I have learned that
the sooner I can come to accept this degree of resistance on
the patient's part, rather than continuing to pound against it
with interpretations no matter how perceptive and saga-
cious, the sooner will come the glad day of his becoming
more collaboratively related with me. The concept of therapeutic symbiosis, which I have discussed in several earlier
papers, is pertinent here.

Importance of the Analyst's Discerning Nuclei of Reality in the Patient's Transference-Images of Him

In my work with the borderline patient, I find that he can
come to accept my help in his achieving a sense of reality
valid for him only after, and to the degree that, I have first
proved able to accept the reality of his transference to me. In
oversimplified terms, he can let me define reality for him
only after he has defined thus my reality. I hasten to explain
that I do not mean that the analyst must have come to accept
the "reality" imposed upon him by the patient's transfer-
ence-image(s) of him as being the analyst's *only* reality; were
that to develop, the analyst clearly would have become a
partner in a *folie à deux*. What I do mean is that the analyst,
before he can help the patient to achieve a valid and durable
sense of reality (one which is consonant, although far from
identical, with the analyst's own sense of reality), must first
have come to sense the impact of the patient's transference-
images of him, an impact having a full reality-value for the

patient, and an impact sufficient to give rise in the analyst to a set of feeling-experiences which become identifiable, over the course of the months and years, as a *kind* of coherent countertransference-psychosis or countertransference-borderline-psychosis—one of intendedly manageable proportions but a nonetheless relatively distinct affect-laden structure in the countertransference.

Once the analyst has become able to experience this impact of the patient's transference-reality, and has become accustomed enough to it to find it tolerable, he will not need to flee in submerged panic from this imposed transference-role by attempting prematurely to interpret to the patient the ego-contents which the latter is projecting upon him. It has seemed to me, in working with one patient after another through such developments, that if I myself am finding the particular transference-role in question to be so intolerably upsetting to me, how can I as yet expect the patient, whose ego-organization is much less strong than my own, to be able to integrate these so-anxiety-laden dissociated ego-components which he is projecting upon me?

The Value, while Interpreting Verbally, of Utilizing the Patient's Own Phraseology and Emotional Tone

Now I shall comment briefly upon the importance, in particularly difficult cases, of utilizing, in one's interpretations, the patient's own phraseology and emotional tone. Of interest here are Marie Coleman Nelson's (1968) and her co-workers' techniques of what they call paradigmatic psychotherapy (a paradigm being defined as a showing or saying by example), for treating borderline and other patients who are inordinately resistive to the usual techniques of verbal interpretation. While I do not embrace paradigmatic techniques in my own psychoanalytic work, primarily for the reason that these involve, for my taste, too much of a deliberate attempt to influence what should be a more spontaneously-evolving transference-and-countertransference process, I find the detailed studies by Nelson and her colleagues to merit careful study.

Something like 25 years ago, Clarence G. Schulz, then a colleague of mine on the Chestnut Lodge staff, emphasized the importance, in work with schizophrenic patients, of giving interpretations which are oriented toward the patient's view of things, rather than one's own (personal communication, 1952). This immediately struck me as sound and, since then, has been very much part of my technique, in working with patients, generally.

Similarly, long ago, I started learning the importance of using, whenever feasible, the patient's own vocabulary in making interpretations, for I have been through many painful experiences of finding that words from my own customary vocabulary which I had assumed to be entirely acceptable synonyms for various of the patient's words proved to have an entirely different, and often very upsetting, meaning to him. One of my most frequent modes of interpreting is to acknowledge the patient's conscious view, using his own phraseology, but then adding a bit of elaboration to this which is intendedly interpretive in effect.

During the past seven years or so, I have learned, similarly, that some of the most difficult patients can hear interpretations only if these are delivered in the affective tone characteristic of the patient's own mode of speaking. This finding is consonant with an impression I have long had, that in early ego development the first-experienced separate object tends to be sensed as a twin of oneself. That is, in work with a highly autistic patient, one may find that he can register one in his awareness, sufficiently to attend to a brief interpretation, only if this is sensed as coming from, essentially, a twin of the patient himself.

For example, in my work with one extremely rigid woman, I seldom found, over the years, occasion for making an interpretation, and found that more than nine-tenths of those I made, over all the years, proved ineffectual so far as I could determine. This woman customarily reported, throughout each session, in a tone (irrespective of the content) of upbraiding me, lecturing me in a domineering fashion, and chronically, in a tone of barely suppressed—nearly uncontrollable—fury. After several years of work with her, I began finding that on those occasions when I made an interpretation which proved effective, I had made it in a tone of barely controlled fury—a tone practically identical with one of her own customary tones.

In my work with this woman, it eventually became clear that, to her, I was alive only when I was speaking in such a tone. In my work with her and with other patients similar in this regard but with illnesses of various diagnoses, I have found the phrase "controlled tirade" to be accurately descriptive both of the patient's daily tone during analytic sessions, and of the needed tone on the analyst's part in conveying interpretations.

More speculatively, I surmise that at different phases of an analysis, interpretations need to be made in various forms and affective tones. For example, when the patient is in a phase of exploring predominantly oral conflicts, interpretations may need to be made in a spirit of feeding; when he is in a predominantly anal phase, in a spirit facilitating of increasingly well-controlled catharsis; when he is in a phase of exploring genital-sexual conflicts, in a spirit of well-sublimated sexual interaction with him. I know this all sounds thoroughly contrived; but what I am attempting to suggest, here, is that the analyst's mode of participating *inevitably will* vary, from one phase of the analysis to another, under the influence of the patient's varying transference-reactions to him; and I am trying to suggest that the more aware we can become of such variations in our own mode of participation, the more capably we can exercise these in a basically non-contrived manner. Surely, the level of the patient's ego-development, at any particular phase of the analysis, will be relevant for the length or brevity of our interpretations, and I believe the affective tones, however subtle, will naturally vary also.

It can be said more confidently, here, that in any case the analyst will be well advised to be attentive to the nature of the patient's varying transference-reactions to his interpretations, throughout different phases of the analysis. Is he unconsciously reacting to one's having given him an interpretation as being equivalent to one's having been giving him to suck at the breast, or as being the equivalent of anal intercourse, or as being a matter of one's holding him in the refuge of one's maternal arms, or as being a disavowal of the emotional oneness which had prevailed just before one launched into the interpretation, or what?

The Patient's Transference-Reactions to, and the Varying Real Aspects of, the Analyst's Silences

Patients' transference-reactions to the analyst's *silences* are, I believe, a relatively neglected area in the literature, and an important one in the work with borderline patients, whose transference-reactions and attitudes are oftentimes so strikingly distorted. It has been no great surprise to me to discover that a patient has been reacting, for months or years, to my being silent as equivalent to my being dead, or my being psychotically immersed in my own fantasy world, or my being senile, or my being an inanimate object of some

sort. But it has been startling to me to find that one borderline patient unconsciously experienced my being silent
throughout nearly all of each session as being a matter of
my incessantly lecturing him in a primly critical and self-
righteously condemnatory fashion. A borderline woman expressed grating rage and fury concerning a male supervisor
whom she found to be outspokenly and verbally critical of
her on frequent occasions. Several minutes later, after I had
continued to be silent, she said, "I guess in your silence I see
you as being that kind of disparaging, mocking, sneering
person."

In the work with a borderline man who digresses endlessly, branching off repeatedly from his own intended main
path in reporting his associations, I have been astonished to
find that he reacts to my sitting there, silently, as being a
matter of my repeatedly interrupting him. It became evident that he felt I should be controlling so closely what he
was saying that, when I silently allowed him to digress, I
was in effect fully and forcefully and verbally interrupting
him, maddeningly, from pursuing his intended main theme.
The fact that he was feeling interrupted by me was not
promptly and explicitly declared by him; it had first to be
inferred from relatively subtle evidence in his behavior,
posture, and vocal tones. In regard to what is going on in the
patient at such a juncture, I think of this as a phenomenon of
one of the introjects' coming in and interrupting the pres-
ently-being-manifested introject, and it requires only a minute sign of the analyst's presence for the interrupting-
introject to be projected upon the analyst. But I have found
such patient-reactions to occur, toward me, even at times
when I was not only silent but motionless, and have found
many times that only a slight variation in the sound of my
breathing is sufficient to evoke the patient's feeling maddenedly interrupted by me.

I surmise that in working with any patient of whatever

diagnostic category, my silence is my most reliably effective therapeutic tool; surely this is the case in my work with borderline individuals. One patient after another eventually comes in course of time to realize that, as one put it with surprise, "Your silence must really be getting to me," whereas all, or nearly all, verbal interpretations have failed to do so.

It is easy for an analyst to maintain an unexamined illusion, about himself, that so long as he is being silent he is functioning in an essentially emotionally-neutral fashion during the session, in the best classically analytic tradition. It is well for us to realize, on the contrary, that patients' diverse transference-reactions to one's silence have, in all probability, some significant basis in the reality of the *kind* of silence one is presenting to them. Just as we find patients' silent demeanors to cover a wide range of feeling-states, from emotional-remoteness to hopelessness to discouragement to sexually-seductive invitingness to paranoid stonewall antagonism to what-not, so we need to be attentive to the circumstance that the particular *kind* of silence we are manifesting, at any one moment, may be anything but dispassionate. It has been difficult but helpful for me to realize, for instance, in my work with one or another borderline patient who was much given to paranoid-antagonistic silences, that my own silence was in all probability being experienced by him, to a degree quite accurately, as being of essentially that same inhospitably stone-wall, or bristlingly antagonistic, threatened and threatening nature. As I have come to see these things more clearly, it has been less baffling to me to find that the patient is having great difficulty in associating at all freely and in reporting to me such associations.

On the more positive side, as to what "kind" of silence the analyst is manifesting—that is, as to what is the specific nature of his non-verbal relatedness with the patient—I have come to believe that, when I have discovered in the patient some largely unconscious conflict concerning which I remain, then, for many months or even some years silent, having reason to know it would be premature, yet, to give the patient an interpretation concerning this conflictual area, my *non-verbal* responsiveness to or participation with him is changed, nonetheless, very significantly as a result of my discovery. For example, if I discover that the patient has an unconscious conflict from negative-oedipal sources concerning me as a parent-figure of the same sex as himself (or herself), I do not doubt that this discovery causes me to behave, in however minute and subtle ways, differently thereafter toward him until his conflict comes sufficiently fully into his awareness to be subject to interpretation and resolution. Whether I behave, meanwhile, in a bit more seductive, or a bit more stand-offish, way—or, more likely, a combination of both, from one time to another—I cannot say; but I am convinced that after the analyst has made such a discovery, even though the patient may hear no interpretation from him concerning this for, say, many months, he has reason to sense, at no matter how unconscious or preconscious a level, that the analyst is responding differently to him. Further, I surmise that this subtly-changed non-verbal participation on the part of the analyst helps to enable the patient to become aware of the feelings and memories in question, and to be able to listen to and integrate verbal interpretations concerning this previously-unconscious material.

What I am endeavoring to do here is to describe, more adequately than one generally finds it described in the literature, what is really transpiring between analyst and patient while the analyst is being silent. It is of fundamental importance for us to become as free as possible from any illusions concerning silence on the analyst's part as being

automatically equatable with neutral, evenly-hovering attention. Surely 90 percent of most analysts' time with most
patients is spent with the analyst's being silent, and in the
work with many a borderline patient, 98 or 99 percent of
one's time involves one's being non-verbal with him.

The videotaping of psychoanalytic sessions, for all the
difficulties so gross a parameter would introduce into the
analysis, would help to bring what I am suggesting here
down from the realm of speculation and into clinically docu-
mented and established form. We need, in this regard,
studies of adult psychoanalysis which are comparable, in
minuteness of detailed observation, to those of Spitz (1957),
of Mahler and her co-workers (1968, 1975) and others concerning the mutual cuing which occurs between a mother
and her infant. Berger (1970) is one of those who are pioneering in videotape techniques which hold considerate
promise for such psychoanalytic research in the future.

Interpretations of the Patient's Identifications

Next, I want to make two points concerning the interpretation of the patient's identifications. First, I wish to emphasize the suicidal-despair-engendering effect of one's interpreting, too early, that much of what the patient has felt to
be the core of his self consists, instead, in large part, in an
unconscious identification (introject) derived from experience with a parent. Patients generally are very resistant,
naturally enough, to discovering that *precisely* that which
they have most assumed to be their very own self is, to a high
degree, comprised of such an introject. A premature interpretation of such an introject, or unconscious identification,
is especially injurious if the analyst gives the interpretation
in a spirit of disavowing implicitly that he himself possesses,

in his own personality-functioning, any appreciable element of the particular personality-traits in question, for an interpretation so given tends to foster the patient's feeling isolated from (a) his usual sense of identity, (b) his parent from whom the introject had been largely derived, and (c) the analyst. Particularly if the analyst is implicitly disavowing of his own part in all this, the patient is likely to be feeling burdened essentially with a projected part-aspect of the analyst's own unconscious, which the patient feels pressured, now, to acknowledge as being his own real identity. All this is comparable with the position in which the analyst so often finds himself, of feeling under intense pressure to acknowledge that the patient's intensely-felt transference image of him is his, the analyst's, only real identity.

In Chapter 5 I describe the analyst as he discovers that his "own" feelings in working with any one patient are comprised in large part, layer under successive layer, of countertransference-elements—comprised, that is, of responses and attitudes which are natural and inherent counterparts to the patient's transference-responses and -attitudes toward him. My second point, now, is an analogous one: namely, that any one area of a patient's identification with a parent has, beneath its relatively superficial layer, successive layers of deeper-lying components, or ramifications, of this identification.

For example, in a recent dream a patient found herself to be living the life of a hermit in a desolate house, the bleakness of which was relieved only superficially by an attractively colorful wall-covering in one of the rooms. The wall-covering was of the same color, she commented, "as this wall-covering" (i.e., in my office). Other associations, from this and other sessions, indicated that behind her superficial cheerfulness, which involved much identification with her mother and which had some counterpart in my own demeanor at times, was a realm of depressive bleakness which

involved, in turn, identification with affective impoverishment in her mother and which has a counterpart, again, in
some of the components of my own personality. That is, the
dream was saying something not merely about colorfulness
on the analyst's (= mother's) part, but also about underlying
loneliness and bleakness.

A patient who suddenly takes a week's vacation, shortly
after the analyst has taken one, can readily be seen to be
doing so on a basis, in part, of a kind of spiteful identification with the analyst. But the particular ways in which the
patient does this need to be evaluated in terms of whether
these also represent less-conscious identifications with the
analyst in terms of the patient's transference-perceptions of
him. For example, it may well develop that the patient's
sudden and spiteful announcement of his own forthcoming
vacation betrays unconscious identifications with the analyst
who is perceived, unconsciously, by the patient as having
given too little notice of a vacation which the analyst was
bent on taking, and taking predominantly as a means of
spiting the analysand.

Further, as I have learned in relatively recent years,
any acting out in which a patient becomes involved during
his vacation is very likely to prove to be based to a significant degree upon identifications with his analyst's vacation-
activities, according to the patient's unconscious fantasies
concerning the analyst—no matter how far-fetched these
initially may seem, in terms of the analyst's and analysand's
conscious images of the former's extra-analytic living.

In closing, I want most to emphasize that an inner
refusal, on the analyst's part, to perceive any reality-basis
in himself for the patient's projection-laden, transference-
linked images of him inevitably boomerangs in rendering
him proportionately ineffective in his analytic work with the
patient. Particularly in work with borderline patients (or
those even more deeply ill), who tend so powerfully to be-

come bearers of the burden of the analyst's projection of his own unconscious self-images as being, say, essentially non-human, or unfit to live, or incapable of caring, or incurably sadistic, or whatever, it is essential that the analyst become as open as possible to acknowledging to himself that even the patient's most severe psychopathology has some counterpart, perhaps relatively small by comparison but by no means insignificant, in his own *real* personality-functioning. We cannot help the borderline patient, for example, to become well if we are trying unwittingly to use him as the receptacle for our own most deeply-unwanted personality-components, and trying essentially to require him to bear the burden of all the severe psychopathology in the whole relationship.

Summary

Although interpretations have a significant role in the analyst's work with the borderline patient, it is a *relatively* minor one by contrast to that of the analyst's non-verbal participation with him. The state of the patient's ego-integration and ego-differentiation is such that he has not yet developed a durable internalized image of himself, or of the analyst, or both. Until such time in the therapy as his ego-functioning has matured further than this, his ability to utilize verbal interpretations is very limited.

The patient's flawed sense of both inner and outer reality tempts the analyst to try to impose upon him what would be only another pseudo-reality and pseudo-identity, and in such an endeavor the analyst would be avoiding, unwittingly, his own full experiencing of the impact upon him of the patient's transference-"reality." Of crucial importance is the analyst's becoming able to discern nuclei of reality in the patient's transference-images of him.

In particularly difficult cases, the analyst's utilization, while interpreting, of the patient's own customary phraseology and emotional tone may be unusually effective.

The nature of the patient's transference-reactions and -attitudes to the analyst's interpretations, and to his silences, is important to note and to explore with the patient insofar as it is feasible.

The analyst is silent in limitless ways which are *in reality* (beyond, that is, the patient's transference-distorted perceptions of these) subtly different. For example, even though he may choose silently to postpone a verbal interpretation of some newly discerned area of conflict in the patient, his non-verbal demeanor toward him is likely to change, nonetheless, in a fashion which helps to prepare the patient, through mutual nonverbal cuing, to become able to utilize, eventually, verbal interpretations concerning this area.

As regards the interpretation of the patient's pathologic identifications, I caution against doing so prematurely in working with these patients, whose sense of an own self is so precariously based. But I point out, on the other hand, the value of coming to explore the successive levels of unconscious identifications which are hidden behind the more nearly conscious levels, such that a more genuine "own self" can eventually come into being in the patient.

The final point in this chapter is that the analyst cannot treat the borderline patient effectively if he, the analyst, is unwittingly using the patient to bear the burden of all the severe psychopathology in the whole relationship.

References

Berger, M. M., ed. (1970). *Videotape Techniques in Psychiatric Training and Treatment.* New York: Brunner/Mazel.

Deutsch, H. (1942). Some forms of emotional disturbance and their relationship to schizophrenia. *Psychoanalytic Quarterly* 11:301–321.

Khan, M. M. R. (1974). *The Privacy of the Self—Papers on Psychoanalytic Theory and Technique.* New York: International Universities Press.

Lichtenstein, H. (1961). Identity and sexuality: a study of their interrelationship in man. *Journal of the American Psychoanalytic Association* 9:179–260.

———(1964). The role of narcissism in the emergence and maintenance of a primary identity. *International Journal of Psycho-Analysis* 45: 49–56.

Mahler, M. S. (1968). *On Human Symbiosis and the Vicissitudes of Individuation. Vol 1: Infantile Psychosis.* New York: International Universities Press.

Mahler, M. S., Pine, F., and Bergman, A. (1975). *The Psychological Birth of the Human Infant—Symbiosis and Individuation.* New York: Basic Books.

Nelson, M. C., Nelson, B., Sherman, M. H., and Strean, H. S. (1968). *Roles and Paradigms in Psychotherapy.* New York and London: Grune & Stratton.

Searles, H. F. (1970). Autism and the phase of transition to therapeutic symbiosis. *Contemporary Psychoanalysis* 7:1–20. Reprinted in Searles (1979a), pp. 149–171.

———(1971). Pathologic symbiosis and autism. In *In the Name of Life—Essays in Honor of Erich Fromm*, ed. B. Landis and E. S. Tauber, pp. 69–83. New York: Holt, Rinehart and Winston. Reprinted in Searles (1979a), pp. 132–148.

———(1972). The function of the patient's realistic perceptions of the analyst in delusional transference. *British Journal of Medical Psychology* 45:1–18. Reprinted in Searles (1979a), pp. 196–227.

———(1973). Concerning therapeutic symbiosis. *Annual of Psychoanalysis* 1:247–262. Reprinted in Searles (1979a), pp. 172–191.

———(1979). (A) Jealousy involving an internal object, and (B) The countertransference in psychoanalytic therapy with borderline patients. In *Advances in Psychotherapy of the Borderline Patient*, ed. J. LeBoit and A. Capponi, pp. 309–404. New York: Jason Aronson. Reprinted as Chapter 5 in this present volume.

——— (1979a). *Countertransference and Related Subjects—Selected Papers.* New York: International Universities Press.

Spitz, R. A. (1957). *No and Yes—On the Genesis of Human Communication.* New York: International Universities Press.

Stierlin, H. (1959). The adaptation to the "stronger" person's reality: some aspects of the symbiotic relationship of the schizophrenic. *Psychiatry* 22:143–152.

Chapter 2

Transference-Responses

It used to be so generally agreed that borderline patients were incapable of developing analyzable transference-responses to the analyst that only in relatively recent years has a modified form of psychoanalysis—that is to say, psychoanalytic psychotherapy—become widely utilized in treating borderline individuals. The question is no longer one of whether the patient can develop powerful and meaningful transference-responses to the therapist, but rather one of whether the therapist can discern those limit-

This is a slightly revised version of the paper which was presented at The Twenty-Eighth Annual Chestnut Lodge Symposium in Rockville, Maryland, on October 8, 1982. It was published in *Psychiatry*, 47:37–49, 1984.

lessly unusual ones which the patient has been manifesting, but unrecognizedly heretofore, toward him.

The Primitiveness of the Patient's Ego-Integration and -Differentiation; Subjectively Nonhuman Phenomena

In a monograph in 1960 (Searles 1960), I discussed the role of the nonhuman environment in normal development and in schizophrenia. A major part of my effort was to show that for any infant and young child, the struggle to become a genuinely human individual involves not only the development and maintenance of meaningful interpersonal relationships per se, but also, and more basically, becoming differentiated from the far vaster nonhuman environment, becoming able to differentiate between human and nonhuman ingredients of one's environment, and achieving emotionally meaningful relatedness with both human and nonhuman realms of one's environment.

The borderline adult, upon entering psychoanalytic therapy, functions in a manner which indicates that he has not come as yet to experience himself as a single, whole, human individual, capable of relating to the therapist as being another, essentially similar, individual.

In Chapter 7 concerning the countertransference with borderline patients, I describe the major roots of the patient's transference-reactions as traceable to a stage in ego development prior to any clear differentiation between inner and outer world, and prior to the child's coming to function as a whole person involved in interpersonal relationships with other persons experienced as whole individuals. Hence the therapist finds that these transference-reactions and attitudes of the adult borderline patient cast him, the therapist, in roles strangely different from those he commonly encounters in working with the neurotic patient, whose transference casts him, say, as a domineering father or a sexually seductive, masochistic mother. Instead, the therapist finds the patient reacting to him in limitlessly extraordinary ways, most of which have a nonhuman, or less-than-fully-human, feel to them. The patient reacts unconsciously to him, for example, as being nonexistent, or a corpse, or a pervasive and sinister supernatural force, or as God, or as being the patient's mind, or some anatomical part-aspect of his mother (her vagina, for example, or her fantasied penis).

As to the etiology of such phenomena on the patient's part, we find that his parent-figures were not predominantly whole, well-integrated individuals, but each was, rather, a collection of poorly integrated, and sometimes seemingly innumerable, introjects, only precariously managed by the parent-figure's relatively weak own self. The patient's own adult personality-functioning comes, in the course of the therapy, to reveal many identifications with such parent-figures, and to reveal, with this, that these introjects were installed within him not only in his unconsciously identifying with these as aggressors, but also by reason of his having been cast, often in early childhood, in the role of therapist whose intended mission in life was to heal his so grievously afflicted actual parent-figures.

The Therapist Must Come to Perceive and Accept Nuclei of Reality in the Patient's Transference-Perceptions of Him or Her

In order for the treatment to be relatively successful, it is essential that the therapist come to experience, and deal with, the patient's strange transference-manifestations as being less a testimony of grievous trauma from the distant past, than as the product of dynamically defensive ego-functioning in the immediate transference-situation. The patient unconsciously splits up psychological processes which belong together, and fuses processes which need to become differentiated from one another. One of the reasons for this is that he is struggling unconsciously to become a fully human individual without relinquishing his subjective omnipotence, omnipotence which would include his nondifferentiating from either the human or the nonhuman surrounding environment. A second reason is that he is struggling to avoid experiencing intolerably intense and conflicting emotions while trying, nonetheless, to become a fully alive and human being who must, if he is to emerge as such out of the background from which he comes, face and experience such emotions.

Scarcely a week goes by, in my work with borderline patients, without my discerning some significant "nonhuman" transference response, as I sit (in my work with most of these persons) behind the couch. I regard it as important that the therapist experience these responses as being of more than merely intellectual interest to him but as having, rather, some degree of felt reality (however metaphorical or otherwise figurative or symbolic) in them, as being responses to some area of the therapist's own subjective identity. Only if the therapist can work in this fashion, I believe, will he come to have the fulfillment (as well as, inevitably, the loss-experience) of finding that, in the transference of the patient, he the therapist has emerged as being a truly human individual, born, as it were, out of the previously undifferentiated human-and-nonhuman surroundings of the patient. I mean to convey here not a once-and-for-all accomplishment, but rather a ceaselessly fluctuating process, fluctuating in terms of maturational processes, over against regressive processes, on the parts of both patient and therapist as the work proceeds.

The Patient's Unawareness of the Therapist May Be a Measure of the Latter's Unconscious Importance (Rather than Insignificance) to Him or Her

Those borderline patients who function, for a long time in my work with them, seemingly obliviously of my individual existence, sometimes remind me (for all the differences in degree of illness) of a chronically paranoid-schizophrenic woman with whom I worked early in my career at Chestnut Lodge. Of her I once wrote:

> The few comments of hers which I shall quote, from among her innumerable "dehumanizing" communications, convey no more than a hint of her very real capacity to make me feel, . . . myself to be, in actuality, something distinctly less than human. . . .
>
> In another hour, during the eleventh month of our work. . . , while the liveliness of our interaction was, overtly at least, approximately equivalent to that which two statues in a room might have, I asked whether she had had some anticipation as to how I might respond to something she had brought up, a few moments before, and concerning which we had exchanged a few words. She replied, flatly [and, to me, thoroughly convincingly], "I don't care anything about the way *you* respond. I care about how *I* respond. *Your* feelings don't mean anything more to me than if you were one of the lines on that wallpaper there." (Searles 1960, pp. 357–59)

It was only in subsequent years that I learned, from my later experience with that woman and with many other patients (in particular, borderline ones), a principle which has stood me in good stead time after time: for such a patient, the therapist is in actuality of such basic importance that the patient cannot allow more than a little bit of the therapist to be perceived as being *outside* the patient.

This is a principle of which I entirely lose sight, however, at times of particularly stressful separations. When I left Chestnut Lodge, one of the four patients whom I left there was a hebephrenic woman with whom I had worked for more than 13 years. She had improved dramatically but only transitorily in two different eras over those years, and was in the depths of grievously severe psychosis at the time I left. I found it most disturbing when, in what I recall as our final session, her eyes did not even focus upon me when she looked toward me; this gave me to feel that, after more than 13 years of enormously difficult and devoted work with her, I had not come even to exist in her awareness. But after some additional years of her work with a succession of three subsequent therapists (which led to her discharge from treatment as, I gather, essentially well), she called me up one day and spoke to me in a way which gave me to know that she remembered me well and fondly; the fond relatedness between us, in that brief telephone call, was such as I had often felt to exist between us prior to the so-premature termination phase of our work. I now understood once again that, at the time of my leaving the Lodge, she had had to identify with me so fully (to have me so entirely within her, or to be so entirely within me) that there had not been enough of a separate-object relationship between us for her eyes to focus upon me.

Over the course of several years of my work with a borderline man, his ego-functioning improved a great deal in many regards; but external circumstances required us to arrange for a termination time, some months hence, before—as we both knew—his treatment would have become reasonably completed. Nonetheless, I was chagrined to find him reporting, in the closing weeks, that so far as he could discern, our erstwhile relationship had evaporated completely, as though it had never been. My shock had much less to do with his words than with his corresponding nonverbal demeanor. Again, it was only some years later, when circumstances enabled him to return for further treatment, that I learned how deeply significant I had become to him: although his conscious reason for returning to treatment was to enable him to effect a separation from his wife, it became evident to me in the first interview, upon his return, that unconsciously he was struggling, at the level of his identity-bearing introjects, to effect a separation—a differentiation—between his own self and his introjected transference-image(s) of me. I now understood, belatedly again, that the relationship between us had evaporated, in the termination phase years before, because, in his unconscious ego-functioning, he and I had become so largely fused, symbiotically. In the original, long period of work with him, I had known him to say such things as (of a sexual partner), "I dissolve into her as though I never were"; but the stress of the termination era caused me to lose that feeling-perspective.

A borderline woman, whose elderly mother was living with the patient and the latter's husband and little children, was raging, in one of our sessions, "My mother, . . . is so *evanescent,* so *insubstantial!*" Years of work with her had convinced me by now, however, that she could not experience her mother as possessing a full, flesh-and-blood reality without her having to relinquish a still-unconsciously-cherished, omnipotence-based image of herself as having been *self-created.* In the transference, I was given by her to feel, for years, essentially devoid of interpersonal, individual significance, until gradually subtle hints emerged that I had become a vital holding environment for her. These hints were almost entirely nonverbal; but on occasion they took a disguised verbal form, as in one session when she was expressing fear lest her husband take a better job elsewhere, she said, "It would mean, for me, the loss of everything— you, my house. . . ." She clearly meant consciously, "You, and my house, and so on," but her tone conveyed the unconscious meaning that I had become, for her, "my house."

The Therapist as the Patient's Symbiotic Identity Partner

A narcissistic woman, although married, would narrate details of her home life by saying that "I" did such-and-such; so rarely, indeed, did she say "we," that one would have thought her to be living entirely alone. I often wondered how her husband was surviving his marriage to this so self-absorbed woman, who year after year gave me very little acknowledgment of any relatedness with her; I found every reason to assume that she was as chronically rejecting toward him as I felt her to be toward me. But then it gradually became evident that "I" included both her husband and herself; he had become as much part of her "I" as was she, herself. I no longer found it paradoxical when she would say, for instance, "Last night, since it was Bill's birthday, I went to see 'Patton,'" a movie which, she had made clear in previous sessions, her husband, Bill, had been looking forward to seeing. I came to realize belatedly that, in the transference-situation as well, when she said, "I," she often was unconsciously including a reference to me as being her symbiotic identity partner.

In Chapter 4, I describe such unconscious dual- or multiple-identity processes as being among the fundamental features of borderline ego-functioning. An understanding of these processes is fundamental to the therapist's awareness of the borderline patient's great involvement in processes of projective (and introjective) identification. The patient's unconscious use of quotes is a rich source of such data. I have learned, for instance, how very frequently, when a patient quotes something which someone else has said to him, *he* is unconsciously saying this quoted comment to the *therapist*.

Another unconscious use of quotes is shown in this vignette. A borderline man, having become much improved over the course of his therapy, was looking back on the early part of it and "Wanting you to say—well, was I psychotic or was I not? . . ." I clearly heard in this the unconscious meaning of, "Wanting you to say, 'Well, was I psychotic or was I not?' . . ." That is, although he had become able to weigh the question of whether he himself had been psychotic or not, he was not yet ready to look at his transference-image of me as wondering whether I had been psychotic or not, for that involved one or more parental introjects yet to be brought in focus in the treatment. He was so resistant to my attempt, at that time, to interpret this, as to give me to know that it was very difficult, still, for him to conceive of *my* having an "I."

The Patient as Mother Who Threatens the Therapist (as Infant) with Abandonment; The Psychoanalytic Process as Involving Regressive Reactivation of the Therapist's Introjects

In an earlier paper (Searles 1970) I described the therapist's sense of how limited and few, if any, are his avenues of relatedness with such patients as these, until relatively far along in the treatment. One can think of it as that the patient strives unconsciously to coerce him into conforming with his introjected image of him, or into personifying one, or a relatively few, of the introjects with which he, the patient, cannot cope otherwise. One woman said of her fantasy-ridden mother, who had settled for a reclusive life elsewhere, leaving the upbringing of her three little children to a maid, "She tried to make everything fit a mold she had in her mind, of what a family should be like, . . . of what children should be like. . . . She couldn't make it *fit*, and it drove her crazy. The only way she could make it fit was to leave, and make it fit in fantasy; so she went off by herself and wrote novels. . . ." I well knew, from the year-after-year impact upon me of her maternal introjects, what she was speaking of here. A borderline man developed, relatively early in our work, an internalized image of me which he found much more satisfactory than he found the flesh-and-blood me to be during our sessions. It was typical of him that, about 15 minutes along in a session in which he had been speaking under considerable pressure, while I had spoken only briefly two or three times, he suddenly interrupted himself, saying with intense impatience and exasperation, "Why can't you be in my head so I don't have to tell you all these things?"

These patients have very powerful identifications with their narcissistic, or otherwise fantasy-ridden, mothers who chronically threatened them with rejection and abandonment. The therapist, under the stress of this work, inevitably (and, I believe, necessarily for the patient's treatment) becomes involved in ego-regression and reactivation of his own myriad introjects. The therapist then comes to feel at first hand, in his work with the patient, that only one or a few of these introjects serve as a link with the patient, who rejects all the others, and threatens totally and permanently to abandon him if he does not continue to provide this link. A borderline man who said, "I don't want you afraid," seemed to think he was conveying a kindly, reassuring image of himself; but I heard the clear, unconscious warning that, were I to become afraid, he would not want me—would reject me utterly. His statement reminded me of one which I heard, innumerable times, from a chronically schizophrenic woman many years ago. She said, always in a conscious attempt to emphasize her family's completely loving concern for her, "My family want me *well*"; but this conveyed, each time, her unconscious realization that they did not at all want her in her actual, very unwell, state. Such patients largely project their own constricting coerciveness upon the therapist, and speak of "my fear of your abandoning me if I don't fit in with your program here."

Dual-Identity and Multiple-Identity Ego-Functioning as Defenses Against Loss

In earlier papers (Searles 1970, 1971) I said that the borderline patient may be functioning, at the beginning of treatment, in a predominantly autistic, or instead a predominantly symbiotic, manner in relation to the therapist. In order to convey here a sense of the subtle, complex, usually years-long, but always inspiring and memorable, metamorphosis whereby the patient who formerly was so oblivious of the therapist is finding, now, his whole meaningful world in the latter, it is necessary to say a bit more about the dual-and-multiple-identity processes which I have mentioned briefly.

These processes, although multidetermined, can often be seen, readily, as unconscious defenses against feelings of loss. For example, a man many years into his second marriage says, "I haven't been able to assert myself with these two wives, and now I am," fully as though his first wife of long ago had not at all been relinquished. A woman who had had some years of analysis, years before coming to me, scarcely ever seemed reminded of that experience. After about three years of working with her, I began to realize that she was reacting, unconsciously, to me as being the former analyst, the loss of whom she had not at all worked through; and in ensuing months, thereafter, she herself came gradually to this realization.

A woman says, "I can remember the house I lived in when I was four and five," a statement unremarkable in word-content alone, but said in such a tone as to convey the unconscious meaning that she had been four and five years of age simultaneously—i.e., that "I" had comprised, simultaneously, a child four years of age, and another child, of five years. That is, I sensed that some unintegrated loss-experience when she was four years of age had prevented her four-year-old self from becoming her five-year-old self. A man's unconscious dual-identity-functioning was conveyed in his reporting of his girl-friend's attempt, the evening before, at a meeting of their minds: "I thought she was, as was I, two mature people, who knew our own minds."

A man who had essentially ignored me for years was moving toward the emergence of his transference to me as being a mother who was, essentially, everyone to him. Recalling his mother, toward whom he (the younger of two brothers) had been particularly devoted, he said, "I had to do the living for both of us. In some ways she was such a recluse—and my father, too, and first wife, too. . . ." It was clear that he meant consciously to indicate that his father and his first wife, like his mother, had been recluses. But what he unconsciously conveyed was that his mother had been not only his mother but also his father and his first wife (and his tone implied, further, that the list of persons his mother had been, to him, was endless).

A man had been treated by a succession of three previous analysts before his coming to me, and for some two years of our work reacted to me with disdain, which I often found stinging and, at times, privately infuriating; he made it abundantly evident, effortlessly, that analysts are (as regards their individual-emotional impact upon one) a dime a dozen. But then gradually, in the third year of our work, I came to sense that whenever, in the course of his free-associating, his reported thoughts went to another person in his current or past living, he spoke that person's name in a tone as though addressing me. Thus, when after a brief pause, say, he would start reporting about "Joan" or "Eddie" or "Murchison" (a girl-friend, a colleague at work, a teacher), and so on, he would say the name in such a tone that I felt an amused urge to say, "Yes?," as though responding to hearing my name called. It appeared that in the *transition* of his thoughts, from their focusing upon one person to focusing upon another person, he had to touch base, as it were, with me—to focus upon me unconsciously as an early mother-figure who represented everyone to him. Such experiences with him reminded me of a chronically schizophrenic woman who delusionally misidentified me as being innumerable persons from her current and past life and who, as I described in an earlier paper, ". . . was looking at my face in fascination as I was making some comment, and exclaimed, 'When you're talking about different people, your eyes become the eyes of whomever you're talking about. It's like a kaleidoscope. I've never seen anything like it before; it's fascinating'" (Searles [1972] 1979, p. 210).

As regards the borderline man whom I was describing a moment ago, in one session he said, "I was thinking of *mother*, and then all of *you* [his emphasis in both instances]—Grace, Louise, Edna [the names of three of his several girl-friends during the course of his experience with me], all of you. . . ." The striking thing about this, to me, was that he said, "all of *you*. . . ." in a way of fully speaking to me, but to me as multiple, comprising Grace, Louise, Edna, and unnamed others. In a session a few months later he said, "Part of the way things have gone for me is punishing you—four analysts for what life has done to me. . . ." When I heard him say, "you," I fully assumed he meant *me* (essentially as I experience myself). Then when he added, after a momentary pause, "four analysts," I had a sense (not a hallucination) of my being four different people. I experienced this with the kind of startlement such as I invariably felt when I would sense that he was unconsciously addressing me as being the "Joan" or "Eddie," or whomever, to whom his thoughts had turned in the midst of a session.

A couple of months later, after we had discussed, very briefly, some bit of news in the headlines that day (something I do relatively seldom in my work), he said, "I do like to hear *you Joan Eddie* [my emphasis], and other people, speak of these things. . . ." It was clear that, consciously, he had omitted any pause (any comma, so to speak) after "you" and "Joan" simply to save time; but he unconsciously conveyed the meaning that I comprised not only myself but also Joan and Eddie and, presumably, "other people" as well.

Transference-Responses to the Therapist's Silence

In Chapter 1, I discussed briefly borderline patients' transference-reactions to the therapist's silences, mentioning that it had been startling to me to find that one unconsciously experienced my being silent throughout nearly all of each session as being a matter of my incessantly lecturing him in a primly critical and self-righteously condemnatory fashion. I have encountered similar transference-phenomena in my work with a number of additional patients. For example, in my work with a woman in whose sessions I am silent nearly all the time, week after week, her saying, "I don't agree with what *you say all the time* [my emphasis]" (by which she clearly meant, consciously, "I don't always agree with what you say"), alerted me to the fact that, at an unconscious level, she was reacting to me as speaking all the time. Another woman, during whose sessions I have been similarly silent, said near the end of a session, "I just had the fantasy that you've been talking this whole session, and I haven't been listening. . . ."

In the instances of some borderline and narcissistic patients, such as the just-mentioned woman, I have found evidence that the patient, while functioning with conscious feelings of distress if he feels that the therapist is not listening to him in deep appreciation of what the patient is saying, unconsciously is convinced that if the therapist *were* to come to listen, deeply and receptively, to him, the therapist would thus be *taking* those verbal contents *from* him. One woman, for instance, said, "—thinking of my mother—how she took my [recent] letter. . . ." It was clear that she was consciously wondering how her mother had reacted to her letter; but her statement conveyed the unconscious meaning that if her mother had been genuinely receptive of and responsive to her letter, at an emotional level, her mother thereby had taken the letter away from her. Upon hearing this, I felt it helped to account for the peculiar sense of her shadow-boxing with me in session after session, not making any tangible and consistent contact or relatedness with me. I had discerned, earlier in our work, a number of other determinants of the nonrelatedness between us; but I felt this to be one of the more important ones. Year after year I had done little but listen to her, and it was becoming clearer, now, how unconsciously threatened she was at the possibility of my really taking in what she was saying throughout the sessions.

In Chapter 4, I describe instances in which the borderline patient's seeming monologue, during the session, is unconsciously a dialogue, in which some of his "own" reported thoughts have the unconscious meaning of responses from the therapist, as a symbiotic-identity partner in the transference.

Here I wish to note that another kind of unconscious

dialogue may be going on, in terms of the patient's reacting to the therapist's *silences*, during pauses in the former's monologue, as being expressive of very specific *verbal communications* from the therapist.

One man, for instance, said in a self-depreciatory tone, "—that sounds crazy, I know." Then he paused for a few seconds, and apparently assumed my continued silence, during that pause, to be fully equivalent to my agreeing, scornfully, "It certainly does," for he then said in emphatic, rather angry protest, and sounding personally offended, "*I* don't think it sounds so crazy!"

Another man, after speaking of various of the usually explored areas of his life, paused briefly, and then said emphatically and defensively, "I'm not trying to find an internist because I've been too busy." This came to me as a complete change of subjects, to one which had not been mentioned in weeks. It was true that I had suggested, some months before, that it would be well for him to have an internist, but had not regarded the matter as being at all urgent. I commented to him, here, "You say that for all the world as though I had just said, 'Why aren't you trying to find an internist?' " He laughed with amusement and readily agreed.

The Impact, upon the Therapist's Sense of His Own Identity, of the Patient's Pre-Individuation Transference-Responses

A borderline man entered therapy with me shortly after the death of his mother; a few years before, his beloved older sister, who had been a significant mother-figure in his childhood, had died. It rapidly became clear to me that his strikingly multiple ego-functioning was serving as a defense against unconscious feelings of both grief and murderousness. Introjects derived from his mother, his sister, and other ungrieved persons from his past were as much a part of him as was any own self, and these were projected into me, in his rapidly developing transference, to a degree that I found disturbing and at times shocking. He would say, for instance, toward the end of the first year of our work, "I guess I still look up to you and my mother," in a tone conveying a striking absence of qualitative differentiation between my living self and his dead mother. A month later, he was saying, "Maybe you fall into the same category, and maybe my mother does, too, of people who don't show enough interest in me." On hearing this I found startling, as usual, his not differentiating my aliveness from his mother's deadness. Further, I privately felt both (a) offended at being so fully equated with a dead person, and (b) aware that he was speaking of his mother as being as fully alive as I am in actuality.

Further, there were moments in our work, during the first two years of the treatment, when I sensed (partly from the content of his words, but more often from their feeling-tones) that he was reacting to me unconsciously as being conterminous with three or more other persons, some of these being living and others (such as his mother and his sister) being dead. The first time I had this eerie experience in listening to him, my sense of myself in response to his transference reminded me of a syncytium, which I recalled from college zoology studies as being a primitive life-form which exists as a collection of joined-together but otherwise individual entities. I find that the dictionary (Webster's 1966) defines "syncytium" as being "a multinucleate mass of protoplasm resulting from fusion of cells (as in the plasmodium of a slime mold)," and "plasmodium" is defined (Webster's 1956) as "a multinucleate mass of naked protoplasm formed by the union of a number of amoebalike organisms." The subjectively dehumanizing effect, upon me, of this form of transference helped me to understand why he still needed the more schizoid aspects of his personality: a developing emotional intimacy with another person required him to confront, basically within himself, such strange, disturbing, and subjectively nonhuman, heretofore repressed and projected, self-images.

A woman whose ego-functioning was again, much like that of the "syncytium" man whom I described made in one of her sessions a slip of the tongue which is relevant here. She was speaking of Bill, a man she had been dating in recent weeks, and of Ralph, a former employer of hers with whom she had been in love. She said, meaning to say, "Bill [or Ralph; I don't recall which name] is one of those men . . . ," "*The women* [my emphasis] is one of those men—did you hear that?" I confirmed that I had. "I said, 'The women is one of those men'. . . ." This slip of the tongue indicated to me, in the context of what she had been saying in this session and in light of what I had learned of her unconscious ego-functioning during about one and a half years of working with her at that point, that whenever a man (such as Bill or Ralph) became sufficiently close to her, emotionally, the man became perceived by her, unconsciously, as being "the women"—introjects derived from part-aspects of her early experience (an emotionally chaotic early experience) with her mother.

As the therapist experiences, with one borderline patient after another, that the intensification of the patient's transference to him causes the patient to become assailed with multiple introjects, many of them bearing a subjectively nonhuman feeling-impact, the therapist comes to realize how poignant is the dilemma in which the untreated patient is enmeshed. The Spanish scholar and novelist Miguel de Unamuno is said (DeVries 1982) to have claimed that his profound love for humankind was best nurtured at the greatest possible remove from it—in solitude. I do not wish to liken Unamuno's reported interpersonal stance to that of the borderline patient, who has no such consistent and well-integrated ego-strength. But I find a useful analogy, here, to the tragic dilemma of the borderline individual, whose own sense of humanness is so precarious, so complexly based upon defenses such as massive denial, splitting, projective identification and so forth, that he risks losing his subjectively human identity if he attempts to have any sustained, at all fully-felt relationship with any fellow human being.

The Patient's History of Living Vicariously; Unconscious Jealousy as a Cause of Unrelatedness; The Therapist's Feeling Irrelevant

It is my impression that a major, if not the major, reason for the borderline patient's typical amnesia for much of his childhood is that he lived during it less as an individual with a strongly functioning ego of his own, than as a poorly integrated aggregation of introjects derived from those persons round about, through whom he was interpersonally relating largely vicariously. This helps to account, further, for the so-frequent finding—at least in my experience with borderline patients over the years—that the transference is in the nature not of a relatedness that had held sway between the patient himself and another family member, but rather of a relatedness which had predominated between *two persons other than* the patient himself—between, for example, the parents; or between a parent and a grandparent; or between a parent and an older sibling.

In Chapters 5 and 8 and an earlier paper (Searles, 1973), I discuss jealousy phenomena in which introjects are

involved, and I wish to show here something of the nonre-
latedness, both intrapsychically and interpersonally, which
results from such phenomena.

A woman said, "I don't behave with people as if I have
no attachment toward them or any feeling for them; I behave as though I do—now, is that all an act? . . . The feeling
part and the thinking part [of herself], they don't get together—they don't have a relationship, . . . because they're
not on the right kind of terms—because those two parts of
myself aren't on the right terms, . . . *I* cannot have the right
kind of relationship with other people—it starts, of course,
with myself; but it seems to me it's because those two parts
are not equal partners—they're not equal. . . ." I suggested
that there were connections between her internal state, as
she was describing it, and the relationship between her two
older brothers. She immediately took this up and elaborated
upon it with conviction as to the validity of my comment.
"Bill and Joe don't talk to one another, have no interest in
one another—each regards the other as impossible, and does
not *want* to have a relationship with the other. I was going to
say that Bill [the eldest sibling] is more beholden to Joe than
vice versa, but I'm not at all sure about that. . . . Bill has
gotten to be of tremendous importance in Joe's life, whether
he [Joe] admits it or not. . . . Joe displaced him when Bill
was a little less than two. . . . Bill was so envious. . . ." This
woman had been troubled chronically by what she felt to be
her lack of genuine attachments to people. The therapy
revealed that these two so deeply-important introjects, derived from her experience with her brothers, each so
jealously demanded her total loyalty that she was largely
unable, for a long time, at a conscious level, to form strong
attachments to persons outside herself.

I have come to realize that the feeling of being irrelevant, which I (as well as other analysts and therapists) typically come to suffer for prolonged periods in the work with

the borderline patient, is one of the criteria which indicate that one has come to represent, in the patient's unconscious experience, the patient's *self* (or a significant part of his self)—a self which feels painfully and hopelessly irrelevant, at an unconscious level, to all those situations and relationships in which he is consciously *involved*, and to which he is referring or which he is describing, in the course of the therapeutic session. It is a measure of the patient's unconscious denial-of-personal-relevance, or emotional relevance, of his "own" daily-life experiences, that the therapist finds himself suffering from chronic feelings of personal irrelevancy to those situations of which the patient is speaking. He feels as irrelevant to these as does the patient's unconscious self feel toward them. I have found it appreciably easier to tolerate these feelings of irrelevancy since I realized this essential point.

As to why the patient tends to be assailed by a feeling of irrelevancy—a feeling maintained largely under dissociation, and projected into the therapist such that the latter comes to feel as I have just described—to his "own" daily-life experiences, and overall life experience, this is partly understandable in terms of family psychodynamics. For example, one woman, the middle child of a highly narcissistic mother and a largely absent father, said, "Why was I there?—I seemed to be utterly superfluous to the operation of that household—Marie [her sister] was the beautiful girl, and Eddie was the pretty boy. . . ." But the patient's unconscious defenses—of pervasive denial of the emotional relevancy and meaningfulness to her of her "own" life-experiences; of splitting, such that emotionally meaningful connections are not experienced; and the operation of other well-known borderline defenses—comprise the most convincing causation of her tending to experience her self as being irrelevant and superfluous to her "own" living.

Most poignant for me, in this regard, has been the

realization that my own so-frequent impulse (while I am feeling irrelevant and superfluous in the session) to ask the patient, "Why are you telling me this?" (an impulse which I usually find it wise to suppress), as well as the patient's not rarely asking, "Why am I here in analysis?"—sometimes asked ruminatively, but sometimes demanded challengingly of the analyst—are traceable to the unconscious question in the patient, "Why am I here on earth?," or "Why am I alive?," or "Why do I exist?"

A man seemed to strive, year after year, to shut me as completely as possible out of the analysis. I was silent in most of the sessions, but spent much time in trying to figure out ways of making interpretations to him which he would accept. Most of the time, however, I could not imagine doing this successfully, so said nothing. He taunted me, on occasion, about my having a "scheming" orientation toward him. Eventually it emerged that one of the determinants of this transference-situation was that he had been reacting to the analysis as being his mother, to himself in the analysis as being his father, and to me in the analysis as being his boyhood self, schemingly bent on sabotaging father's relationship with mother and stealing mother from him. He came to realize, for example, "I always feel strange when I'm alone with my mother, because I always have the feeling that I'm trying to steal her from my father." There were, incidentally, at least equally important negative-oedipal determinants at work in this case.

About ten months later, there emerged another heretofore-dissociated oedipal-rivalry determinant of this man's still-formidable resistance to the analytic process. After detailing some of the ways in which his functioning in his career had been changing for the better in recent months, he said, "I've always been puzzled by the apparent lack of connection between changes" in his daily life, on the one hand, and "what happens in the session," on the other hand.

"The two are linked; but I can't see a relationship between them—or, at least, an obvious one. . . ." I commented, "'The two are linked; but I can't see a relationship between them'—might you have said that, perhaps in childhood, in reference to your parents?"

He—who still, at this stage of our work, promptly rejected as invalid a high percentage of my comments—instantly and emphatically confirmed this. "My parents—yes. Always—when I was seventeen, for instance—I always remember wondering why my parents got married; they didn't seem to love one another, and there didn't seem to be any obvious bond between them. I always wondered how they met one another. . . ." Later in the session he revealed that he had long wondered "whether the sessions have *any* influence upon" his life outside the sessions, and he said this in such a way as to indicate that he was still not sure whether they did. But in the closing minutes of the session—a session during which much else occurred—I felt that it had been the most tangibly collaborative one we had ever had in our more than four years of work together. It appeared that—to describe this in an oversimplified way—in the analytic sessions his identifications with one parent were predominant, whereas in his daily life his identifications with the other parent held sway, and his oedipal jealousy decreed that there be no relationship between these two largely introjective selves of his.

Review of Relevant Literature

The relevant literature—to mention only a few of the authors and their works—includes Winnicott's concepts of transitional objects and phenomena (1951) and of the holding environment (1941); Segal's (1964) *Introduction to the Work of Melanie Klein*, who first described (Klein 1946) projective identification; Khan's (1974) further development, in *The Privacy of the Self*, of some of Winnicott's concepts; Modell's (1968) concept of the therapist as becoming a transitional object for the borderline patient; Mahler's (1968) tracing the crucial trauma, in the borderline patient, to the rapprochement subphase of separation-individuation; Kernberg's (1975) *Borderline Conditions and Pathological Narcissism*; Little's (1966) paper entitled, "Transference in Borderline States," and her book (1981), *Transference Neurosis and Transference Psychosis*; Boyer and Giovacchini's (1967) *Psychoanalytic Treatment of Schizophrenic, Borderline and Characterological Disorders*, and Giovacchini's (1979) *Treatment of Primitive Mental States*; Masterson's (1976) discussion of the rewarding and withdrawing object-relations part-units, in his *Psychotherapy of the Borderline Adult*; Volkan's (1976) *Primitive Internalized Object Relations—A Clinical Study of Schizophrenic, Borderline, and Narcissistic Patients*, and his 1981 study of complicated mourning, entitled, *Linking Objects and Linking Phenomena*; Kohut's discussion of selfobjects and of mirror transference, in his 1971 volume, *The Analysis of the Self*, and in his 1977 volume, *The Restoration of the Self*; Langs' (1976) discussion of projective identification and introjective identification in his *The Bipersonal Field*; Grotstein's (1981) *Splitting and Projective Identification*; and Ogden's (1982) volume entitled *Projective Identification and Psychotherapeutic Technique*.

Conclusion

Many forms of borderline transference are difficult to discern because they are strangely different from those of the predominantly neurotic patient. Since these transference-responses are developmentally referable to a stage in ego development prior to differentiation between human and nonhuman, many of them cast the therapist in what he senses as nonhuman transference roles.

It is essential that the therapist come to experience the patient's transference-reactions as having in them nuclei of reality—as being in part realistic reactions to areas of the therapist's own subjective identity.

The patient who gives the therapist to feel that the latter scarcely exists in the patient's awareness may be in actuality so largely fused, unconsciously, with the therapist that very little of the so-indispensable therapist can be allowed to exist, as it were, outside him.

Dual- and-multiple-identity processes are fundamental features of the patient's ego-functioning, such that the therapist develops the transference-status of a symbiotic identity partner to the patient, within the latter's unconscious sense of "I."

In terms of the patient's identifications with the rejecting aspects of his parental figures, the therapist comes to feel threatened lest, if he fails to make available those introjects or identity-components of his own which the patient demands of him, the patient as the narcissistic or borderline mother, for example, will abandon the therapist as the child or infant.

Multiple identity-functioning, although multidetermined, can be seen relatively readily as an unconscious defense against loss. In the transference, the patient comes to react to the therapist as a mother who is everyone to him—is all the succession of mother-figures the loss of whom, over the years, the patient has not worked through.

A variety of typical transference-reactions to the therapist's silences have been described, and I have discussed some of the emotional impacts upon the therapist of the patient's reacting to him as multiple and as not differentiated from dead persons or nonhuman entities.

The transference often takes the form of a relatedness which held sway between two persons in the patient's past, other than the patient himself. His unconscious jealousy, involving one or more of the introjects within him, is seen to be among the causes of various forms of unrelatedness in the transference.

The therapist, in feeling irrelevant much of the time in his work with the patient, personifies in the transference the patient's own self: the patient himself feels, at an unconscious level, irrelevant to the daily-life experiences which he is recounting to the therapist, and basically to his "own" life as a whole.

References

Boyer, L. B., and Giovacchini, P. L. (1967). *Psychoanalytic Treatment of Schizophrenic, Borderline and Characterological Disorders*. New York: Jason Aronson.

DeVries, P. Wodehousehold. *New Yorker*, August 23, 1982.

Giovacchini, P. L. (1979). *Treatment of Primitive Mental States*. New York: Jason Aronson.

Grotstein, J. S. (1981). *Splitting and Projective Identification*. New York: Jason Aronson.

Kernberg, O. (1975). *Borderline Conditions and Pathological Narcissism*. New York: Jason Aronson.

Kahn, M. M. R. (1974). *The Privacy of the Self—Papers on Psychoanalytic Theory and Technique*. New York: International Universities Press.

Klein, M. (1946). Notes on some schizoid mechanisms. In *Envy and Gratitude and Other Works, 1946–1963*. New York: Delacorte Press/Seymour Lawrence. London: Hogarth Press and The Institute of Psycho-Analysis, 1975.

Kohut, H. (1971). *The Analysis of the Self*. New York: International Universities Press.

——— (1977). *The Restoration of the Self*. New York: International Universities Press.

Langs, R. (1976). *The Bipersonal Field*. New York: Jason Aronson.

Little, M. I. (1966). Transference in borderline states. *International Journal of Psycho-Analysis* 47:476–485. Reprinted in Little (1981).

—— (1981). *Transference Neurosis and Transference Psychosis.* New York: Jason Aronson.

Mahler, M. S. (1968). *On Human Symbiosis and the Vicissitudes of Individuation.* New York: International Universities Press.

Masterson, J. F. (1976). *Psychotherapy of the Borderline Adult—A Developmental Approach.* New York: Brunner/Mazel.

Modell, A. H. (1968). *Object Love and Reality.* New York: International Universities Press.

Ogden, T. H. (1982). *Projective Identification and Psychotherapeutic Technique.* New York: Jason Aronson.

Searles, H. F. (1960). *The Nonhuman Environment in Normal Development and in Schizophrenia.* New York: International Universities Press.

—— (1970). Autism and the phase of transition to therapeutic symbiosis. *Contemporary Psychoanalysis* 7:1–20. Reprinted in Searles (1979d).

—— (1971). Pathologic symbiosis and autism. In *In the Name of Life—Essays in Honor of Erich Fromm,* ed. B. Landis and E. S. Tauber. New York: Holt, Rinehart and Winston. Reprinted in Searles (1979d).

—— (1972). The function of the patient's perceptions of the analyst in delusional transference. *British Journal of Medical Psychology* 45:1–18. Reprinted in Searles (1979d).

—— (1973). Concerning therapeutic symbiosis: the patient as symbiotic therapist, the phase of ambivalent symbiosis, and the role of jealousy in the fragmented ego. *Annual of Psychoanalysis* 1:247–262. Reprinted in Searles (1979d).

—— (1977). Dual and multiple-identity processes in borderline ego functioning. In *Borderline Personality Disorders: The Concept, the Patient, the Syndrome,* ed. P. Hartocollis. New York: International Universities Press. Reprinted in Searles (1979d).

—— (1978). Psychoanalytic therapy with the borderline adult: some principles concerning technique. In *New Perspectives on Psychotherapy of the Borderline Adult,* ed. J. F. Masterson. New York: Brunner/Mazel. Also reprinted as Chapter 1 in this volume.

—— (1979a). The countertransference with the borderline patient. In *Advances in Psychotherapy of the Borderline Patient*, ed. J. LeBoit and A. Capponi. New York: Jason Aronson. Also reprinted as Chapter 7 in this present volume.

—— (1979b). Jealousy involving an internal object. In *Advances in Psychotherapy of the Borderline Patient*, ed. J. LeBoit and A. Capponi. New York: Jason Aronson. Also reprinted as Chapter 5 in this present volume.

—— (1979c). The analyst's experience with jealousy. In *Countertransference*, ed. L. Epstein and A. H. Feiner. New York: Jason Aronson.

—— (1979d). *Countertransference and Related Subjects—Selected Papers*. New York: International Universities Press.

Segal, H. (1964). *Introduction to the Work of Melanie Klein*. New York: Basic Books.

Volkan, V. D. (1976). *Primitive Internalized Object Relations—A Clinical Study of Schizophrenic, Borderline, and Narcissistic Patients*. New York: International Universities Press.

—— (1981). *Linking Objects and Linking Phenomena*. New York: International Universities Press.

Winnicott, D. W. (1941). The observation of infants in a set situation. In Winnicott (1958).

—— (1951). Transitional objects and transitional phenomena. In Winnicott (1958).

—— (1958). *Through Paediatrics to Psycho-Analysis*. New York: Basic Books.

Part II

Disturbance in Ego-Functioning

Chapter 3

Non-Differentiation of Ego-Functioning in the Borderline Individual, and Its Effect upon His Sense of Personal Identity

I n earlier papers I (Searles 1965) have discussed some of the impairments of ego-integration and -differentiation which are manifested by schizophrenic patients in the course of their psychoanalytic therapy. Here I shall explore some aspects of ego-non-differentiation which I have encountered in working with borderline individuals. For brevity's sake, I shall not attempt to discuss these patients' comparable difficulties with ego-integration.

This chapter was originally presented at the Sixth International Symposium on the Psychotherapy of Schizophrenia, in Lausanne, Switzerland, on September 28, 1978. Published in *Psychotherapy of Schizophrenia: Proceedings of the Sixth International Symposium on the Psychotherapy of Schizophrenia, Lausanne, September 28–30, 1978,* edited by C. Müller; Amsterdam: Excerpta Medica, 1979.

The ways in which the borderline patient manifests his difficulties with ego-differentiation are fascinatingly subtle, in this regard, by contrast to the relatively manifest struggles of schizophrenic patients. Typically, it is only after several to many months of therapy that we begin to see how pervasively unable he is to differentiate, at a more than superficial level, between nocturnal dreams or daytime fantasies on the one hand, and perceptions of outer reality on the other hand; between memories of the past and perceptions of the present; between emotions and physical sensations; between thoughts (and/or feelings) and behavioral actions; between symbolic and concrete levels of meaning in communications; between himself and the other person; between himself and the whole outer world; between human and nonhuman, animate and inanimate, ingredients of the outer world; and so on. We become accustomed to hearing him say, as one woman reported several years along in her therapy, "I woke up this morning with a feeling that I couldn't remember whether it was a dream, fantasy, or real. I'm referring to my daughter's telling me, 'Grandpa called this morning, and said that he and Grandma are coming for a visit.' I think I dreamt it or imagined it, but I wish it were true."

The Subjective Experience of the Patient Who Has Not Yet Achieved Enduring, Internalized Images of Himself and of the Therapist

It usually requires years of therapy for the borderline patient to achieve a durable, internalized image of himself and of the therapist. Prior to the achievement of this degree of differentiation in his ego-functioning, he experiences the therapist's physical absence in outer reality as abolition of the therapist's total existence, from within the patient at the level of mental imagery as well as from outer reality. Also, as I (Searles 1976) have described in an earlier paper, when the patient has become involved with a newly-developed, deeply cherished, internalized mental image of the therapist, the actual therapist in the patient's outer reality may come to feel pitted, paradoxically, in jealous odds with that very mental image of him, with "whom" the patient has become so enthralled.

A man who had been in psychoanalytic therapy with me for several years said something which helped me to understand why borderline patients tend to be so audience-oriented during their treatment sessions—why, that is, instead of their being oriented toward discovering what thoughts, or other internal experiences, occur to them during the course of the session, and verbally reporting these insofar as possible to the therapist, they are concerned instead with the therapist as an ever-present audience whose needs (to be kept interested, or entertained, or whatever) must be kept constantly in the forefront of the patient's attention. This man said, "The only way I know a person is there—that a person exists—is, I have to keep a person in mind, or the person dies, the person disappears." He then referred, by way of example, to a session a week previously during which, for the first time in his therapy, "I completely forgot about you, and when I thought of you again I had no way of knowing that you were alive . . . unless I could see you again and know you were there and get you back in my mind. That's the only way you exist, is in my mind."

It was evident that, at this stage of his treatment, he had not yet established a durable internalized image of me, an image differentiated as such from his perceptions of me in outer reality. Thus, the recurrent loss of his tenuous internalized image of me—a loss occasioned by lack of perceptual reinforcement of that image, while he was lying on the couch and I was sitting silently behind him—tended to have, for him, the impact that I had actually died.

Another man said, at the beginning of a session following my having been out of town for a day, "I really missed you," and went on to say that he never had missed me before at times when I had been away. He explained that previously, at such times, "Everything felt unreal, and I felt unreal; but I didn't connect it with your being away. This time, I missed you, but everything didn't feel unreal this time." Hearing this, I made a note to myself (without interpreting to him) that "It is evident that I am no longer everything to him; I am a separate person to him. He is just growing out of a phase in which I am [i.e., have been] the whole world—all of reality, including the reality of himself, such that the loss of me causes [i.e., has caused] him to experience a feeling of unreality about 'everything' as well as about his 'I'."

The Distortions in the Patient's Sense of Identity, and the Confusion, Traceable to His Non-Differentiation Between His Human Self and His Nonhuman Environment

In a monograph in 1960 entitled, *The Nonhuman Environment in Normal Development and in Schizophrenia,* I (Searles 1960) described human maturation as involving the individual's struggling to achieve and maintain a sense of identity as being human and as being differentiated, thus, from the nonhuman realm of his environment. I described the schizophrenic individual as having failed in this struggle and as having a fundamental need, therefore, for the therapist to help him to achieve this in the long and oftentimes stormy course of psychoanalytic therapy. In a paper in 1972 entitled, "Unconscious Processes in Relation to the Environmental Crisis," I (Searles 1972) commented that over recent decades we have come from dwelling in an outer world in which the living works of nature either predominated or were near at hand, to dwelling in an environment dominated by a technology which is wondrously powerful and yet nonetheless dead, inanimate. I suggested that in the process we have come from being subjectively differentiated from, and in meaningful kinship with, the outer world, to finding this technology-dominated world so alien, so complex, so awesome, and so overwhelming that we have been able to cope with it only by regressing, in our unconscious experience of it, largely to a degraded state of nondifferentiation from it. I suggested, that is, that this "outer" reality is psychologically as much a part of us as its poisonous waste products are part of our physical selves (p. 368).

In my therapy of borderline patients, I find that these persons' subtle and largely unconscious, but pervasively important, incomplete differentiation between their human self and their nonhuman environment gives rise to as frequent and varied distortions, in their own sense of identity and in their transference-perceptions of the therapist, as was so profusely evident in my work with frankly schizophrenic patients at Chestnut Lodge between 1949 and 1964. To give but one example here, a borderline internist commented, concerning a medical colleague with whom he was working in a clinic, "That's a despicable situation, that Powell [entirely as though the person, Powell, were a situation and not at all a human individual]. . . . Probably I'm unfit to be a physician. I realize a *physician of all things* should not feel so much contempt." His tone, as well as his words, in saying, "a physician of all things" clearly referred to a physician as a *thing*. Further, I could glimpse here an unconscious identity-aspect of himself as being a physician to, or for, all things everywhere.

The borderline individual has so much difficulty in

integrating feelings concerning change and loss that we find
in him, although relatively subtly manifested, the kind of
confusion as regards geographic location which is compara-
tively conspicuous in the chronically schizophrenic person.
In a paper concerning my nearly seven years of intensive
psychoanalytic therapy with a chronically schizophrenic
woman, I (Searles 1972) reported that during the first year
of her treatment, I had come to see that, instead of her
missing anyone or any experience from her past, she instead
reexperienced the past in such vivid detail that she tended to
become lost in it—immersed in the past. It became evident
that her walking about on the hospital grounds followed a
very complex pattern indeed; there were many areas of the
grounds which she avoided because they tended to remind
her of grief-laden areas of her past. I came to see that it was
not simply that entering into those areas would cause her to
experience grief, but that she had to avoid becoming actually lost in those areas of the past (p. 41).

A woman whose long-chronic schizophrenia had sub-
sided, after much therapy, to a borderline level of severity
said at the beginning of a session, getting toward summer,
"it is so *hot* on Wisconsin Avenue, and then when you turn off
it and walk down Oliver Street, there's *such* a cool breeze,
it's like you're in a different city!" She said this in such a tone
as clearly to indicate that it was hard for her to be sure that
she was not actually in a different city. That is, she tended to
feel really confused, disoriented in place, by encountering
the cool breeze. I am reminded, here, of the experiences
which Proust (1927) chronicled in *Remembrance of Things
Past.* This woman's life was lived, for a long time as she
gradually moved more and more fully outside of and away
from the sanitarium, in such a way that each of three places
became central to her sense of identity: the sanitarium, her
apartment in the city, and my office where she had therapy-
sessions several times a week. It became evident to me that

she had often to struggle, behind a relatively self-possessed demeanor, to keep clear whether at any one moment she were in my office, or rather in the sanitarium or her apartment. There were undoubtedly many times when she was in all three, simultaneously, at a largely but not entirely unconscious level.

He Unconsciously Reacts to His Thinking, and His Thoughts, as Being Omnipotent

I find fascinatingly subtle the borderline individual's manifestations of his unconscious conviction that his thinking possesses an omnipotent power. This subjective omnipotence of thinking is based in an incomplete differentiation between inner and outer reality. In my paper in 1962 entitled, "Scorn, Disillusionment and Adoration in the Psychotherapy of Schizophrenia," I (Searles 1962) noted that the child's too early, too great "disillusionment"—a repressed and incomplete process, rather than a completed one—with the mother, occurring before differentiation between inner and outer reality has solidly occurred, leaves him with the unconscious conviction that the emotion of disillusionment, if one permits oneself to feel it, destroys the other person (p. 49). That is, such an individual would feel not merely that his formerly idealized *image of* the mother has been destroyed but that the flesh-and-blood mother *in outer reality* has been destroyed in the same process—for he cannot differentiate between the internalized image and the corresponding person in outer reality.

In Chapter 6, which deals with borderline thought disorder, I report on, among various determinants of this disorder, a subjective omnipotence of thinking, on the following basis. This man's thought disorder, at perhaps its deepest level, included a *lack of qualitative differentiation between inner and outer reality*—between mental images and verbal thoughts, on the one hand, and the corresponding objects in outer reality. This reification of his thoughts greatly complicated his ability to think freely, for he feared the tangible power of thoughts to do harm either to himself or to others (see also Searles 1969, p. 661).

One man was saying, ". . . I was thinking in my *head* of all sorts of different things, . . ." said fully as though he does some of his thinking *elsewhere*. My impression, based upon long work with him by then, was that he unconsciously regarded changes in the outer world as equivalent to, or as caused by, his thinking. Another man whose treatment I supervised for many months mentioned, similarly, to his therapist, ". . . I've been thinking in my mind that . . ."

A woman said, in reference to her long-depressed mother, who had died several years before, "The more I think about my mother, the more it seems that she was depressed." I had had enough experience with her, by now several years along in her therapy, to hear in this superficially unremarkable comment a subtle hint of her unconscious conviction that her own thinking possessed the power to have caused her mother to become increasingly depressed, and even dead. Significantly, it was extraordinarily difficult, for years, for me to help her to resolve her resistance to allowing her thinking really free rein in the free-associational process.

A man made a comment, during one of his sessions, very similar in nature to the one I have quoted from the just-mentioned woman. He said, while reminiscing about his mother and maternal grandmother, ". . . Probably if I looked at pictures of Mom and Grandma, they would be *quite* similar. . . ." This sounded to have an unconscious meaning that he could cause the two actual persons to come to appear quite similar to one another, by looking at pictures of them.

A woman commented, thoughtfully, "The things of the past—the physical things of the past—are no more as I think of them, . . ." This statement, again superficially unremarkable, seemingly expressive of a growing realization that various things of the past were now irretrievably gone, was said in such a tone as to convey her unconscious conviction that her very thinking of the things of the past had destroyed them.

Omnipotent-Based Disillusionment, and Denial of Much of Outer Reality as Protective Defense Against That Disillusionment

The previously-mentioned woman who had been chronically schizophrenic, and was now borderline, was expressing disillusionment with doctors; she spoke, for example, of a news item about doctors' politically agitating, in a convention in Atlantic City, for some selfish goals. She went on to express disillusionment with people in general for being so untidy; she described in detail, for example, how littered with papers and other refuse was the area about her apartment building. She said, with intense feeling, "it's awful to think that people would be so untidy! . . ." I had become, by now, long used to knowing what violence such a kind of thinking, on her own part, wrought upon her most cherished, idealized images of herself, and clearly heard an unconscious meaning, here, of "It's awful *of me* to think that people would be so untidy!" It was becoming increasingly evident, in other words, that a long-maintained, unconscious denial on her part, a denial of large sectors of outer reality (including the reality of most of what had gone on in her parental home during her formative years), had had to be sustained for the major reason that the sheer perceiving of any "outer" ugliness, and the sheer thinking in acknowledgment of that, brought with it a comparable denigration of her own formerly idealized image(s) of herself—a self still so incompletely differentiated from that "outer" reality.

Some two years later, this same woman, commenting upon the recent blackout—general failure of electricity—in New York City, said, "It's awful to think that anything like that would happen, . . ." She was sitting (rather than lying) on the couch, as she often did, and as she said this I could see on her face a look of horror. Her facial expression, coupled with those words, conveyed the unconscious meaning, as many times before, "It's *awful of me* to think that anything like that would happen."

A few months later, in the closing minutes of a session during which she had spoken, as usual, of many things, she said, "I got some very sad news." She went on to describe that a saleslady who had often waited upon her, in a fashion shop, and whom she had found very helpful over the years, had been robbed and beaten so severely by some teenagers that she had had to be hospitalized. She said, "I'm very worried about it; *it's terrible to think* [my emphasis] that anything like that would happen." I immediately felt that this linked up with her having given evidence, earlier in the session, of dissociated rage toward her social worker, a lady whom she ordinarily found helpful to her but who had had to cancel her most recent weekly appointment with the patient. It appeared that rather than her becoming aware of a rageful fantasy of beating her social worker, she instead felt intensely self-condemnatory for even thinking of the other lady's (upon whom her unconscious rage was displaced) having been severely beaten. Very characteristic of her had been her describing the cancelled appointment in such a way that, while conspicuously free from any manifested outrage herself, she had put me under intense pressure to become outraged at the social worker on her behalf. Specifically, although remaining silent, I had felt under intense pressure to feel and say, "You mean she didn't even let you *know?*—Why, that's *outrageous!*"

I have been trying here to show that, in borderline ego-functioning, sometimes the disillusionment may be experienced as destroying predominantly the person in *outer* reality, whereas, on other occasions, it has a predominant impact, through the individual's introjection of that disillusioning other person, of a real diminution of the patient's own *self.* Thus, just as one individual could speak of a time when he had become disillusioned with his father's athletic prowess by saying, "When my father's athletic ability vanished," so can another individual say, of a person whom she has come to despise, "Just *seeing* her makes me feel diminished."

One woman was clearly in a general state of disillusionment and was expressing this in regard to, for example, the quality of our public schools, and of those in Maryland more specifically. "This whole state, I guess, is bullshit when ya think about it," she said, in such a tone as to convey the unconscious meaning that one's thinking about Maryland causes the whole state to become, literally, bullshit.

A man speaking, very similarly, of his mother whom he had visited recently and with whom he was feeling, currently, deeply disillusioned, said, "I think of my mother being a stupid whore—*in my mind* [his emphasis; all this said with startling concreteness, as though his mother in his mind were a flesh-and-blood, stupid whore there], . . . a mess of garbage, that's what I feel like. . . ." It was clear that he was so largely undifferentiated from his mother that disillusionment with her brought with it disillusionment with himself, and *vice versa*; and, further, that each side of this disillusionment served, momentarily, as a defense against his experiencing the fullness of the other side of it.

One woman while free associating spoke, by parapraxis, of her eldest brother, Ben, while intending to speak of her eldest son, Bill; she said, "Ben—Bill—Why do I mix *them* up? . . . I know from the way *I confuse people* [this emphasis mine] that I have no appreciation of people in their own right. . . . I just don't differentiate between people at all—they just don't exist as separate people. . . ." The way she said, "I confuse people" here conveyed the unconscious meaning that she confuses not only her mental images of people, but also people in outer reality. That is, as with disillusionment, so with confusion, the borderline individual unconsciously experiences his own confusion as causing this same confusion in the outer world. The just-mentioned woman persisted, through several years of therapy, in experiencing herself as endowed with witchlike powers, including the power to sow confusion in the world around her, and was variously delighted with and terrified of these subjectively suprahuman powers.

The Power of the Patient's Transference Makes the Therapist Conform Appreciably to It

A major reason for the borderline patient's persistent difficulty in becoming able to differentiate between an internal, mental transference-image of the therapist on the one hand, and the therapist himself on the other hand, consists in the fact that his transference-reactions and -attitudes are so powerful in their effect, over the long course of the therapy, as to mold the therapist's actual feelings and behavior, during the sessions, into conformity with those transference-images. This basically delusional-transference impact is so effective that the therapist himself comes to have great difficulty in perceiving the element of the transference, differentiated as such from the reality of his usual sense of his own identity.

In this connection, the treatment of the borderline individual presents difficulties only somewhat more moderate in degree than those I (Searles 1965) have described as true of the work with the frankly and chronically schizophrenic individual.

When I left the staff of Chestnut Lodge, about 15 years ago, I had been working for several years with six chronically schizophrenic individuals, four hours per week in each instance. It was only some few years later that I came to realize, in retrospect, how important in my collective work with all these patients had been his or her transference, from the outset of the treatment in each instance, to me as being a basically ineffectual mother. I had felt realistically ineffectual, with each of them and all of them collectively, to such a very high degree that it was only now, after the interim of these years, years during which my self-esteem had been finding greater support from various sources, that I could achieve a better-differentiated perspective upon that Chestnut Lodge experience. I now discerned clearly, in retrospect, that I had been unable fully to differentiate, and maintain as differentiated, these patients' *transference-* based, unquestioned assumptions that I was an ineffectual mother, as distinct from my own then-current-experience-based perceptions of my own effectiveness or ineffectiveness in the actual work of the therapy, day after day and year after year.

The Ramifying Effects of the Borderline Individual's Inability to Differentiate Clearly Between His Self and the Surrounding World

It is generally agreed that denial is one of the major unconscious defense-mechanisms in borderline ego-functioning. The main point I wish to make in this paper is that unconscious denial of all sorts of aspects of "outer" reality has, as one of its major determinants, the unconscious inability to differentiate clearly between the self—including the sense of personal identity—and the outside world. The woman who had conveyed unconsciously the conviction that it was *terrible of her* to think of the recent blackout in New York City was threatened with an unconscious image of herself as *being* the frightening blackout with its looting and other chaotic aspects. Linked with this dissociated image of herself as omnipotently malevolent was a contrasting image of herself as limitlessly vulnerable, totally impotent, in face of an invading outside world which had the power thus to mold her sense of identity, dependent only upon the changing conditions in the "outside" world. Whereas at one extreme she unconsciously believed her own thinking (and fantasying) to control omnipotently the outer reality, at the other extreme she experienced her internal world, including her sense of personal identity, to be totally controlled by that outer reality.

During the past two or three years I have come to see more clearly why such a patient needs so desperately to maintain, perhaps for many years in therapy, her denial. It is not merely that she is failing to perceive and take full account of some important *aspect* of *outer* reality. Far beyond that, she is struggling to preserve her familiar sense of personal identity, which otherwise would be replaced by that denial-encysted sector of "outer" reality. She is threatened unconsciously lest her familiar sense of identity as a human being be replaced by, for example, a sense of identity as nonhuman and omnipotently malevolent.

In a paper in 1975 entitled, "The Patient as Therapist to His Analyst," I (Searles 1975) included a clinical vignette which is relevant here. The patient, here called Miss J., is the previously mentioned woman who, formerly chronically schizophrenic, has been functioning for some years now at a predominantly borderline level. An important part of this woman's history consisted in her having come to occupy the parental-family role of caretaker to her emotionally disturbed mother.

I described that the last room-mate she had had, for about a year before moving to an apartment of her own in Washington, was a highly psychotic woman whose verbal and physical behavior was often highly disorganized. Miss J. would describe it that Edna was being, once again, "in a whirl." In one of her analytic sessions with me during that year, she asked me whether it would be all right with me for her to go to New York City on the following Sunday, to visit her female cousin there, and to miss her Monday hour. I said that it was all right with me; for reasons I shall not detail here, I did not respond in an analytic-investigative manner, as I would do in working with a neurotic patient. She then said something about not being sure she could do it—i.e., make the trip to New York City alone. "I feel so little in New York. . . . I guess I always think of New York as a big city in a whirl. . . ."

The idea which struck me, upon hearing this, is that she projected onto New York City her own still-largely-repressed confusion, and tended to feel responsible—a responsibility overwhelmingly awesome to me as I sensed it—for the whole gigantic, perceivedly confused city. Her psychosis had first become overt, many years before, shortly following a visit to this cousin in New York City, and I felt that here I was being given a brief glimpse into the nature of her psychotic experience then. Later on, in looking over my notes on this session, I realized that New York City was unconsciously equivalent, for her, to her overwhelmingly confused mother, for whom the patient felt so totally responsible.

About two years later, in a relatively recent session, she was describing to me her weekly visit to her current social worker at Chestnut Lodge, a woman toward whom Miss J.

has a mother-transference which involves, amidst clearly ambivalent feelings, a great deal of admiration, fondness of a sisterly sort, and a maternal caring for the social worker. She said, "Recently she's been so busy, her office looks like a whirl!", making an illustrative whirling gesture with her arm as she said this.

This same woman, in a session about two months later, manifested some of the psychodynamics of her confusion which are relevant here. Although continuing to maintain herself in her apartment in Washington, she had not become able to drive a car, but had to rely upon buses to get to her therapy-sessions with me four hours per week, and to attend unit meetings on her former sanitarium-ward once or twice a week.

She began the session by speaking of her "confusion" in "going from one place to another." She was detailing, by way of example, her bus-trip to Rockville (the suburb where the sanitarium is located) yesterday, and the ward-unit meeting she attended, all of which evidently had proved confusing to her. The confusion of which she spoke was manifest in her demeanor, and it was evident to me that her having come, even, from my waiting room into my office, a few moments before, had contributed to her confusion. It became apparent within the first few minutes that this confusion resulted from an unconscious need on her part to dissociate both (a) her fury at the change (a new insight to me in this connection) and, as I had known for many years to be true of her, (b) her feelings of loss evoked by the change. Both these kinds of dissociated feelings were evident in her facial expressions as she sat on the couch and talked.

She had said about a week previously that "I suppose if I were driving a car I could be many places in a day." This statement conveyed to me an unconscious meaning that she would be in many places *simultaneously* in one day. I realized, more clearly than before, that she felt threatened, unconsciously, lest she would become confused by driving a car—would come confusingly to experience herself as being in many places at once.

In a subsequent session, she complained that "The bus I got on was so shaky, I almost fell over. . . ." She then added, "It made me very nervous, to be such a shaky bus." Although it was clear that she consciously meant something to the effect that "Because the bus proved to be such a shaky one, I became very nervous," her statement clearly conveyed an additional, unconscious meaning to the effect that "It made me very nervous to become such a shaky bus." Incidentally, my (Searles 1960) monograph concerning the nonhuman environment contains many comparable examples of patients' unconsciously feeling at one with various nonhuman ingredients of their surroundings.

Another woman struggled, for years, with a conflict as to whether to continue living in the Washington area or to return to Chicago, where she had spent the first 25 years of her life. She projected this conflict, and with it much of her unconscious sense of her personal identity, upon these two cities to a striking degree. On occasion, she spoke in a tone as though the two huge cities were at war with one another. In one session when she said, "I think I mentioned to you, when I was talking about *the New York–Chicago conflict* [my emphasis], . . ." this was said in such a tone as to conjure up, in my mind, an even vaster conflict, one of interplanetary dimensions, à la H. G. Wells.

The woman I have mentioned several times was planning, at one point relatively early in her out-patient living, upon a rare visit to her cousin in New York City. One concern of hers was that the smog in both cities was, as attested by the news-reports, very bad. As the time for her trip drew near, she said that, because the smog in New York was worse now than that in Washington (confirmed by the newscasts), she didn't know whether she would be making the trip after all, and she indicated that her cousin had become exasperated with her for being so indecisive. "I can't guarantee anything," she said protestingly. I had been saying nothing; yet she seemed unsure whether I expected some guarantee from her. "Betty [her cousin] is very annoyed and angry [said in such a context, and so ambiguously, that I was not sure whether she meant that Betty was angry at her, or at the smog in New York] . . . I told her [during one of their many telephone calls] I can't help it; it'll depend on whether the smog gets less—*I* can't help it that the smog is so bad. . . ."

Parenthetically, I had encountered an abundance of data from her, over the years, to indicate that her parental-family members did indeed tend to hold her responsible for innumerable events and situations which were far beyond the realistic control of any human individual. Surely, she had been given to feel, from very early childhood on, an uneasy sense of total responsibility for the unpleasant, obscure, vaguely threatening emotional climate, so to speak, of the family home. Throughout many years of my work with her, she clearly tended variously to feel responsible for the weather, or to project upon me such a responsibility.

Later in the session which I have been detailing, she said, "Well, maybe things will clear up," consciously referring to the smog in New York, but unconsciously conveying the additional meaning, "Well, maybe things will clear up between Betty and me."

It turned out that she did make the trip in question, and upon her return felt that she had done relatively well during it. She commented that the weather had been good, "So *that* went pretty well," she said, in a tone implying that this had been one of her own more successful accomplishments during the visit.

In a later session she commented, ". . . I was glad to stay in my apartment yesterday. . . . I noticed the air wasn't good yesterday—*I didn't know if it was me or the air* [my emphasis], but they [i.e., the T. V.] did say it was very polluted."

The sense of personal identity, in some of these patients, is projected upon the outer world to a very striking degree. One woman, for instance, spoke of a

". . . feeling that everything outside of myself has more value, is more me, than I am, . . . my surroundings; so I try to control all of it, because if something's happening to my surroundings, it's happening to me—not as *though* it's happening to me, but it *is* happening to me, . . . I'm the shell, but the content of me is all outside of myself: . . . You're part of it and this room is part of it, and a lot of other people are part of it—Ed [her husband], of course, and my children, and my house. . . . I'm just a lifeless shell that walks around among these things, that imagines it's alive. But it isn't; I'm really not—being in a coffin, as mother was. . . ."

In the instance of one woman whom I treated for several years, I came to see with considerable clarity, relatively late in the work, that she had had a powerful transference to all of outer reality as personifying, in her unconscious experience, a dominating, withholding mother whose power she was determined to minimize and whose existence, in fact, she strove insofar as possible to deny. I had never seen this particular kind of transference-attitude, with this degree of clarity, in my work, years before, with hospitalized, chronically schizophrenic patients, and I immediately felt that this transference-phenomenon helped, in retrospect, to account for their so massive, and so long maintained, unconscious denial of outer reality. Time does not allow me, here, to spell out some of the transference-events which helped me to see this in the instance of this woman. Suffice it to say that she, similarly to the far more ill, long-hospitalized patients, had

shown heretofore, year after year, a maddeningly high degree of self-containment, of imperviousness to the outer
world which included myself and my attempts at interpretation.

Summary

In this chapter I have emphasized that the borderline individual's signs and symptoms of ego-non-differentiation are
fascinatingly subtle, by contrast to the frankly schizophrenic patient's relatively conspicuous difficulties in this
area. His tenuous internal image, if any, of the therapist is
easily lost in the absence of much perceptual feedback from
the latter. In that event, since the internal image is not well
differentiated from the object in outer reality (the therapist), he reacts as though not only the image but the therapist himself has gone out of existence.

His sense of personal identity is not well differentiated
from his surroundings—not only the human but also the
nonhuman environment. Geographic moves thus tend to
cause him confusion and loss of his sense of personal identity.

His incomplete ego-differentiation between inner and
outer reality causes him to react to his own thinking, and
various aspects of his affective life, as having an omnipotent
power over external reality. Experiences of disillusionment
tend to make him feel that not merely has his image of the
disillusioning person now changed, but that he has destroyed that actual person in outer reality. Similarly when
he becomes confused, he reacts unconsciously in terms of his
having sown confusion, omnipotently, throughout his outer
world.

Denial, which is widely agreed to be among his major
defenses, is one of the bulwarks of his tenuous sense of

personal identity. Admission into awareness of that area of outer reality which has long been encapsulated by denial brings with it, for him, two enormous threats. First, because *perceiving* is unconsciously equated with omnipotently *causing*, he feels overwhelming guilt at perceiving such things as illness and death and damage in the world. Secondly, his incomplete differentiation between inner and outer reality tends to make him experience this newly revealed realm as being predominantly in the nature of a horrifying and strange inner world, in which his personal identity is, if not limitlessly weak and vulnerable, then malevolently omnipotent.

I have touched, also, upon some of the inherent difficulties in the therapist's working with borderline individuals, such as his becoming unable to differentiate between the patient's transference-distorted images of him, and his usual sense of his own identity as being relatively healthy and competent; and his vulnerability to becoming jealous of the patient's newly-established and enthralling internal image of him.

References

Proust, M. (1927). *À la Recherche du Temps Perdu, VII, Le Temps Retrouvé*. Paris: Librairie Gallimard. Published in English in 1970 as *Time Regained*. London: Chatto & Windus, Ltd. Also published as *The Past Recaptured*. New York: Random House.

Searles, H. F. (1960). *The Nonhuman Environment in Normal Development and in Schizophrenia*. New York: International Universities Press.

—— (1962). Scorn, disillusionment, and adoration in the psychotherapy of schizophrenia. *Psychoanalysis and the Psychoanalytic Review* 49:39–60. Reprinted in Searles (1965).

—— (1965). *Collected Papers on Schizophrenia and Related Sub-*

jects. London: Hogarth Press. New York: International Universities Press. See especially papers 10, 11, 18, 19.

—— (1969). A case of borderline thought disorder. *International Journal of Psycho-Analysis* 50: 655–664. Reprinted in Searles (1979), pp. 109–131. Also reprinted as Chapter 6 in this volume.

—— (1972). Unconscious processes in relation to the environmental crisis. *Psychoanalytic Reveiw* 59:361–374. See especially p. 368. Reprinted in Searles (1979), pp. 228–242.

—— (1972). Intensive psychotherapy of chronic schizophrenia: a case report. *International Journal of Psychoanalytic Psychotherapy* 10(2):30–51. See especially p. 41. Reprinted in Searles (1979), pp. 243–266.

—— (1975). The patient as therapist to his analyst. In *Tactics and Techniques in Psychoanalytic Psychotherapy, Vol. II: Countertransference,* ed. P. L. Giovacchini, p. 95. New York: Jason Aronson. Reprinted in Searles (1979), pp. 380–459.

—— (1976). Jealousy involving an internal object. Presented at New York Conference on Borderline Disorders, New York City, November 20. Published in *Advances in Psychotherapy of the Borderline Patient,* ed. J. LeBoit and A. Capponi, pp. 347–403. New York and London: Jason Aronson, 1979. Also reprinted as Chapter 5 in this present volume.

—— (1979). *Countertransference and Related Subjects—Selected Papers.* New York: International Universities Press.

Chapter 4

Dual- and Multiple-Identity Processes in Borderline Ego-Functioning

Due in part to a too literal interpretation of some of Erikson's (1956) early writings concerning ego identity, I long thought the sense of identity in a healthy person to be essentially monolithic in nature, comprised in large part of well-digested part identifications with other persons. But in more recent years, especially in the course of exploring the psychodynamics of the border-

Presented at the International Conference on Borderline Disorders, at The Menninger Foundation, Topeka, Kansas, March 20, 1976.

Reprinted from *Borderline Personality Disorders* edited by Peter Hartocollis, M.D., Ph.D., by permission of International Universities Press, Inc. Copyright 1977 by International Universities Press, Inc. Reprinted on pp. 460–478 in *Countertransference and Related Subjects — Selected Papers* by Harold Searles, M.D. New York: International Universities Press, 1979.

line patient, in whom the sense of identity coexists simultaneously in two or more internal objects, I have come to see that the healthy individual's sense of identity is far from being monolithic in nature. Rather, it involves myriad internal objects functioning in lively and harmonious interrelatedness, all contributing to a relatively coherent, consistent sense of identity which springs from and comprises all of them, but does not involve their being congealed into so unitary a mass as I once thought. I have come to believe that the more healthy a person is, the more consciously does he live in the knowledge that there are myriad "persons"—internal objects each bearing some sense-of-identity value—within him. He recognizes this state of his internal world to be what it is—not threatened insanity, but the strength resident in the human condition.

Examples of the Patient's Phraseology as Subtly Revealing of Multiple-Identity Functioning

Often the content of a patient's remark seems ordinary enough, but the feeling tone conveyed gives the analyst a glimpse of the patient's unconscious functioning in terms of a dual or multiple identity. A married woman comments, "I suppose the most tolerable compromise with these hungers of mine is to go with another couple, so I'd have a chance to share ideas with another man." Here she reveals both her unconscious image of herself as a man, as well as that of her being a couple. On another occasion, she describes, "One time when I was smoking some grass, and *Bill were* [my italics] having—and Bill and I were having an argument . . ." Her slip here reveals her unconscious image of Bill as being two persons (a projection of her own internal state). A male patient makes a similarly meaningful slip in speaking of one of his several cousins, "He's the *ones* [my italics]—the one who's a lawyer." An attorney says of his opponent in a forthcoming case, "He's filled with vindictiveness; he's determined to *kill me off* [my italics] during the trial." Common usage tends to confine the phrase "kill off" to doing away with multiple foes, rather than a single one.

A woman patient reproaches me with, "You *overran* [my italics] me yesterday," unconsciously projecting on me her own multiple-ego functioning in alluding to me as though I were a herd of stampeding horses, or a horde of insects. Another woman states, "My mother has a large head, y'know." This seems mundane enough in content, but it was said with an intonation that conveyed the unconscious meaning, "My mother has a large head, *among other* heads in her possession." This reminds me of a frankly psychotic woman's delusion that either her head, or mine, was replaced by a succession of other heads on innumerable occasions in the course of our sessions.

Within another woman's ordinary-seeming statement that "I feel terribly uneasy in my family, in my marriage, in my home" is a feeling tone which reveals the existence, at an unconscious level, of three separate identities in her—one having to do with her family; a second, with her marriage; and a third, with her home. A much-traveled woman says, "I feel more disturbed in England than I do in other countries. . . . I feel more comfortable in Italy; I feel more comfortable in France. I used to feel all right in Canada." Again, this innocuous-seeming statement is said in a curious manner that conveys the unintended meaning that, at an unconscious level, she is living simultaneously as several different selves, in England and in other countries, including Italy and France.

Many patients who habitually and frequently add parenthetically, in the course of their reporting, "Y'know" imply the unconscious meaning that "You know, because you are having or have had the same experience; your experience is always a twin of mine."

Equally frequent is the patient who, in reporting some recently past incident, expresses puzzlement about some aspect of his own behavior, either implying or, much less often, explicitly stating that, "It wasn't like me to react as I did." Here is an allusion to the presence of another "me," this one unconscious, who governed his behavior in the past incident. This is a muted variation of the frankly paranoid person's delusion that occult forces were governing his mind and behavior. One paranoid patient was convinced for years that innumerable "doubles" of herself existed, and that supernatural forces unpredictably replaced her self with one or another of these doubles, which then carried out destructive behavior for which she herself was later held accountable. A borderline young woman revealed a subtle hint of paranoid reaction to one of her internal objects when, having found herself uncharacteristically late for her college classes, she said, "So I wonder if there's something cooking." Clearly she meant here, something at work in her own unconscious, but with the unintended, paranoid-flavored allusion to the possibility that external forces were influencing her. She added, in the same vein, "I wonder if there's something going on. It's not like me to be late for classes. . . ."

The Patient Who Doesn't Know Where to Begin

It may not be deeply significant if a patient occasionally begins a session with the statement, "I don't know where to begin." It may be simply a realistic attempt to cope with, for example, the fact that much has been happening around him and within him of late. But I began to realize some two years ago that the patient who more often than not begins the session with this statement (or some variation upon it) is unconsciously saying, "It is not clear which one of my multiple I's will begin verbally reporting its thoughts, its feelings, its free associations, during this session." That is, it is not basically that there are too many competing subjects for this "I" to select among to begin the reporting, but rather that there are too many "I's" which are, at the moment, competing among "themselves" as to which one shall begin verbalizing. One such patient explained, after an initial silence in which his physical demeanor was expressive of "I don't know where to begin," that during that silence he had been feeling partly like Jimmy, a boyhood friend who was given to temper tantrums—and, evidently, partly like a much more adult, and quite different, person. A woman, who had become able, over the course of her analysis, to integrate into her conscious sense of identity many previously warded-off part identities, began a session by saying, in a manner which I felt expressive of much ego strength, in a kind of confident good humor, "Now let's see; which one of my several identities will materialize today?"

Certain Significances of the Use of the Word "We"

Some patients' reminiscences about childhood are expressed not in terms of "I," but rather in terms of "we." Such a patient almost invariably recalls that "we" used to do this or that. He scarcely ever says "I" in this connection, and the analyst is left largely in the dark as to whom "we" is meant to include. My impression is that the patient's sense of identity is essentially symbiotic in nature (as was true of each of the patients mentioned here), with the sense of identity being either dualistic or multiple, and with an ever-changing shifting of the symbiotic partners in that sense of identity.

Several years ago I encountered comparable data in a supervisory session, in which the female supervisee was describing her work with a hospitalized, frankly psychotic man who showed an extraordinarily severe problem in terms of multiple-identity functioning and, by the same token, of symbiotic interpersonal relatedness. Time after time, as the supervisee herself reported to me that "We decided to meet on the sun porch," or "We talked for a few minutes about that," it was impossible for me to know whether "We" referred to the supervisee and the patient, to the supervisee and one of the ward-staff members, or to the supervisee and the whole ward-staff collectively. I began to realize how impossible it was for the deeply confused patient to discern with whom he was dealing in the supervisee who was immersed in such an ambiguous and shifting "we"-identity.

A few weeks ago, in my third session with a male patient who was still occupied mainly with presenting details of his history, I suddenly realized that he was using "we" with the significance I am describing here. I had already become accustomed to his presenting himself more as a married couple than as an individual. He spoke of his wife nearly as much as he did of himself, so that it was as though the wife were ever-present in our sessions. In this third session I noticed that he would describe the events over a relatively long stretch of the marriage—detailing what "we" had done during that time, mentioning relatively briefly that his mother-in-law had intruded briefly but disruptively on the scene, then resuming his narrative that "we" had moved to another part of the country, detailing at length what "we" had done there, mentioning a brief affair he had had, then resuming his narrative of what "we" had done in subsequent years. I am oversimplifying here, but, in essence, I realized that at an unconscious level, "we" did not refer consistently to his symbiotic identity comprised of himself and his wife. Rather, at the time when the mother-in-law arrived on the scene, she had replaced his wife as his symbiotic partner. The "we" who had moved to another part of the country had been, in his unconscious experience, himself and his mother-in-law. Similarly, later on his mother-in-law had been replaced by his mistress; it was a symbiotic himself-and-his-mistress, not a symbiotic self-and-his-wife, who had participated in the things "we" had done in subsequent years. These were simply three among many symbiotic partners whom he evidently had had at an unconscious level.

Patients' use of "we" as having an unconscious symbiotic-*transference* significance is a phenomenon I find particularly valuable to note—privately, that is. I do not recommend an early interpretation of this phenomenon, lest premature interpretation interfere with the development of the nondefensive, healthy-identification aspects of this phenomenon (those aspects which relate to the patient's development of a constructive introject of the analyst).

A female patient, for example, comments at the beginning of the session, "Why did you move that plant over there?" After a very brief silence (my having made no reply), she goes on "*We* [my italics] were invited out to a Chinese dinner with some people last evening, and went to the Kennedy Center afterward." "We" consciously refers to herself and her husband, as from long-established custom I was assumed to know. But unconsciously it refers, as I had come to realize from this and other transference data, to herself and me (a father-figure in the transference) as a symbiotic-marital partner.

A male patient details for several moments, at the beginning of a session, his feelings about what he experiences as the combative relatedness between us of late, making a number of references to our session of the preceding day. After a pause of only a couple of seconds, he goes on, "I was thinking about yesterday *we* [my italics] took the children to the zoo." Later in the session, referring to a girl friend he had had in California prior to his meeting his wife, he says, "When I think about her, and then I think about myself *here* [my italics], married and with three children. . . ." Data from many sessions substantiate my impression that the "we" who had taken the children to the zoo is, at an unconscious level, himself and me as his transference-mother.

Another male patient characteristically asked at the end of each session, "Time to go?", with such an intonation as to convey, "Time for us to go?" It had become clear to me that he carried an internal image of me within him between (as well as during) our sessions. He frequently began sessions by saying that "We" did thus-and-so with the children over the weekend, or that "We" had another nasty argument last night. It became more and more evident to me as the analysis went on that these communications, like his beginning a session with, "Night before last we had sex," contained unconscious references to me as his symbiotic-identity partner. In the transference, I represented mainly aspects of his symbiotically-related-to mother.

The psychodynamics described by Freud (1917), including the phenomenon of identification with the lost object, and the venting of hostility on the self as a representative of that ambivalently loved-and-hated lost object, when applied to the symbiotic transference phenomena described here, help to illuminate innumerable instances of patients' acting out. One female patient, for example, says, near the beginning of a session, "If I seem relatively unanxious to you this evening—I don't know whether I seem so to you or not; I feel relatively unanxious—it's probably because *we* [my italics; this ostensibly refers to her and her husband] didn't do any acting out [any tirading at their poorly disciplined children] last night."

In dozens of instances from my work over the years, it has been apparent that a patient's acting out (during my or his vacations, or in the usual interims between scheduled sessions) in the form of reckless driving, excessive drinking of alcohol, or self-detrimental behavior at work represents, to a significant degree, his rageful subjecting not of himself but of me, his symbiotic-transference identity-partner, to such punishment. Sometimes such a patient is conscious of his trying to emulate the analyst (or, in some instances, someone ostensibly outside the analytic situation), but then, time and again, he feels unable to carry through the identification successfully; he keeps falling on his face. He represses the fact that at an unconscious level, it is not that he is so much "unable" to maintain the identification, but rather that he keeps on, as it were, burning the other person in effigy within himself; he keeps throwing the internalized analyst upon the latter's face, within himself.

The Analyst's Feelings and Fantasies as Clues to Dual- or Multiple-Identity Functioning

In a discussion in 1973 of the role of jealousy in the fragmented ego, I wrote, concerning my work with a schizoid patient, that for several years I found this man infuriatingly smug. But the time came when, to my astonishment, I realized that what I was feeling was jealousy; *he* so clearly favored his *self* over *me* that I felt deeply jealous, bitterly left out of this mutually cherishing and cozy relationship between the two "persons" who comprised him. In retrospect, I saw that I previously had not developed sufficient personal significance to him to sense these two now relatively well-differentiated "persons" in him and to feel myself capable of and desirous of participating in the "three"-way, intensely jealousy-laden competition. It is my impression that such schizoid patients usually prove so discouragingly inaccessible to psychoanalysis that the analyst and the patient give up before they have reached this lively but disturbing stratum in which the patient's ego fragmentation becomes revealed and the nature of the transference becomes one of a murderously jealous "three"-way competitiveness (pp. 256–257).

Since then I have collected many examples, largely from my work with borderline, schizoid, and narcissistic patients, concerning this phenomenon, which I have thought of as "intrapsychic" jealousy, or jealousy involving an internal object in one or the other of the two participants in the analytic interaction. Recently, for instance, when a woman suddenly interrupted her own reporting by telling herself with intense impatience and exasperation, in an appreciably different tone of voice, "Oh, *shut up*, you *idiot!*", I experienced that by-now-familiar feeling of jealousy of this idiot-"person." Her tone, despite all its furious impatience, was filled with possessive fondness. The "idiot" to whom she spoke was clearly mother's cherished little idiot.

I often sense that one or another patient is functioning unconsciously in a multiple-identity fashion when I feel not simply intimidated or overwhelmed by this overbearing patient but, curiously and more specifically, *outnumbered* by him. With one woman, relatively far along in her analysis, I had the thought, accompanied by a feeling of gratification and fulfillment, "She is moving." But along with this freely conscious thought and feeling, there emerged in me an entirely unbidden fantasy: in my mind's eye, I saw some 50 to 100 people on foot in a caravan, moving in a straggling, undisciplined but clearly peaceable fashion across a landscape—all going essentially together in the same direction. They were clearly all related to one another, and it later occurred to me that the word "tribe" described that relationship. The fantasy was accompanied by a distinct sense of awe at the realization that, evidently for a long time, I had been perceiving, unconsciously, this woman as comprised of so many "persons."

During the long years of analysis before so coherent an internal object relatedness had developed within this patient, she unconsciously defended against the recognition of this internal state, partly through the projection of this or that internal object on the analyst at the slightest opportunity, as it were. As the analyst, I felt that I was somehow interrupting her train of thought, even when I was totally silent. It eventually became clear to her that if I "allowed" her to digress from her intended main path, I was thereby guilty of interrupting her. If I moved slightly in my chair, this tiny sound was reacted to as a gross interruption. She reacted fully as though a third person had come upon the scene, or as though this were the surreptitious sound of a copulating couple (another form of unconscious relatedness of her own internal objects), or, at times, as though a part of her own body-image had suddenly and dismemberingly separated itself out from the rest of that body-image.

Such patients are, in my experience at least, by no means rare. The intensity of their projection of the internal objects which interfere, at an unconscious level, with their more conscious ego-identity functioning tends to have a severely constraining effect on the analyst's functioning at all overtly as an analyst during the sessions. One such patient implies that I am an enormous interference with his attempts to free associate. I often think of his silent and agonized demeanor as being that of a fly imprisoned in amber, and, further, I have noted privately that more often than not, when I venture some intendedly liberating brief interpretation, it is as if the fly in the amber now manages to appear, somehow, even *more* cramped than it was before.

As the patient becomes more aware that the interrup-

tions come primarily from within, he speaks, for instance, of
". . . what I was going to tell you when I was interrupted by
that remembrance of the fantasy I had on the way here," or
he may explain that the reason he is silent so much of the
time is "because I can't stand the sound of my own voice.
. . . It is so grating; it sounds exactly like my mother's
voice. . . ." Such patients make clear, on some of these occasions, that their "own" voice is experienced by them as thoroughly alien, fully equivalent to that of an antagonizing and
entirely separate other person.

Defensive (Transference-Resistance) versus Ego-Integrative Aspects of These Phenomena

Any of these clinical phenomena, when it appears in the
context of the transference, needs to be evaluated in terms of
whether it is predominantly a defensive phenomenon—an
instance of the patient's characteristic borderline, symbiotic
mode of ego functioning in relation to other persons over the
years—or whether it is a predominantly healthy development, signifying (among other things) the patient's having
managed to develop a healthy internal object representation
of the analyst in the latter's own right, beyond his transference significance to the patient. Presumably any one
vignette represents to some degree a mixture of both kinds
of elements.

     As for the defensive functioning of these phenomena,
much of the clinical material presented in my first published paper (Searles 1951), concerning incorporation, is
relevant. That material shows patients' unconscious utilization of incorporation as a mode of defense to maintain under
repression, for example, feelings of hostility and rejection.
On the other hand, most of the examples of dual- and multiple-identity processes described here are of essentially the

same nature as those encountered in what I (Searles 1961) have termed the phase of ambivalent symbiosis, a phase I have described as one traversed by the schizophrenic patient in the course of his improving ego integration. To my way of thinking, the ambivalently symbiotic, dual- and multiple-identity processes so characterologically typical of the borderline patient give way, over the course of psychoanalytic therapy, to better integrated functioning on the patient's part only if the therapist becomes able to function during the sessions in a fashion that allows the ambivalent symbiosis in the transference to become replaced, gradually, with a therapeutic symbiosis, the characteristics of which I have described elsewhere (Searles 1965, 1973).

Space allows me to touch only briefly upon the defensive aspects of the processes under discussion. Time after time in my work with borderline patients, I find that the patient's not responding to my greeting upon his entering the office has come to infuriate me so much that I no longer greet him either. This is one of the ways in which we come to function as alike or as one. Such behavior on the analyst's part is clearly a fostering of symbiosis (or a succumbing to the patient's coercion toward symbiosis), but of a symbiosis which is defensive against antagonism.

A patient who says that "Yesterday when I walked in, you looked as if you were afraid I was gonna attack *me* [my italics]" is clearly fusing with me, unconsciously, at the moment of this slip, as a defense against his anxiety concerning his perception of me as being afraid of him. It is less threatening to him, unconsciously, to be the attacked than the attacking one.

A married man showed, relatively early in his analysis, a multiple-identity mode of ego functioning at an unconscious level. In reminiscing about his childhood, for example, he described the struggles that took place between his alcoholic uncle and his three older brothers, who had attempted to keep the uncle from drinking. *"I can remember fighting with him* [my italics]—not me personally but my three brothers. . . ."* The italicized portion was said *fully* as if he personally had fought with the uncle; it was clear that "I" included his three brothers as well as himself. Incidentally, I was reminded, upon hearing him say this, of a chronically schizophrenic woman who had two sisters, two and four years younger than herself. She once said, in reminiscing about something in her childhood, "When I was six, four, and two," then corrected herself, "When we were six-four-and-two. . . ." The man whom I was just discussing soon established, in the treatment sessions, a defensively symbiotic mode of ego functioning which proved for years highly resistive to analysis. He essentially presented himself as a couple comprised of himself and his wife. This had, of course, various genetic roots; for one thing, he was identifying with a mother who had functioned in his upbringing as both mother and father. It gradually became clear that he was enormously threatened, at an unconscious level, lest I replace his wife as his symbiotic-marital partner, which would mean that I would become not merely, so to speak, his mate in a truly separate object relation, but that I would become the other half (so to speak) of the only ego identity he possessed.

A woman patient came, over the course of many months of analysis, to tell me during one of our sessions, "You are my self," in a way which I found very moving. She then added, with a kind of small-child shyness, the qualification, as though not to frighten me, "not *all* the time." The affective quality of this communication was such as to make me feel that it was not predominantly treatment-resistive in nature, but rather a manifestation of healthy growth in her, made possible partly by my no longer needing to shy away from a more therapeutically symbiotic mode of transference relatedness with her.

In my work with each of several patients, after a number of years the patient has finally asked me, with unusual simplicity and directness, "What's the matter with me?", or "What's wrong with me?" In each instance this question seems consciously expressive of feelings of futility, helplessness, mystification, exasperation, discouragement, and so on, because of various tenacious treatment-resistant symptoms. But in each instance, the question proves to have been expressive, at an unconscious level, of oedipal longings. The patient in this regard is asking me why he or she still does not qualify, in my eyes, to become my romantic and sexual partner. But at a still deeper level the question conveys the meaning, "Why have you still not accepted me fully as your symbiotic identity partner, and by the same token surrendered fully your individual identity and entered fully into a symbiotic identity with me?"

The Patient's Monologue as Being, Unconsciously, a Dialogue

In 1972 I devoted a paper to reporting a few of the developments in my pyschoanalytic therapy with a deeply schizophrenic woman with whom I have been working for 23 years at this writing. For at least 15 of those years I have been accustomed to her spending the bulk of many of her sessions in dialoguing vehemently with one or another part of herself, thus shutting me out to a high degree from talking at all directly with her.

In about 1962 I heard M. A. Woodbury describe, during a staff presentation at Chestnut Lodge, that the auditory-hallucinatory experiences of a chronically schizophrenic woman with whom he was working functioned, during the therapy sessions, to provide her with responses from another person, so to speak, at a time when he was not supplying any comments to her. A paper of mine (Searles 1976) contains comparable data from another patient of mine, much less ill than the one mentioned above, but who has experienced auditory hallucinations for many years. One time this woman came into a session deeply worried about the persisting, and apparently undiagnosed, illness of a cousin. She asked, "What do you think Paul has, Dr. Searles?" I made no direct answer, but endeavored to evoke more of her thoughts in this regard. Within a few seconds, she reported, seriously, "I heard the voices say, 'It's a reaction.'" She quoted the voices as speaking in an explanatory tone, as if providing, authoritatively and decisively, the explanation she had sought in vain from me.

But many years of experiences such as those mentioned in the preceding paragraph did not lead me to recognize, until a very few years ago, how frequently the borderline patient's monologues during the session prove to be, on closer examination, unconscious dialogues—dialogues between two parts of the patient's self, one part being comprised of the introjected analyst, a symbiotic-identity partner, at an unconscious level, in the transference. I emphasize that the fact that he is involved in a dialogue is genuinely unconscious to the patient.

It is important that the analyst become aware of what is happening primarily because otherwise this symbiotic transference functions as a powerful resistance to further analysis. In addition, from the analyst's observing in detail the nature of the dialogue role he is unconsciously being assigned, he can see whether the patient tends to perceive him as being, say, an enthusiastically interested parent or a parent ridden with futility and having essentially nothing to offer him.

In one instance after another, subtle shifts in the patient's tone, as he vocalizes first one side of the dialogue and then the other, help one to detect that this unconscious dialogue is occurring. I shall present a few among a great many available examples, examples which emerge in relative profusion in any average working week for me.

A woman reports a dream in some detail. I say nothing, as usual. After a few seconds of silence, she comments in the tone, now, of an interested observer, "Rather interesting dream," and goes on with her seeming monologue.

Another woman complains, ". . . the *boredom* of the analysis is what gets me down . . . I wonder [tone of discovery] if that's why I've been getting into all these social activities lately?" Then, after a momentary pause, she says in a rather different tone of voice—one now of an interested rejoinder—"Hm! Could *be!*" I distinctly feel that in saying these last three words, she has been functioning unconsciously as though she were I, an interested symbiotic mother in the transference, responding with vocalized interest and acknowledgment of an interesting new idea on her part.

A man reports a detailed précis of a play he attended the previous evening, and which he found very interesting. After having completed this précis, he is silent for a few moments, during which I say nothing. He then gives an interested-sounding, emphatic grunt, and resumes his seeming monologue.

Another man speaks animatedly throughout the session, as usual, while I say little or nothing. Near the end of the session, he pauses briefly, then says in a tone which is now relatively unanimated, futile, and empty, "I don't really know what to say." I sense, here again, that in saying this he is speaking unconsciously as me in the transference—me as the personification of his own schizoid-depressed, mother-identification qualities.

I can merely touch here on the matter of interpreting these symbiotic-transference phenomena to the patient. In general, I do not attempt to interpret them at all early. In line with my concepts about therapeutic symbiosis, it seems to me essential that the analyst come to recognize that these phenomena are representative not merely of unconscious defenses on the patient's part, but also of a need on his part for an appreciable degree of symbiotic relatedness with the analyst, relatedness having both reality as well as transference aspects. A too early attempt at interpretation tends to make the patient feel dismembered. In one instance I suggested to a patient, "When you say '_____,' are you speaking for me?" She replied, "For *you?* [her tone clearly indicating that she found this suggestion preposterous]. *No;* I have enough trouble speaking for *myself.* Why should I speak for *you,*" she added, not really asking a question, but making a bluntly decisive statement. But a few moments later she showed interest in my suggestion. "You mean that if you don't answer, I have to supply an answer?" I replied, ambiguously, "Mm." She did not go further with this matter directly, but within a few moments said, in reference to her brother, "Ed is *torn in two* [my italics] these days about whether to move to Massachusetts."

Conclusions

This chapter is written with the assumption that unconscious dual- or multiple-identity processes are among the fundamental features of borderline ego functioning, and with the additional, implicit assumption that such processes can be found to some detectable degree in the analysis of any patient with an illness of whatever diagnosis. Most of the patients whose clinical material is included here were functioning, to a superficial view, as normal neurotic individuals; their dual- or multiple-identity functioning was at first subtle indeed.

Work with patients such as these has helped me to realize that the normal neurotic individual may be unconsciously reacted to by the other person as comprising, and may unconsciously experience himself as comprising, two or a group or a tribe or a multitude of persons. In the same process, I have also realized that individual psychoanalysis and sociology are, at base, essentially one field of study. This psychoanalytic work has given me a deeper appreciation of the multifarious creativity of the human being's unconscious than I possessed even a few years ago.

References

Erikson, E. H. (1956). The problem of ego identity. *Journal of the American Psychoanalytic Association* 4:56–121.

Freud, S. (1917). Mourning and melancholia. *Standard Edition* 14:243–258. London: Hogarth Press, 1957.

Searles, H. F. (1951). Data concerning certain manifestations of incorporation. In Searles (1965), pp. 39–69.

—— (1961). Phases of patient–therapist interaction in the psychotherapy of chronic schizophrenia. In Searles (1965), pp. 521–559.

—— (1965). *Collected Papers on Schizophrenia and Related Subjects*. New York: International Universities Press.

—— (1972). The function of the patient's realistic perceptions of the analyst in delusional transference. *British Journal of Medical Psychology* 45:1–18. Reprinted in Searles (1979), pp. 196–227.

—— (1973). Concerning therapeutic symbiosis. *The Annual of Psychoanalysis* 1:247–262. Reprinted in Searles (1979), pp. 172–191.

—— (1976). Transitional phenomena and therapeutic symbiosis. *International Journal of Psychoanalytic Psychotherapy* 5:145–204. Reprinted in Searles (1979), pp. 503–576.

—— (1979). *Countertransference and Related Subjects—Selected Papers*. New York: International Universities Press.

Chapter 5

Jealousy Involving an Internal Object

In one of the popular songs of my high school years, a lover is giving expression to his possessive jealousy of all that impinges upon his beloved. He sings, for example, of his jealousy of the moon that shines above, and ends with the rueful realization that "I'm even getting jealous of myself."

Earlier versions of this chapter were presented at the Department of Psychiatry of the University of Wisconsin, Madison, Wisconsin, October 4, 1974, and at the New York Conference on Borderline Disorders (under the auspices of the Advanced Institute for Analytic Psychotherapy) in New York City, November 20, 1976. This chapter previously appeared in *Advances in Psychotherapy of the Borderline Patient,* edited by J. LeBoit and A. Capponi, pp. 347–403; New York: Jason Aronson, 1979.

This romantic ballad in no way prepared me for the discovery, conveyed to me by various of my patients decades later, that one's jealousy of one's "self," and analogous experiences of jealousy which are related to such an internal object within either oneself or the other person in an ostensibly two-person situation, are at the heart of a great deal of severe and pervasive psychopathology and account, in psychoanalytic treatment, for much of the unconscious resistance, on the part of both patient and analyst, to the analytic process.

This "internal-object jealousy" is a significant element in the psychodynamics of patients of whatever diagnosis, and therefore cannot be considered specifically characteristic of borderline patients. But psychoanalytic therapy with these latter individuals provides the arena *par excellence* for the study of this jealousy. In Chapter 4, I described those processes as being among the fundamental features of borderline ego-functioning. The type of jealousy I am describing in the present chapter is a major factor in maintaining the disharmony of the borderline patient's internal-object world and in preventing him, therefore, from experiencing a single, whole, and continuous identity.

My first clinical experience of this strange jealousy-phenomenon occurred in the course of my work, about 30 years ago, with a young man whom at the time I regarded as suffering from nothing more severe than an obsessive-compulsive neurosis, but whom I now know to have been manifesting a borderline schizophrenic degree of impairment of ego-functioning. During one session he began venting intense jealousy in the process of describing, with much hatred and bitterness, that his mother frequently conversed aloud, in a spirit of warmly adoring intimacy, with a hallucinated image of Jesus Christ. The patient's jealousy of her hallucination was unmistakable.

After the session I was left with a sense of how strange

was the nature of his jealousy: when one considered that her hallucination was a projected component of her own unconscious contents,* one saw that he was essentially jealous of her relationship with a part of herself.

Some years later, in the course of my work at Chestnut Lodge with a hebephrenic young woman, I felt an even more strongly memorable impact of her saying, on one occasion, "I guess I'm jealous of myself." She confided this to me partly in the spirit of a painful confession; but it went far deeper than that. It clearly had a connotation of a split in her functional ego, with her ego being in two parts, her "I" and her "myself," equal in valence and in a state of hopelessly jealous odds with one another.

My first remembered experience of feeling within myself jealousy of essentially this same nature—jealousy involving an internal object, in this instance an internal object in the other person, precisely as had been felt by the borderline schizophrenic young man I first mentioned—occurred some years later still, in my work with a hebephrenic middle-aged man. This man had been hospitalized constantly for about 15 years when my work with him began, and for many months his demeanor was marked mainly by silent dilapidation and apathy, punctuated only by sudden and brief streams of vitriolic cursing, seemingly at the world of people around him, as when he was impelled to leave the couch at the end of the corridor, where he customarily reclined during the day, to walk rapidly to the nurses' station for a cigarette.

But after several months of four-hour-per-week psycho-

---

*In more recent years I have come to believe that a hallucination is referable, in significant degree, not only to the patient's projection of his "own" unconscious personality-components, but also to his unconscious perceptions of actually outer reality, perceptions which take the form of the hallucination. But for the purposes of this chapter, that does not diminish the relevancy of the early clinical vignette mentioned here.

therapy (which for the first one and one-half years of my experience with him was conducted in a four-person situation, involving two therapists and another chronically psychotic patient in addition to himself), the daily nurses' reports indicated that Eddie (as he was commonly known) was sleeping poorly, waking up repeatedly during the night and cursing furiously for prolonged periods at, evidently, hallucinatory figures. During the therapy sessions, however, his continued apathetic silences, while the other patient conversed volubly, were among the factors which led to the abandonment of the four-person treatment endeavor, and I went on working with Eddie on an individual basis, for an overall period of nine years.

As those years went on, he became more and more alive in the sessions, with, however, from my point of view, an oftentimes frightening unpredictability, for his aliveness consisted in his suddenly becoming involved, time and again, in trading curses, insults, and belligerent threats with, evidently, one or more hallucinatory figures. For many months after this development had come to dominate the sessions, he seemed still so oblivious of me that I was given to feel part of the woodwork or, one might say, a passerby who sees and hears, in a nearby phone booth, a man wholly immersed in a loud and vitriolic telephone conversation, and utterly unaware of the passerby. On one occasion during this era, when I pressed more strongly than usual to make my presence felt, with some loud comment to him, he retorted in absolute fury, "Shut up! I got company!" and immediately re-immersed himself in his only momentarily interrupted, and very lively, dialogue with the hallucinatory figure(s).

But as the months and years wore on I came gradually to know, from innumerable largely indirect and nonverbal cues, that I was of real interpersonal significance to him. It was in this new era—lasting at least several months—that I found myself prey to the strange jealousy which is the focus of this chapter. He had become by now relatively verbal in speaking directly to me, and on those many occasions when he would turn away suddenly and start conversing with one or another hallucinatory figure who had more powerfully wrested his attention from me, I was left feeling helplessly jealous of his hallucination(s). In the closing two years or so of my work with him, I had become so sure of my personal significance to him that it was easy to perceive data indicating that his hallucinatory experiences, during the sessions, were secondary to the vicissitudes of the relationship between him and me, such that I no longer felt susceptible to jealousy, and was able to work with him concerning his hallucinations as being (as, of course, I knew intellectually they had been all along) transference-based psychotic symptoms, rather than quasi-real rivals of mine. Perhaps I should make plain that at no time did I hallucinate during our sessions; but during the era when I was feeling jealous I had the strange and unsettling *sense* that there were several— not merely two—persons in the room. In the instance of a chronically schizophrenic, severely ego-fragmented woman with whom I have worked for many years, the feeling-atmosphere of the sessions has been, on more than a few occasions, that of a group-relatedness, precisely as was the case for a time in my work with Eddie.

The experiences with these few patients, each of them more than merely neurotically ill, have served for me as a springboard into innumerable subsequent experiences with more subtly-evidenced, but nonetheless centrally pathogenic, manifestations of this same kind of jealousy in schizoid and neurotic patients. I have described earlier in this volume (see pp. 87–88) my work with a schizoid patient— that is, a patient whose degree of illness is common in an office practice. I described that, in this instance, I realized that what I was feeling now was jealousy; *he* so clearly favored his *self* over *me*.

With this mushrooming accumulation of clinical experiences in more recent years, I have come to see that the jealousy-phenomena with which the analyst is accustomed to working, namely, those occurring in a context of three whole persons, are merely—to resort to Breuer's (1893–1895) metaphor for the predominance of unconscious over conscious living—the tip of the iceberg, of which the far greater portion, invisible to a surface view, is comprised of those vastly more frequent and varied jealousy phenomena which involve but two actual persons and an internal object in one or another of them, an internal object which is invested with the feeling-significance (often if not always on a transference-basis) of an actual whole and separate person.

These jealousy phenomena are so varied, and their childhood etiology so diverse, that I can present only a few typical examples. As regards the diagnoses of those patients whose analyses have yielded the clinical vignettes which follow in this chapter, it is not to be assumed that their illnesses were of a *preponderantly* borderline-schizophrenic order of severity. Several of these patients were functioning in a largely normal-neurotic manner. In my experience, significant *areas* of splitting of ego-functioning come to light in the analyses of patients of whatever diagnosis, just as does the "internal-object" jealousy which is based upon such splitting. I share Fairbairn's (1952) opinion that everyone has schizoid factors in his personality. As he puts it:

> . . . The fundamental schizoid phenomenon is the presence of splits in the ego; and it would take a bold man to claim that his ego was so perfectly integrated as to be incapable of revealing any evidence of splitting at the deepest levels, or that such evidence of splitting of

the ego could in no circumstances declare itself at more superficial levels, even under conditions of extreme suffering or hardship or deprivation . . . (p. 8).

Jealousy Involving a Body-Part or Whole Body Upon Which an Internal Object Is Being Projected

One category includes instances wherein a part of one's own body is, at an unconscious level, not a part of one's body image but is reacted to, instead, as being a separate person to whom one reacts with intense jealousy. By now I have become convinced that a male patient's jealousy of his own penis is a frequent, if not regular, factor in the dynamics of men who suffer from sexual impotence and castration anxiety. In the histories of such patients, one learns after some years of their analyses that, in each instance, in childhood his penis had been involved in, as it were, an adoringly intimate relationship with the mother, a relationship from which he had felt jealously excluded, much as though his own penis were a favored younger sibling who had displaced him. Further, in such a patient, his penis, when erect, proves in the analysis to have a transference-significance to him as being the personification of the rigidly autocratic qualities of one or both his parents. The analysis comes to reveal these heretofore unconscious determinants of the symptoms only when the analyst has become approximately as important to the patient as is the latter's penis, and the analyst finds to his astonishment that he is feeling jealous as regards the patient's intimate and fascinated relationship with the latter's own penis. The analyst, that is, first comes to feel as his own the jealousy which the patient himself has dissociated for so many years, jealousy referable to his mother's relationship with his penis.

Frequently indeed, a woman patient will prove after long analysis to have been repressing jealousy of her own breasts, breasts which at her puberty—or in some instances, at the level of the parent's mental imagery, even at her birth—had been the object of such exclusively-focused interest on a parent's part that the girl herself had felt jealously excluded from that intimate "interpersonal" relationship between the parent and the girl's biologically own body-parts. Similarly, a woman's unconscious jealousy of her well-turned legs which are the focus of men's fascinated interest to the large-scale exclusion of the rest of her body (not to mention the non-somatic aspects of herself), may interfere with her integrating these legs into a whole body-image. Again, it is inherent in the successful analyzing of this "intrapsychic" jealousy that the analyst become able to experience it *vis-à-vis* the relationship between the patient and the body part(s) in question, before the patient can be expected to become aware of, and integrate, this strangely jealousy-ridden relationship between herself and one or another introject represented by the body part(s) in question.

One borderline woman, whose body image was composed of a number of different parts in at times murderously jealous war with one another, said of a personnel manager whom she had seen in a job interview, "He kept looking at my *legs*," in a tone implying that all the rest of her had felt largely ignored. The course of her analysis brought to light a kind of dismembering, largely internalized, jealousy in her which was at times of frighteningly self-destructive proportions.

Just as the analyst's becoming aware of feeling jealousy toward a patient's penis, for example, can provide an indispensable clue to a major determinant of the patient's sexual impotence, so can the analyst's recognition of his own jealousy of the patient's *whole body* help in understanding the patient's symptom of depersonalization—his sense of not really inhabiting his own body but of experiencing it, rather, as being an external object alien to him. The unconscious jealousy in the patient which is keeping that body alien from him is first experienced by the analyst.

I first became aware of the role in depersonalization of internal-object jealousy during my supervision of a female therapist's treatment of a chronically schizophrenic woman. It became evident, through the therapist's demonstration to me of the patient's posture and gestures in their largely-silent treatment-sessions, that the patient was offering tantalizingly to the therapist the former's body, not predominantly in an adult-Lesbian sense, but rather in a far more primitive sense, as a physical housing for the therapist's self to occupy. Various of the patient's symptoms of chronic schizophrenia became relatively understandable in terms of the hypothesis that her mother thus had dangled tantalizingly before her, as it were, the mother's body to psychologically inhabit, as the indispensable context for the girl's (as infant and young child) establishment of her first human identification, while at the same time (because of the mother's own emotional difficulties, probably including depersonalization) being unable really to share her body, psychologically, with the daughter for the kind of infant–mother symbiosis which occurs in healthy infancy.

Another way in which a body-part proves to have had a fundamental role in the childhood-etiology of a wide variety of clinical symptoms is through the child's being given reason to feel jealously excluded from the relationship between a parent and one of the latter's own body-parts (entirely as the analyst may come to feel jealous, as described previously, of a patient's relationship with the latter's own penis). The hypochondriacal parent who nurses for years a chronically-ailing stomach or limb, for instance—a body-part having the unconscious significance, for the parent, of a possessively loved transference-parent in turn—is typical of the parents in the histories of such patients, as becomes revealed in the evolution of the transference and corresponding countertransference.

Jealousy Involving a Mental Image as the Third "Person"

In a second broad category of these jealousy-phenomena, it is not a body-part but a mental image which is the third "person" involved in the jealousy-laden transference-countertransference relationship in which patient and analyst come to participate—a mental image within either patient or analyst. In the examples previously given here, mental images have been involved, of course—unconscious mental images of internal objects, mental images which are being projected upon, for instance, a body-part. But this category is comprised of instances wherein the mental image in question is relatively readily recognizable as such, in consciousness, by the person in whom it exists.

The etiologic sources from which such images derive are of limitless variety. For example, it developed that the father of one male patient had given the boy to feel jealous of the middle-aged father's own idealized, youthful "self," still so tangibly alive in the father's nostalgic preoccupation. This same patient subjected my analyst-"self" to such incessant derision, while expressing admiration of my author-"self," that I experienced uncomfortable stirrings of jealousy of the relatively admired author Searles whose works this scornful man was sure I could not possibly have written or, had I done so, then the brain cells which had made this possible had long since died in my skull. Another patient was placed in jealous competition, as his boyhood and young manhood proceeded, with his parents' and older siblings' remembered images of his own baby-self, a self with whom he felt now, as a result, more at jealous odds than in any really well-integrated oneness. His mother never tired of saying fondly, "You were the cutest baby I've ever seen," and this made him feel less cherished and appreciated, in the present, than rejected and jealous of this "cutest baby" she had in her mind's eye.

Not infrequently, so patients' histories and transference-evolutions indicate, a frank psychosis has been precipitated in a setting of the patient's coming to realize that he is not, after all, at the center of the life of a mother or father who had appeared, heretofore, selflessly devoted to him. He now realizes that the parent's interest in him has been, all along, essentially narcissistic and that, to the extent that he has been a truly separate person at all to the parent, he has been not cherished but, rather, the object of covert, intense jealousy. He himself must now cope with his own jealous realization that the parent has a self, after all, a self "who," in fact, is far more beloved to the parent than is he.

When I wrote of this development in an earlier paper (Searles 1962), I had not yet come to see the element of internal-object jealousy. I described that the schizophrenic illness first becomes manifest, typically, in a setting of the individual's coming face to face with overwhelming disillusionment. Specifically, he is no longer able to maintain a symbiotic relatedness with a parent, a relatedness perpetuated into chronological adulthood, long past the time when the mother–infant symbiosis is normally resolved, perpetuated partly in the service of maintaining intense scorn, and other negative emotions, under repression. He now becomes confronted with a weight of evidence which can no longer be denied, evidence showing that the parent's ostensibly altruistic interest in him has been basically narcissistic in origin—that this interest has been invested not in him as a real and separate person, but in him only as an extension of the parent's self.

Early in my work with a middle-aged borderline-schizophrenic man, I became aware of jealousy of his intimate, buddy-buddy, comfortable-old-shoe relationship with his "self"; this "self" of his proved to be an introject with multiple childhood-derived transference-significances referable to his relationship with his mother and older brother. Not only did he give me to feel, during the sessions, that in his daily life he was on far more companionable terms with his "self" than I felt to be with him—for I felt walled out, and incapable of making any personal impact upon him, a very high percentage of the time—but also, he seemed to treat himself, all things considered, with a kinder intimacy, for all his roughly blunt ways of talking to himself in his daily-life internal dialogues, than the far harsher condemnation and vilification I commonly vented privately upon myself over those years of his analysis.

As the analysis wore on, he came to dialogue, internally but consciously, in daily life between sessions, oftentimes and in loving leisure, with an idealized image of me, such that during the sessions I came to feel, on more than one occasion, jealous of my "self"—of, that is, the Dr. Searles with whom, in fantasy, he often talked between sessions, talked in entirely the same intimately companionable spirit in which he had long been accustomed to dialoguing with his "self," while continuing, during the analytic sessions, to maintain the same wall of resistance to my own efforts. This phenomenon I have encountered sufficiently often, in my work with borderline patients, to convince me that it is typical indeed for the analyst of the borderline patient to come to find himself pitted in jealous competition with such a transference-derived introject, or image, in the patient, of the analyst "himself."

In the instance of a narcissistic woman whom I had known socially, but relatively distantly, for some years before she entered analysis with me, I quickly found that an intense and seemingly ever-present jealousy was at work within her character structure, and I came to have the odd experience of finding that my analyst-self was vulnerable to feeling jealous of my social-acquaintance-self *vis-à-vis* the patient. In one session, for instance, in which I found myself experiencing a kind of tension that had become very familiar to me over the course of my work with her, she was making clear that she had made her boyfriend jealous by holding in his presence a prolonged telephone conversation with a male co-worker of hers, and had made another male co-worker jealous by some other means. Before the end of the hour I had become convinced that she tended to cause me, as *analyst*, to feel jealous of my*self* ("my*self*" consisting in the non-analyst, social acquaintance aspects of myself). This came about, I saw then, partially through her so-characteristic large-scale ignoring of slips of the tongue (causing me to feel *neglected* as her analyst), and in her usual social-chatty way of reporting during the session, talking to me much as she would with *any* social acquaintance or friend.

Since my discovery of this kind of countertransference-jealousy phenomenon in my work with this woman, I have recognized the same phenomenon in my work with a number of other borderline patients—patients who foster this split in the analyst's subjective ego-functioning, such that he feels that the patient either warmly accepts him, or is quite ready warmly to accept him, as social acquaintance or social friend (or as fantasied lover), but makes him feel jealously excluded and depreciated in the identity-area which he occupies, subjectively, by far the majority of the time—as analyst.

I have seen evidence that, in a marriage in which one or both persons is in analysis or psychotherapy, either partner's developing the paranoid suspicion that there is "someone else" is his or her way of experiencing the impending realization that the spouse is developing, for the first time, a separate *self*—is becoming an individual person for the first time—and is no longer selflessly devoted to him or her. He or she perceives this self of the spouse as displaced onto some delusionally or quasi-delusionally suspected rival. This phenomenon is essentially the same as that which I described years ago concerning the young person's realization, at times so shattering as to precipitate psychosis, that the "selflessly devoted" parent has, after all, a self, and a highly narcissistic one at that.

In a paper in 1964, I reported upon another dimension of this same symbiotic-marriage phenomenon. I described that in a number of married patients who were bent on divorce, I had seen that the patient's determination to "get a separation from" the marital partner consisted basically in a striving, long unrecognized as such by the patient, to achieve a separation at an *intra*psychic level, to achieve a genuine individuation *vis-à-vis* a wife or husband with whom a symbiotic mode of relatedness had been existing. In such instances, the marital partner had been responded to not predominantly as a real other person, but rather as the personification of the unacceptable, projected part-aspects of the patient's self, or, one might say, as the personification of his own repressed self-images. Thus the patient does have a need, however unrecognized as such, to achieve a separation between those repressed and projected aspects of himself, on the one hand, and, on the other hand, the marital partner as a real and separate person.

I have learned that patients can be expected to come to manifest jealousy, in the context of the analytic session, of *whomever* they themselves have come, seemingly at their own initiative, to spend much of the session in discussing. One sees this particularly readily in work with borderline patients, and most often when the patient talks incessantly of his or her spouse. That is, during those phases of the analysis in which the patient spends much of the analytic time in reporting to the analyst details about the patient's marriage (and I refer here not merely to details about the couple's sexual adjustment, but to details about whatever marital interactions), the patient in this analytic situation is unconsciously being a jealous child, reacting to his actual spouse as being one of his parents (his mother, say), and to the analyst as being the other parent (his father, say)—the patient being jealous, at this unconscious level, of how much of the analyst–father's interest is being devoted to this image of the spouse-mother.

Such patients function in such a manner, during the sessions, as powerfully to give the analyst to experience the jealousy toward the spouse which the patient is striving unconsciously to keep under repression. One such man, for instance, had said something to which he was apparently hoping for a response from me, and I had maintained my usual silence. He then went on, after a brief pause, "One thing, in my *relationship* with *Margaret*, . . ." His intonation was so smug and jealousy-engendering as to imply that, whereas I have no relationship with him, his wife Margaret and he *do* have a relationship. He was still successfully defended, unconsciously, against the awareness of his jealous feeling that Margaret (to whom so much of his analytic time was being devoted) and I have a relationship with one another, whereas he has none with me.

In reality, I never met this man's wife. Since the patient's spouse on the one hand, and the analyst on the other hand, rarely if ever have set eyes upon one another, and remain year after year miles apart, it is at first startling to discover how powerful is his transference-reaction to these two as being his two parents. But, in one instance after another, it becomes clear, as the childhood-origins of this transference-distortion are brought to light, that his parents had been perceived by him as being, in psychological terms, fully as remote from, as unrelated to, one another as are his spouse and his analyst, geographically and in other regards, in his adult life.

The wishful aspects of such a perception of his parents, on the child's part—beyond a generous basis in reality for this perception, particularly on the part of the more ill patients whose parents were, indeed, highly schizoid—are largely a product of the child's unresolved positive and negative oedipal ambitions. His largely unconscious, rageful jealousy gives rise to an unconscious denial, on his part, of the relationship, sexual and otherwise, which the parents in actuality have with one another.

There is an additional form which the patient's unconscious, oedipal jealousy takes, in the analytic situation, which I find to be frequent indeed and a powerful source of resistance to the analytic process: he unconsciously fosters, and obstinately maintains between himself and the analyst, the gulf of unrelatedness which, so his oedipal ambitions—both positive and negative—dictate, held sway between his two parents.

Such a form of transference-resistance to treatment is one of the phenomena which render work with borderline patients extremely difficult, and work with chronically psychotic patients next to impossible. A chronically psychotic woman with whom I have worked for many years (Searles 1972) has conveyed an image of her father as being a Pharaoh of Egypt, existing in a time-dimension thousands of years earlier than that of her mother, the latter being a queen of various different European countries. Thus a seemingly unbridgeable gulf, as regards time as well as distance, is maintained. In the transference-situation, the most difficult among many difficult aspects of the treatment is the high degree of unrelatedness which prevails, most of the time, between us (she being largely fused with the mother and I, with the father) and which, as has become increasingly clear, is serving for her as an unconscious defense against remarkably intense oedipal ambitions (both negative and positive) and terrors, from various sources, which attend those ambitions.

A woman with whom I have worked for many years was, during the first several of them, chronically schizophrenic, but in more recent years has been manifesting a borderline degree of impairment of ego functioning. She has long been subject to experiencing auditory hallucinations, both during and between her treatment-sessions, and I have been given to feel on occasion jealous of her hallucinations, as in the instance of the hebephrenic man whom I mentioned near the beginning of this chapter. In my work with this woman I discovered a different form of these jealousy phenomena than I had seen before.

I had long known that her parental family had had idealized images, ostensibly of her but in actuality of themselves, images which, evidently largely unconsciously, they had imposed harshly upon her and to which they had tried coercively to make her conform. I had long known, too, from my own work with her what a sadistically disappointing person she is. She is a person of little accomplishment by any conventional standards. Time after time I would sense, or clearly visualize, a larger, healthier, more capable, more intelligent, more mature, more talented, more loving and lovable person, nascent or latent in her, than the relatively ineffectual and colorless one she was presently being. But time after time, my hopeful efforts to help her to realize these capabilities which I perceived in her met with bitter disappointment as she failed, once again, to take this or that forward step into greater maturity of functioning, either within the sessions or in her daily life between them.

The unconscious-jealousy component of these failures

did not come to my attention until the following seemingly trivial incident occurred in one of the sessions. I was shortly to go on a modest summer vacation. While sitting on the couch as she often did, she said, looking at me, "You'll get tanned, won't you, Dr. Searles? . . . attractive . . . bronzed . . ." I felt, as she talked, that she was clearly visualizing my looking so, in her mind's eye, and this definitely tended to make me feel jealous of the attractively bronzed image of me which she was visualizing, quite tangibly, as she gazed at my face. That experience with her left me well able to believe that similar jealousy was mobilized within her on occasions when she sensed that I was visualizing her as being a person capable, for instance, of driving a car, of becoming married, and so on.

As regards the hebephrenic man I mentioned early in this chapter, during the course of the work with whom I became aware of jealousy of his hallucinations, he broke one of his usual silences, after several years of our work together, by saying reproachfully, "You're jealous of my shadow." At the time, long accustomed by now to my feelings of jealousy in our work, I nonetheless heard "my shadow" only in its literal meaning, and was unaware of any jealousy of his shadow itself. I was not aware of any feelings of jealousy during this particular session, nor had I been conscious of any for several months; things had been progressing slowly but well in the work with him during those months, and I was feeling relatively content. But, in retrospect, I surmise that "my shadow" was his only way of conceptualizing the tenuous individual self which was developing in him as a result of his labors, mine, and those of the innumerable other persons who had endeavored to help him during his years in the sanitarium. I think he was quite correct that, much as I was consciously endeavoring to help such an individual self to emerge in him, I did indeed react with jealousy to his relationship to this new and still-shadowy presence. On another occasion, when I broke the silence by asking what he was thinking or feeling, he explained, touchingly, "I'm playin' possum, tryin' to catch myself."

In my work with one narcissistic woman, who was enrolled in a doctoral program in psychology, it became evident that her functioning during the analytic sessions for years was the equivalent, at an unconscious level, of the two parents in copulation with one another, while I was cast as the personification of herself as a child, torn by jealousy on both negative oedipal and positive oedipal bases. She had had several years of largely unsuccessful analysis prior to coming to me, and I quickly and enduringly found her to be extremely resistive to the analytic process. Her character disorder contained readily discernible narcissistic and sadomasochistic features as defenses against—among other conflicts, of course—her repressed homosexual strivings. It was evident, from the nature of the daily-life material which she reported, that she functioned in that setting, as she surely did in the analytic one, in an intensely jealousy-engendering fashion—a defense, of course, against her own largely-repressed feelings of jealousy. She proved highly resistive, year after year, to experiencing in awareness this jealousy, or of being able to discern her characteristic jealousy-engendering ways of relating, either outside or within the analytic setting. My own expressing to her, repeatedly, the jealousy engendered in me by our work together, helped to bring all this relatively much into her awareness before our work together ended. But for years the sessions had a highly sadomasochistic quality, and only after several years did it become evident to me that her usual tortured demeanor on the couch was in part a reaction-formation against the unconscious copulatory pleasure being enjoyed by the two "persons"—parental introjects—within her.

In a session late in the analysis she reported a dream in which she unwittingly intruded into a situation wherein her parents were having intercourse, with the mother on top of the father, and the patient feared her mother's wrath at this intrusion. The analytic work had progressed sufficiently far, despite many difficulties, that I was able to interpret—although with only limited effectiveness—her wish to be overpowered and raped by her phallic mother, who was equivalent, I interpreted, to the university, toward which the patient was more than a little paranoid and by which she felt chronically wronged, after her several years of still-unsuccessful attempts to gain a Ph.D. there.

As this session went on she spoke, in reference to the dream, of her fear that she would be beaten up by her powerful mother "if I intruded upon her pleasure." Upon hearing this I immediately thought that it nicely described the way I recurrently still felt intimidated, more often than not, from "intruding upon" the analysis, lest she become exceedingly wroth (over some interpretation which would prove premature) and beat me up—*literally*; I still found reason for such physical fear of this woman who, like her mother, was powerfully built. I did not tell her of this thought, which in my mind was associated with early-childhood fear of my perceivedly phallic mother. Nor did I call her attention to her implied assumption, in the dream, that if she were to be further intrusive, her mother would in a sense *prefer* beating her up, to going on copulating with the father; in this sense, the daughter apparently assumed that her mother would find her more arousing (even though to a form of sexual involvement disguised as aggression) than the father was being. No doubt my own chronically intimidated manner of functioning in the analytic work sprang from similarly unconscious, masochistic homosexual longings toward her (with her being equivalent, as my just mentioned associations suggested to me, to the phallic mother of my early childhood, whose beatings of me with a yardstick were commonplace; my father's much less frequent, and relatively unfeared, spankings were done with a simple foot-long desk ruler).

As I have been exploring these jealousy-phenomena with one patient after another more and more deeply, year after year, I find it more understandable why a male patient is so vulnerable to feeling jealous of "Edith" (the name of his wife, whom I have never met). It becomes more and more clear, in this and comparable cases, that "Edith," of whom he talks endlessly in the sessions (talks, in, usually, an intensely condemnatory, rejecting, hateful spirit) is essentially, in the context of the analytic interaction, not predominantly a reference to his wife in outer reality, but rather is a projected image of his own subjectively feminine self. I have found, long since, much reason for compassion toward and appreciation of "Edith" and I have many times felt, privately, that, for all his vituperation against "her," "Edith" is a basically more lovable "person," in my view, than is the patient "himself" ("himself" being those conscious identity-components which are subjectively masculine and need not be projected into "Edith"). He is in a sense realistic in feeling jealous of the esteem which "Edith" enjoys in my eyes, for I do find, increasingly, his subjectively feminine self ("Edith") to be a gentler, more loving and lovable "person" than his so hypermasculine, ruthless, rejecting "self" is being, during our sessions. It is unnecessary to detail, here, that this image to which he refers as "Edith" is comprised to a generous degree, as well, of components of his repressed transference-images of the analyst.

The Role of These Jealousy-Processes in Negative Therapeutic Reaction

I have been discussing here jealousy-phenomena which, when maintained under repression or dissociation on the part of either patient or analyst, undoubtedly contribute importantly to many otherwise-inexplicable instances of negative therapeutic reaction. I surmise that in many an instance wherein the analytic work founders, both patient and analyst have proved unable to integrate their unconscious jealousy of the patient's (and analyst's, as well) potentially healthier "selves."

An attorney in his late 20s, who in the course of his analysis gave me cause many times to feel anxiety lest he commit suicide, was reminiscing about his first attempt to obtain counseling. As a senior in high school he had "decided to see someone about myself" and had gone for an interview with the minister of the church his family attended. "He was used to seeing people who were in really grievous situations, and I guess I was one of the few he'd seen who had been so successful in school and all. I sat there in his study, and all sorts of intellectual insights came out of this murk [that is, the "murk" which prevailed in his head whenever he was severely depressed] that I hadn't known I knew. . . . He said [at the end of their interview, in a brisk and admiring tone], 'Well, you surely do have an excellent grasp of what's troubling you!'" The patient went on to say that what he had been saying, to the minister, had seemed entirely unreal to himself. All this seemed to me a beautifully-expressed example of a person's ostensibly healthiest, most capable ego-aspects' functioning, in actuality, on the basis of an unintegrated introject which does not feel to be part of the patient himself, and thus does not enhance his self-esteem.

This young man's analysis revealed that he tended to feel murderously jealous of the so much more successful person, so to speak, within him. It seemed to me not coincidental that, later in the previously mentioned session, he commented upon a recent item in the news, concerning an unusually gruesome suicide on the part of someone who evidently had been, as the patient put it, "bound and determined to die." His own analysis brought to light much evidence that his suicidal urge consisted, in large part, in an unconscious determination to kill the jealously-hated, intellectually successful but emotionally remote mother-introject within him. This kind of clinical material, concerning repressed jealousy involving an introject, is relevant to the literature concerning imbalances in the development of various ego-functions (James 1960, Ross 1967).

A man in his thirties, who had worked for several years with a previous analyst, said early in a session with me, "I had a dream last night. I *have lots* of dreams; *my* trouble is that I can't *remember* my dreams. It's an uncooperative part of me that I resent, because they [i.e., his dreams] say things more clearly and succinctly than *I* do when I digress throughout my sessions." He had expressed furious exasperation toward both himself and me, innumerable times, for making—so he felt—little constructive use of our time together; he recurrently found it maddeningly difficult to express cogently his voluminous free associations. It seemed to me strongly implied, in what I have quoted here, that he was unconsciously jealous of his dreams, as equivalent to persons more articulate than himself; his difficulty in remembering his dreams apparently was based, in part, upon this unconscious jealousy of them.

A woman who frequently manifested, during her sessions, the sudden onset of transitory headaches (clearly linked with the threatened derepression of explosive rage, and other unconscious affects), said on one such occasion, "I sorta envy the headaches, because they seem to belong to another existence, and not to the life I'm trying to lead. . . ."

A woman whose resistance had withstood largely intact several years of an eventually seven-year analysis commented, at the beginning of a session, that she felt that each of us had greeted the other, in the waiting room, with "disinterest. The analysis was what I was looking forward to, and what had brought me here today," adding that I had seemed to feel uninterested in her, as she had felt toward me, and that she had "assumed that your thoughts would turn toward my *associations*, rather than toward *me*. . . ." She said all this in a thoughtful, largely dispassionate tone; but I sensed an underlying feeling of hurt in her, and an underlying feeling, also, of jealousy of her own associations—her own analytic productions, so to speak. I heard this as linking up with her childhood experiences of (for example) enormous interest on the part of her mother during the piano lessons to which she daily had subjected the daughter.

This same woman said, many months later, that she had been hurt, during and following the previous day's session, by my having said so little during it, and in this session she repeatedly expressed wishes to kill me; parenthetically, for years she had expressed toward me, on innumerable occasions, murderousness of a paranoid-delusional intensity which I often had found very threatening. On this occasion, she went on (without comment from me) to concede, however, that "It may be very beneficial for the analysis that, . . . you don't respond to everything I talk about. . . ." This last statement I heard as conveying, significantly, a hint of her unconscious jealousy of the analysis. On another occasion, when she ruminated, "It's weird how different I feel in here, than I feel outside the analysis, . . ." I heard this comment as revealing that she evidently was equating, at an unconscious level, "in here" (my office) with her analysis—as though her analysis were confined to my office and did not participate, as it were, in her life elsewhere. Her unconscious jealousy of the analysis would help account for her isolating it thus—her refusing to let it share the rest of her daily living, but her leaving it behind, instead, every time she left my office at the end of a session.

A woman whose intense homosexual longings were largely defended against by paranoid mechanisms ended some characteristically contemptuous, bitter statement with the derisive word ". . . *psychoanalysis!*" and added, in an assertive, competitive, triumphant flourish, "—*my ass!*"

The tone and sequence of her words clearly indicated that she unconsciously experienced her ass to be in competition with psychoanalysis (including her own psychoanalysis) and that once again, for the nth time, she had demonstrated the primacy, in the competition, of her ass. There had emerged, in the earlier years of our work, abundant material to support this formulation. It had become evident how strong a resistance she had against receiving *analytic* help from me, since this would constitute unmistakable evidence of my being able to resist the lure of her ass sufficiently to enable me to function as an analyst to her.

In more general terms, and widening the focus to include extra-analytic situations also, it had become evident that she functioned, in many interpersonal settings, in terms of her brain's having to compete (as regards the arousing of the other person's interest in her) with her body. For example, she many times reported to me, in analytic sessions, that in the most recent seminars in her master's-degree program in nursing, she had scarcely begun to express the many theoretical and clinical observations which she was eager to contribute, before all the others present (most of whom were women) had "jumped on me" or "descended on me."

Not rarely, the analysis itself proves to have become for the patient, as I have already mentioned in brief, the personification of the jealously-fought internal object. One borderline woman made an ordinary-seeming, but highly significant, comment about "my attempts to link up things [i.e., daily-life events] *with you, or with the analysis* [italics mine]." As the session went on, she provided data which indicated a transference to *me* as mother (relatively interpersonally-responsive, accessible, tangibly *there*), and a simultaneous and contrasting transference to the *analysis* as father (an extremely emotionally-remote person, for the most part, in the patient's childhood—inaccessible, impersonal, enigmatic). Even though jealousy did not emerge into awareness during the session, either in myself or, so far as I could discern, in her, I knew this to be the kind of splitting of the transference, as between the analyst on the one hand and the analysis on the other hand, which typically enables the dissociated internal-object jealousy to emerge, in course of time, from dissociation, as I had found, and continue to find, to occur quite explicitly in my work with a number of patients, work wherein the analysis emerges as a jealousy-engendering rival for either patient or analyst.

One man said ruefully at the end of a session during which, bored as usual, I had said little or nothing, "I've done it again. I've filled up the hour with grinding boredom. I've rendered the hour ineffective. I've rendered the analysis ineffective. . . ." Our work together had given me reason to hear, in these ordinary-seeming expressions of futility and discouragement, an important oedipal-jealousy significance. It was becoming increasingly clear to me that the analytic hour, the analysis generally, and the most formal-analyst components of myself, represented to him, at an unconscious level, an oedipal-rival parent (either father or mother, varyingly), while the less formally analytic, more simply and spontaneously personal, aspects of me were equivalent to the oedipally-desired parent (again, either mother or father, varyingly, so the genetic data indicated). Thus, for example, in such a session as that just ending, he apparently had been involved in an unconscious effort to unman the father-components of the analyst ("the hour," or "the analysis") and possess, sexually, the mother-components of the analyst. It eventually became clear that there was not only a transference but also a countertransference component in this, for I discovered in myself a certain submerged appeal, for me, in his remaining rocklike, immune to my analytic efforts, with the implicit promise, as I tended to experience it, that he would eventually wear down my analyst-defense and possess me sexually in a setting of my surrendering my long-sustained attempt to analyze him successfully.

All this seems to me relevant to the literature concerning the "real" relationship between patient and analyst, and concerning, similarly, the therapeutic alliance (see Greenson 1965, Greenson and Wexler 1969, and Stone 1967). From my experience with such patients as this just-mentioned man, it seems to me highly illusory to think that there is much of any extra-transference, "real" relationship between the two participants until relatively late in the analysis, after the patient's oedipal conflicts have largely emerged from repression and become integrated. Prior to that time, the so-called "real" relationship between the two is all too likely to be comprised, to an appreciable if not predominant degree, in the patient's unconscious experience of it, of a transference-relationship to those pertinent aspects of the analyst's functioning as being equivalent to one parent, and the more formal-analyst components of the analyst equivalent to the other parent, referable to the patient's unresolved-oedipal era of development.

Still another form of transference-jealousy, which I have seen most readily in schizoid and narcissistic patients, is one in which the patient reacts to the analysis as being a parent whom the patient is determined to keep all to himself; whenever the analyst does succeed in participating perceptibly in the analysis, the patient reacts with jealous rage against this perceivedly sexual rival for the beloved parent.

In ostensible contrast to the phenomenon I have just cited, but on closer scrutiny an example of that phenomenon, is the following instance of a patient for whom the analytic process proved to be the unconscious equivalent of the many-years'-long medical-nursing process, in his parental home, centered upon a slightly younger sister who had been born with a serious cardiac-valvular disorder. He re-

membered in detail, many times during the analysis, how
greatly the treatment of this sister, carried on primarily by
his mother but largely dominating the life of his whole
family, had cast a shadow over his own whole remembered
upbringing. His jealousy of this grievously afflicted sister
was, of course, difficult for him to face and integrate. But
what I wish to emphasize here is some of the evidence that
his erstwhile-unconscious competitiveness had not only to do
with the sister herself but, farther from the conventionally
human realm, with the *care of* this sister.

In one session he was saying, "There was *nothing* about
the care of Esther in our home that did *any*thing to rally our
family together. . . . It was a *destructive* thing. . . . It was
just a nightmare from beginning to end." Because what he
said, here, reminded me of how he had spoken frequently of
the analysis (which he often had come close to stopping), I
interrupted him, asking, "If you were to stop the analysis at
this point, and were to look back on it, I wonder to what
extent this would serve to express one of your feelings about
it: 'There was *nothing* about the analysis that did *any*thing to
rally our family [here meaning his marital family, as I felt
sure was clear to him] together—it was a *destructive* thing—
it was just a nightmare from beginning to end'?"

He replied promptly, thoughtfully, and convincingly, "I
wouldn't the last part; but the rest of it I would," and went
on to say that the analysis—like, he implied, the care of
Esther during his childhood—is "Something that keeps you
[referring consciously to himself; it was maddeningly difficult to bring him to see that the 'you' indeed referred, unconsciously, to me] in turmoil. No matter how much you try
to wall it off, it's always present, it's always a source of
contention."

I thought of this man's unconscious resistance to the
analysis as being equivalent to "the care of Esther in our
home. . . . a destructive thing . . ." when on a later occasion I

was interviewing, in the presence of a group of residents, a borderline schizophrenic woman. About this woman, both at that hospital and the previous one from which she had been transferred, there had been unusually diverse opinions concerning her diagnosis, and it seemed to me that this uncertainty was related to her clearly severe identity-uncertainty. During the interview she asked me if she were "a guinea pig," which of course was not an unusual question from a patient being interviewed in such a setting; later on she said, uneasily, "I wonder if I'll walk out of here feeling like a piece of liverwurst." But what particularly reminded me of the previously-described man was this patient's next question, "Am I a teaching process?" —"teaching process" being so much on a par, in its bizarrely nonhuman-identity connotation, with "the care of Esther."

The patient whom I was interviewing in the hospital had had (like, in certain regards, my analytic patient) childhood experiences clearly relevant to her presently poorly-established identity as a human being. In her childhood she had lived under the serious threat that she would be given to the Negro ice man—who, she told me, "beat his horse"—and, after the ice man died, to the garbage man. She tried repeatedly, and equally seriously, to give away her baby brother, whom the mother left much in her care. By the time of my interview with her she had had the experience of working for two years as a prostitute, during which time she had obtained an abortion of an eight-and-one-half-month-old fetus.

One point which I wish to emphasize here is that patients whose own sense of identity is so distorted—patients who at an unconscious level have self-images as being various nonhuman entities, such as a *process* of one sort or another—are entirely capable of developing transference-reactions, in the treatment setting, to various aspects of the situation in addition to the analyst himself, transference-reactions in which the particular identity-component in question is being projected upon the nonhuman object or process in question.

In the instance of a middle-aged woman with a narcissistic character disorder, whose upbringing had involved a father who had been only tangentially and elusively present on the scene, psychologically, and a mother with multiple sclerosis which had caused her to become progressively disabled over the years of this daughter's growing up, I discovered an element in her resistance to the analytic process of which I had never been aware in my work with any patients before her: she clearly was manifesting a *transference* (tenacious and multirooted) *to transference*. That is, to the whole realm of transference-phenomena, of whatever childhood-origin, she reacted with certain unconscious, and therefore automatic, reactions which made her conscious recognition of these phenomena extraordinarily difficult. For her, at an unconscious level, transference-phenomena were equivalent, by reason of their elusive and subtle presence on the scene, to her elusive father, for whom her contempt and antagonism were enormous. Further, any transference-reaction on her part, toward the analyst, implied a three-person setting—herself, the analyst, and the childhood-predecessor of the analyst—and three-person situations inherently were imbued with intense jealousy for this woman, whose narcissism was serving as a defense against (among other emotions) much paranoid jealousy.

Jealousy Toward Nonhuman Objects

In these jealousy phenomena which involve an internal object in one of the two actual persons, that internal object frequently is projected upon some nonhuman thing (as I have indicated earlier here) which thereby acquires the psychological impact of a third person in the jealousy-ridden triangular relationship. It is not rare, for example, to discover that the analytic patient is jealous of a plant in the analyst's office, a plant reminiscent of those to which the patient's mother had devoted loving care, plants which had represented, for the mother, unconscious transference-objects, the externalized representations of internal objects with which she had been involved in intimate and loving relatedness, to the jealous exclusion of the child himself.

The involvement, here, of an ingredient of what is in actuality the nonhuman environment is traceable to an incomplete differentiation, in the ego-developmental history of one or both of the two persons involved, from the nonhuman environment. That is the subject to which my first book (Searles 1960) was devoted; in it, I tried primarily to portray how manifold are the human strivings or emotional conflicts which are given expression through, or defended against by, identification with or non-differentiation from the nonhuman environment.

A borderline woman's statement, "I felt very envious of their house" (referring to the new home of a couple who were friends of her and her husband's) is typical of the phraseology which, no matter how commonplace in its grammatical usage, betrays the speaker's unconscious lack of differentiation between animate and inanimate, and her unconscious longing to *be* the inanimate possession of the persons who are, at a conscious level, the objects of her envy for the possession of it. In other words, the phraseology reveals that although the speaker *consciously* envies the other person for possessing the object in question (the new house, in this instance), *unconsciously* she wishes to be not the human possessor of that inanimate object, but the object itself, possessed and cherished by the other person(s). Unconsciously, the envy is based on a far more primitive identificational longing than appears on the surface to be the case.

Experiences with many patients have convinced me that, in this admittedly commonplace phraseology for the expression of envy ("I envy his new car," "I envy her new dress," and so on), we are dealing not merely with a grammatical shorthand to obviate the necessity for the more cumbersome, "I envy him his new car," or "I envy her her new dress." In many instances, such seemingly-mundane comments have served to alert me to the fact that this or that patient has an important if not predominant realm of his personal identity existing, at an unconscious level, in the form subjectively of an inanimate object, or other nonhuman entity, in envious competition not with other human beings—for subjectively, he has not achieved a predominantly human ego-identity—but with actually nonhuman ingredients of the world about him.

In general, it seems to me, the envy-dominated patient is less far along, in achieved differentiatedness from the nonhuman environment, than is the jealousy-dominated patient. The patient who envies a colleague's new *car*, for instance, is a patient who tends to feel so akin to his nonhuman environment, so far from feeling established as a human being among his fellow human beings, as to feel readily thrown into competition with cars, and other material possessions, of the human beings about him. On the other hand, the patient who is envious *of his colleague for possessing* a beautiful car, and even more, the patient who is jealous of an acquaintance for "possessing," so to speak, a beautiful wife, is reacting in terms more of burning to be the *person* who possesses these; his human identifications, and with these his identity as a human being, are stronger than is the case with the former patient whose identifications are relatively more with various ingredients of the nonhuman world.

Space does not allow me any comprehensive discussion of the determinants of a patient's having developed a sense of identity based more upon kinship with the nonhuman environment than with the human environment; my monograph (1960) concerning this subject explores that topic at length. Here I want simply to mention that as regards external causes for this, a child's seeing his parent to be lovingly related more with plants, animal pets, the furniture of the household, and various cherished material possessions, for example, than with the other human members of the family, tends to pit the child in competition with these nonhuman ingredients of his childhood surroundings. A frequent internal cause has to do with the child's attempt to take refuge from the world of people in his environment, an interpersonal world perceived by him—undoubtedly in part realistically, not merely through projection—as being permeated with murderously jealous competition, fleeing into identifying with the less frightening, more stable, nonhuman world about him—by being or remaining, for example, part of the woodwork in the home, rather than taking any identifiable part in, for instance, violent arguments between his parents, or competition with feared, or parentally much preferred, siblings. This flight into such a refuge tends—as one can see most clearly in schizophrenic patients—eventually to boomerang, to greatly worsen the patient's situation, for the nonhuman environment itself comes to personify, for him, the menacing objects of his jealous rivalry, such that the whole nonhuman world may come to feel terrifyingly inimical to him.

The ego-functioning of a woman in her late forties remained, over a very considerable number of years of analysis, essentially schizoid, with her emotionality being of a contrived, "as-if" quality. The only emotions she manifested which seemed to me indubitably real were a relentless, grinding rage, admixed at times with self-pity; and even these emotions she herself seemed not to acknowledge within herself as being a part of her identity. The point relevant for this chapter is the dénouement, after many years of analysis, that a long-repressed jealousy of all of outer reality (as epitomized by the world outside the parental/marital home), experienced as being a sexual rival of hers in her oedipal striving for her father, was one of the determinants of this flaw in her relatedness with reality. Her denial of outer reality was, at this level of ego-functioning, tantamount to massive depreciation of this oedipal rival.

Near the beginning of her analysis, she made clear that her father had suffered throughout her upbringing, and still suffered, from a number of phobias—of flying, of traveling at all far from his house, and so on—which rendered his life largely constricted to the house itself; it was clear to me, and I felt sure that it was to her also, that his need to repress promiscuous sexual impulses, as well as rageful impulses, was one of the major causes of his phobias. It was early clear, that is, that the world outside her father's home had represented, in his unconscious, a tempting but frightening myriad of ragefully-uncontrollable sexual objects.

The patient herself loved gardening. It became clear early in her analysis that her chronic, diffuse rage was expressed, on the innumerable occasions when it became unbearably intense, in a stereotyped urge to "carve up a rose-bush," an urge which she had carried into action on many occasions over the years. Many times during the analytic sessions, when this always-tense woman was feeling even more tense than usual, she would become immersed in a vivid fantasy of slashing a rose-bush into bits with a sickle.

Incidental to the present point, but by no means unimportant, at a deeply pregenital level this woman also manifested powerful "prehuman" identifications with her father, experienced here as a mother, and these identifications became manifested, about two months prior to the session I shall shortly discuss, in a self-image as a beautiful rose-bush covered with blooms, an image I found both esthetically beautiful and emotionally moving.

In the pertinent session two months later, about fifteen minutes along in it she was surmising that "It's envy or jealousy that makes me want to carve up rose-bushes." She went on to say that one time in New Hampshire, where she and her marital family had lived before moving to the Washington area, her husband (who, like her father, was subject to severe phobic anxiety) had come to feel very frightened of the overgrowth of shrubbery outside the house into which they had just moved, and had said something fragmentary, and not fully intelligible, about his mother; the husband's parental home was not far away. The patient went on to speak of the jealousy she had felt in that setting. Her jealousy clearly had a reference to her husband's relationship with his mother; but, of particular interest here, she hinted strongly that her jealousy had been of the shrubbery also. She all but said that she had been jealous of the shrubbery for its evoking a more intense response (of phobic anxiety) in her husband than she herself had felt capable of evoking. Relevant here is the fact, long known to both of us, that throughout her upbringing she had felt maddenedly unable to compete successfully with her father's adored image of his long-dead mother. In adult life she felt chronically belittled and ignored by her husband, just as she had felt treated in childhood by her father.

She went on to say, during the same session, that the "ferocity" with which she carved up rose-bushes, with the sickle, would frighten her husband and two young sons. Parenthetically, some of the most stressful of our sessions had a kind of impending-axe-murder atmosphere, an atmosphere so undemarcated by any firm ego-boundaries that on occasion the murderousness felt to be not localized clearly within either one or the other of us, but to be permeating the room.

Still later in this same session which I have been detailing, she went on to say, without any intervening comments from me, that sometimes it seems to her that she is, in her head, having dialogues with herself, and "perceiving the world in the third person."

Obviously, I cannot prove incontestably here an hypothesis, based in important part upon clinical intuition, which proved pertinent and useful in my work with her. But it does seem to me that the previously-mentioned fragments of data, taken together, strongly suggest that she long had been reacting, at an unconscious level, to the outer world as being a person, a person the object of her murderous jealousy and therefore attempted denial, because this "person" represented to her oedipally-striven-for father his own sexually desired but tabooed mother, with whom the patient was furiously unable to compete successfully. I am reasonably confident that my records of my work with frankly schizophrenic patients can yield much analogous data, pointing toward essentially the same kind of contribution of oedipal conflicts to the later development of psychosis in many patients.

I have encountered closely comparable data in appreciably less ill patients also—patients whose ego-functioning was of a predominantly normal-neurotic variety—in the depths of their analyses.

The Loneliness of the Analyst's Work

The strange emotions against which borderline and frankly schizophrenic defenses are maintained are, by definition, too stressful for the patient's relatively weak ego to tolerate in awareness. In the analyst's work with such a patient, the analyst's own relatively strong ego must become able to admit into awareness these emotions before the patient can become able, partly through identification with the analyst, to do likewise. Intrapsychic jealousy is one of these strange emotions.

As regards the difficulty, for the analyst, in coping even with the more obvious forms—the three-actual-person forms—of jealousy, it should be seen that the loneliness, in reality, of the analyst's work is such as to make him highly prey to feeling reality-based jealousy in the analytic setting. This lonely nature of one's work as an analyst is an immensely powerful reality-factor which tends to require one to repress the feelings of jealousy to which the work renders one so vulnerable—including feelings of jealousy of that partially split-off aspect of *oneself* which enjoys, transitorily at least, relatively close communion with the patient, as one or another of the clinical examples given here have detailed.

Far more than by the ritualized structuring of the analytic situation, structuring which prohibits or severely limits any usual social intimacy, the analyst is rendered lonely by his necessarily predominant attunement to aspects of the patient which are unconscious, yet, in the latter, and which may not emerge into relatively full awareness for years. As regards the patient's conscious self, the analyst is, to the degree that he is attuned to these unconscious components of the former, alone in the office. Moreover, to the extent that the patient concomitantly is related, during the session, with a projected transference-image which the analyst feels to have little basis in his, the analyst's own, subjective personal-identity, he feels unrelated-to by the patient. Still another factor in the analyst's loneliness may have to do with the probable fact that, oftentimes, the greater part of his analytic work is being carried on at an unconscious level in *himself*—at a level of ego-functioning which is relatively split off from, and therefore inaccessible as any potential working companion to, his lonely consciously-functioning ego-aspects.

Many patients spend their analytic sessions as though the analyst were a diary in which to record the daily-life events which have transpired since the previous session. It has seemed to me that one of the underlying affects which impel the patient compulsively to do this is his anxiety lest the perceivedly recluse-analyst feel barred out from even this vicarious living-through-the-patient, and become murderously jealous of him.

Quite beyond the matter of any predominantly *symbiotic* transference, *any* analytic situation in which the transference-neurosis or -psychosis has become well established, leaving the rest of the patient's daily living relatively undisturbed by his most intense emotional conflicts, now safely focussed predominantly in the transference-relationship, is a setting in which the patient tends to feel threatened by the analyst's presumed readiness to feel jealous of him. The patient's extra-analytic daily life is now relatively enjoyable, whereas the analytic sessions—the only aspect of the analyst's daily living which the patient has an opportunity to perceive—are relatively filled with anxiety and conflictual feelings. Thus the patient tends to fear that the analyst, who leads—as judged by this immediate sample—so difficult and unpleasant and perhaps highly anxious a life—is jealous of him for the gratifications which the patient's life outside the analytic sessions has come to provide him.

Under such circumstances as I have just been describing, the following typical comment came from a married woman who had been in analysis for several years. Upon arriving ten minutes late she said, after having lain down upon the couch, "I hadn't tried to be late; but I hadn't tried not to be late, either. It seems like something of a paradox: I feel like I'm doing very well in general, and at the same time it seems like it's more difficult to come here. . . ."

Four months later this same woman, predominantly schizoid in her personality-functioning, mentioned, "My birthday is coming up on Wednesday; I'll be thirty. It is twenty years since my mother died. Somehow that seems very striking to me—that I've been living twice as long, since her death, as the number of years I lived when my mother was living. . . ." At the juncture when she said, "Somehow that seems very striking to me," I found myself wondering whether—and very much doubting that—she had *ever* felt equally struck by *any*thing *I* had ever said to her, and I began sulking in jealousy, even though I felt sure that she was vigorously fostering this reaction in me. I said nothing as she went on speaking, and a few minutes later she was saying in a semi-amused but otherwise dispassionate tone, "I feel like we're running a small hospital—Bill [their toddler-age son] with his broken leg, Marjorie [their four-year-old daughter] with her eye infection, Eddie [their eight-year-old son] with his recent tonsillectomy . . ." She was saying this from her customary posture of lying comfortably curled on her side on the couch, staring absently toward the nearby window. By the end of the session, I was left feeling that this had been one of those innumerable sessions in which she had functioned in a maddeningly, infuriatingly aloof manner, a manner which often fostered my feeling bitterly left out and deeply jealous of the contrastingly lively interaction among the personality-components (introjects having the subjective identity value, and interpersonal impact, of persons) within her. The family, so to speak, of her unconscious introjects were often projected, during sessions such as this one, upon the other members of her marital family—persons who in daily life may have found reason, as often as I, to feel jealously shut out of what was going on within her.

In a paper in 1971 concerning pathologic symbiosis and autism, I reported that in both my own analytic (i.e., therapeutic) work and in doing supervision, I had encountered many instances of the patient's functioning as though he were the only link between the analyst and a real world where there are real people who are living, who are involved in doing things and experiencing feelings. In short, the patient functions as though he were the analyst's aliveness, as though the analyst could gain access to living only vicariously, through the patient's own living outside the office.

I described that to some degree this is a realistic reaction on the part of the patient to the sedentary aspects, the recluse aspects, of the analyst's living as the patient can only limitedly know it. But it is more significantly a transference reaction to the analyst as personifying the more schizoid, detached, preoccupied components of one or another figure from the patient's early life, and as personifying, by the same token, the patient's own detachment from living. That is, the schizoid part of the patient himself, the part which participates little in his own daily living, he projects upon the analyst.

Thus the patient, I noted, in his recounting of various daily-life incidents, communicates these in a fashion which tends to make the analyst feel a recluse, in this garret, secretly jealous of all the living the patient is doing; or secretly guilty because he cannot be filled, as he feels he should be filled, with altruistic joy on behalf of the actually narcissistic patient immersed in this recounting; or secretly grateful to the patient for speaking in a fashion which enables him to share the "reliving" of the incident. Neither the subtly schizoid patient nor the analyst may realize that the former was not at all fully living the original incident now being "relived"—that he is only now really living it for the first time, in this setting of "reliving" it in connection with the analyst who symbiotically personifies his own unconscious and projected schizoid self.

The symbiotic, pre-individuation, ego-developmental aspect of the analyst's jealousy, as described in the foregoing paraphrase of my 1971 paper, is evident enough. But it seems to me probable that, as in the clinical example of the woman who repeatedly experienced urges to "carve up a rose-bush," there is a determinant of this jealousy from, also, the oedipal level of ego-development. That is, just as in that woman's girlhood all of reality outside the home had been reacted to by her, unconsciously, as being an oedipal rival favored by the father, so the analyst as I have described him in the above passage is being given by the patient to feel unconsciously jealous of the patient's extra-analytic reality as being an oedipal rival of the analyst, a rival favored by the patient.

Commentary Concerning Psychoanalytic Technique

The clinical vignettes already presented have served, I hope, to emphasize the importance of the analyst's becoming open to experiencing, during the analytic session with the patient, moments of intrapsychic jealousy such as I have described. As the years have gone on in my own work with patients, I have found increasingly frequent occasions for reporting to the patient, moreover, my inner jealousy-experience, as data of importance to be shared with him in our mutual exploration of what is transpiring between us and thus, most importantly of course, within him at less than conscious levels. Whereas at the beginning of my psychoanalytic career it would have been unthinkable to me to reveal to a patient that I was feeling jealous in any regard, this has become a relatively commonplace occurrence in my work and, particularly if I have already begun to form at least some tentative impression of the nature of the transference-context in which I am experiencing this, and if I reveal this affective experience of mine in a relatively unanxious, non-guilty, non-accusatory fashion but rather in an interested-collaborator fashion, the patient will find this response to be, in a very high percentage of instances, predominantly illuminating and helpful rather than disturbing.

It may well be that my psychoanalytic technique in general, in my work with non-psychotic patients, involves a marked degree of under-interpretation of the analysand's productions; certainly more than one of my training analysands has thought so. But, whereas it might be thought that one's discovery of the vastness of this realm of intrapsychic jealousy, so frequently glimpsed now in one's daily work, would provide one with a profusion of opportunities for making interpretations—interpretations not of the transference in the usual sense of post-individuation object-relatedness between patient and analyst, but interpretations, rather, concerning aspects of the interrelatedness between, or among, different parts of the patient's self—in actual practice I do not find this to be the case.

I still find that it requires a great many hours of predominant silence on my part before the patient can achieve a sufficient degree of object-relatedness with me to be able to experience me as being an entity at all separate from him and an entity, at the same time, of sufficient significance to warrant his (a) hearing what I can convey to him, in verbal interpretations which are a product of my thoughts and my feelings; (b) listening attentively to what I am saying; and (c) associating constructively to what I have said to him. Prior to such a phase in the analysis, the final paragraph of my previously-mentioned 1971 paper still seems to me valid. I was discussing, here, not only the blatant autism so evident in patients suffering from schizophrenia of whatever degree of severity, but also the subtly-present autism that emerges in the depth of any neurotic patient's analysis. I described that as the months and years of the analyst's work with the autistic patient wear on, the analyst is given to feel unneeded, incompetent, useless, callous, and essentially *nonhuman* in relation to his so troubled and beseeching and reproachful, but so persistently autistic, patient. It is essential that the analyst be able to endure this long period—a period in which, despite perhaps abundant data from the patient, transference interpretations are rarely feasible—in order that the patient's transference regression can reach the early level of ego development at which, in the patient's infancy or very early childhood, his potentialities for a healthy mother–infant symbiosis became distorted into a defensively autistic mode of ego-functioning. At that level of ego development, the infant or young child had not yet come to achieve a perceptual and experiential differentiation between himself and his mother, *nor between his mother and the surrounding nonhuman world.* When in the evolution of the transference that early level of ego-functioning becomes accessible, then it is possible for therapeutically symbiotic processes to occur between patient and therapist, and be interpretable as such. In due course, this phase of therapeutic symbiosis will subsequently usher in the phase of individuation.

In other words, as regards this present chapter's thesis, it continues to be my experience, concerning psychoanalytic technique, that it is predominantly silence on my part—a silence which involves as high a degree of accessibility as possible to communications from my own unconscious as well as from that of the patient (a silence which involves, for example, my relatively freely becoming aware, within me, of such intrapsychic-jealousy phenomena as this paper reports)—which facilitates the patient's coming to experience his internal objects, and me in the transference-relatedness, as being of approximately equivalent psychological significance to him.

Once this degree of therapeutic symbiosis has developed in the transference-relationship, the analyst has achieved a position, in the patient's eyes, from which he can make powerfully effective interpretations concerning the interrelatedness among the patient's internal objects and the analyst as a transference-object. Prior to the emergence of this primitive level of ego-functioning in the evolution of the patient's transference-regression in the analytic situation, the analyst's utilization of verbal interpretations, no matter how accurate their content may be, still seems to me to have the effect, more often than not, of a temporary severing of such symbiotic relatedness as has been developing between patient and analyst and a postponing, therefore, of the establishment of the necessary degree of therapeutic symbiosis. All too often, that is, the analyst's delivering a highly-perceptive-seeming, highly intelligent verbal interpretation is in actuality a predominantly unconscious-defensive response on his part, impelled by his unconscious need to demonstrate to himself that he has not lost his individuality—that he and the patient are not fully at one.

In the instance of one narcissistic or schizoid patient after another, I have come to realize, as the analysis has come to reveal the splits in the ego which at the beginning of his analysis had long been sealed over, that at the outset of the analysis he had been so powerfully defended against feeling consciously dependent upon me not simply for the reason that he would be exposing himself otherwise to the risk of feeling rejected, hurt, disappointed, angry, and so forth but, far more, for the reason that he would be exposing himself to the tangible danger that he would become psychotic. One way of construing this risk is that, having exposed himself to symbiotic relatedness with the other person and then having lost the other person, he thereby loses him*self*. One can say, as well, that he is defended against the inner danger of being torn to pieces by intrapsychic jealousies which become intensified in a setting of increasing intimacy with a real other person, the analyst.

It is the task of the analyst, as over the years of the analysis the patient's regression deepens in the increasing intimacy (partly transference-intimacy but partly real intimacy also) of the analytic work, to foster the emergence of these previously buried ego-splits in a controllable, ego-integratable manner, partly through the analyst's being able to go ahead steadily, while the patient is projecting his own ego-fragmented inner state upon the analyst. The analyst's going ahead steadily, in this process, involves his being able both to experience in awareness, and maintain under analytic scrutiny, such intrapsychic jealousy as had been in part responsible for the maintenance, heretofore, of the splits in the patient's ego-functioning—responsible, that is, for the fact that the patient's internal object-world has been permeated by jealousy-ridden disharmony.

In the instance of one highly schizoid woman, it required nearly ten years of analysis for her to become aware of feelings of jealousy toward anyone; the realm of her own dissociated feelings of jealousy became accessible to her through the avenue of my becoming aware of jealousy toward her legs, with which she had developed an overt, intimately-cherishing fondness, as comprising essentially a person separate from her. Such tenacious dissociation of the realm of jealousy-feelings suggests to me how essential it is for the analyst to become open to experiencing jealousy of the patient's relationships with the latter's introjects, in order that the patient, in turn, will become able to emerge from her interpersonal autism, through starting to face and experience the intense jealousy against which (among other dissociated emotions) the autism had been maintained as an unconscious defense.

A point I made a couple of paragraphs before seems to me sufficiently important to warrant restating in somewhat different terms. As I have encountered more and more intra-psychic-jealousy phenomena, in diverse forms, in my work with patients, I have come to have what seems to me a fuller appreciation of what before had seemed to me a relatively simple repression of dependency-needs in many patients. I now understand that a schizoid man, for example, functions in an emotionally sealed-off manner not so much to keep dissociated his dependency needs (and attendant frustra-tion-rage, and so on) toward the outer world *per se* as, rather, to keep dissociated his intense intrapsychic jealousy which increasing intimacy with the outer world would tend to activate, and which tends to tear him apart into the component internal objects which comprise his "self" and which (paralleling the mother's internal state in his early childhood, and paralleling the state of the unconscious inter-personal relationships in the childhood family as a whole) have been existing in a state of defensively distant nonre-latedness from one another within him. In the work with such a patient, I come to see that his childhood-family psy-chodynamics had involved the family's living, over the years, on a powder-keg of collectively-dissociated jealousy. When the analyst is working with a patient who is inti-mately involved in relatedness with (for example) a halluci-nation, and the analyst is consciously content to be treated as insignificant to that relatedness, he, the analyst, is—just as in the instance of the walled-off schizoid patient—uncon-sciously defending himself against the fear or terror of be-coming torn to pieces by jealousy from intrapsychic sources.

In addition to many clinical experiences of finding how devastating to the patient had been his realization that his mother had a separate self, I have encountered instances in which it had seemed hardly less devastating to discover that the mother and father, formerly perceived unconsciously as one fused parent-figure, were in actuality two separate persons, who were involved in a relationship—a relationship very jealousy-engendering for him—with one another. Such analytic material is of essentially the same nature as my description, quoted early in this chapter, of my coming to perceive the two "persons" intimately involved with one another in my jealous view, who comprised the schizoid man who previously, in his impact upon me, had been a maddeningly walled-off but single, non-jealousy-engendering, individual.

I am mindful that a patient's unconscious perception of the analyst as being comprised of the two parents not fully differentiated from—that is, safely fused with—one another, has, as one of its determinants, the unconscious need to defend against both positive and negative oedipal strivings toward the parents. More than eight years ago, in my supervisory work with a psychiatric resident who was treating a young borderline schizophrenic woman, it became evident that, for her, individuation carried with it the threat of fulfillment of incestuous strivings, such that she unconsciously clung to a transference-image of her therapist as being both parents, safely fused together in sexual union. I do not doubt that the analytic data presented above is expressive of this determinant also.

Melanie Klein (1932) stated that fantasies of "the combined parent figure" normally form part of the early stages of the Oedipus complex. She reported later (1957; see pp. 197–198 in version reprinted in 1975) that

I would now add that the whole development of the Oedipus complex is strongly influenced by the intensity of envy which determines the strength of the combined parental figure. . . . The influence of the combined parental figure on the infant's ability to differentiate between the parents, and to establish good relations with each of them, is affected by the strength of envy and the intensity of his Oedipus jealousy. For the suspicion that the parents are always getting sexual gratification from one another reinforces the phantasy—derived from various sources—that they are always combined.

For the analyst to become aware of the whole multifarious world of internal objects within the patient and within himself—to become aware of this at a more than merely intellectual level—requires him to allow himself to experience again at least a sample of what was, for him as for all human beings, his earliest and greatest loss, the loss (through large-scale and decades-long-maintained dissociation) of the so-largely-non-integrated world of very early childhood, a world comprised of a mother experienced in some such largely non-integrated and non-differentiated manner as Winnicott repeatedly has conceptualized, as here (1945) for example: "In regard to environment, bits of nursing technique and faces seen and sounds heard and smells smelt are only gradually pieced together into one being to be called mother. In the transference situation in analysis of psychotics we get the clearest proof that the psychotic state of unintegration had a natural place at a primitive stage of the emotional development of the individual" (p. 150).

The adult's unconscious resistance in this connection must be based in major part upon his unconscious unwillingness to open himself up, once again, to the loss he experienced in early childhood at having largely to give up (repress or dissociate) this predominantly non-integrated and non-differentiated world, as the price of his coming to function, in his daily waking life, as a single and whole human individual. The kind of gratification he has had, in this process, so largely to relinquish becomes manifest, in my experience, in the therapeutically-symbiotic phase of the individual patient's psychoanalysis and, similarly, in a comparable phase in the family therapy of schizophrenic patients. In both settings, the participants come to experience, among less comfortable emotions, a kind of gratifying playfulness relatively unfettered by adult stability of ego-boundaries, playfulness permeated by an overflowing affection and *joie de vivre* which are, at least in my experience, at best tangential to adult daily life—except for the adult's relatively common but largely vicarious pleasure of this sort in watching, say, little children or puppies at play with one another.

Review of Relevant Literature

The literature concerning jealousy is in large-scale agreement that jealousy is found in a context of three (or more) persons, in contrast to envy, which occurs in a two-person context; Sullivan (1953), Farber (1961), Pao (1969), and Spielman (1971) are among the writers who have made that point.

Between 1971–1975 I wrote the rough draft of a monograph on this chapter's title-subject, and only very late in the writing did I discover that anyone else had done any appreciable work in this field before me. I came across Melanie Klein's little book, *Envy and Gratitude* (1957), then out of print but subsequently (1975) republished.

This chapter presents relatively few examples of the myriad of constellations in which jealousy is at work in a context of two actual persons, with a third "person" in the triangle consisting of an internal object within one of the two actual persons.

In that book, Klein draws the usual distinction between

envy and jealousy, in stating that "envy implies the subject's relation to one person only," whereas jealousy "involves a relationship to at least two people" (pp. 6–7 in 1957 version). But in her writing of what she terms the primary envy of the mother's breast, and the consequences of that envy, she makes a fundamental contribution to the subject to which my present chapter is addressed.

Klein cites Joan Rivière as having introduced, in a paper entitled, "Jealousy as a Mechanism of Defence" (1932), the concept that envy in women is traceable to the infantile desire to rob the mother of her breasts and to spoil them. According to Rivière's findings, jealousy is rooted in this primal envy. Klein reports, similarly, that "My work has taught me that the first object to be envied is the feeding breast, for the infant feels that it possesses everything he desires and that it has an unlimited flow of milk and love which the breast keeps for its own gratification" (p. 10).

Klein further points out that

> We find this primitive envy revived in the transference situation. For instance: the analyst has just given an interpretation which brought the patient relief and produced a change of mood from despair to hope and trust. . . . This helpful interpretation may soon become the object of destructive criticism. . . . The envious patient grudges the analyst the success of his work. . . .
>
> Destructive criticism is particularly evident in paranoid patients who indulge in the sadistic pleasure of disparaging the analyst's work, even though it has given them some relief. . . . What happens is that the patient has split off the envious and hostile part of his self and constantly presents to the analyst other aspects that he feels to be more acceptable. Yet the split-off parts essentially influence the course of the analysis,

which ultimately can only be effective if it achieves integration and deals with the whole of the personality. . . .

In these ways envy, and the defences against it, play an important part in the negative therapeutic reaction . . . (pp. 11–13).

Of her experience with one such patient who became, as Klein puts it, "able to experience the analytic session as a happy feed," the author reports that "It was by enabling her gradually to bring the split-off parts of her self together in relation to the analyst, and by her recognizing how envious and therefore suspicious she was of me, and in the first place of her mother, that the experience of that happy feed came about. This was bound up with feelings of gratitude" (p. 46).

Klein found, as have I, that ". . . to enable the patient to face primary envy and hate only becomes possible after long and painstaking work" (p. 70).

I do not find, in Klein's book, an appreciation of the power and depth of splitting such as I experience in my own work with patients. She reports a patient's *dream*-material as showing the analyst to be two different, split figures (p. 57); but one looks in vain, in her material, for clinical vignettes which document, in a tangible way, that the patient is reacting to the analyst as being two (or more) different persons *during the analytic session*, although she mentions this phenomenon (p. 57). Part of the explanation may be that Klein did not treat patients as ill as have been some of those whom I have treated (for example, see my previously-mentioned 1972 paper). Further, Klein's writing reports relatively little of what the analyst feels in doing analytic work; I could find no instance of her becoming aware, herself, of experiencing jealousy during a session with a patient.

Herner (1965), in a paper entitled, "Significance of the Body Image in Schizophrenic Thinking," reports his having found that

> The split body image observed in schizophrenic patients is the introjected, disorganized, interpersonal relationships perceived by the infant to whom the family is the world. In therapeutic work with such a patient, unsolved problems of relationship to immature parents are delineated. He struggles for liberation from these maleficent figures, who appear in his dreams and hallucinations. In the course of treatment, the incomprehensible symptoms can be explained and a unit [i.e., unity] of the split body image effected. It is possible to meet the crippled and weak ego of the schizophrenic in a new way (p. 465).

I have worked with a considerable number of patients who manifested such disturbances of body-image formation, and disturbances of childhood-family interpersonal milieu, as were entirely consonant with Herner's to me convincing hypothesis.

If the first installation of internal objects occurs, in the child's development, in a setting or atmosphere (in the relationship with the mother and in the family as a whole) of intense jealousy, then presumably this emotional connotation attaches to any subsequent elaboration of the internal world, any subsequent installation of new internalized objects. The whole process of internalization becomes laden with unworked-through jealousy, which interferes with the internal assimilation and integration of these internal objects. Here again, we get some glimpse of the extent to which the present and future welfare of the adult analytic patient's whole internalized world is dependent upon the degree to which the analysis helps him to gain access to, and thus become better able to integrate, this affective realm of intrapsychic jealousy.

In my paper, "Concerning Therapeutic Symbiosis" (1973), in a subsection entitled, "The Role of Jealousy in the Fragmented Ego," I made my first published report on an aspect of this chapter's title subject, and in 1974 made my first oral presentation concerning the present subject as a whole, under this chapter's same title, "Jealousy Involving an Internal Object" (see footnote on page 99).

Scott (1975), in a lengthy paper, "Remembering Sleep and Dreams," entitles the eleventh sub-section of his paper, "Self-envy and Envy of Dreams and Dreaming." Scott presents a number of ideas and clinical findings which have precisely to do with the subject of this chapter. He presents from his analytic practice an example of self-envy:

> His associations seemed to make it clear that the part of himself which had been anxious and incapable in the past was now envying the ego which had developed [during the course of the analysis thus far], just as this same part had previously envied his father, first the external father, later the internal one. . . . His old symptomatic anxious and reproachful self now envied his capable ego . . . (pp. 335–336).
>
> His father had also been envied. The patient's developing ego had now new assets which were identified with the envied aspects of his father . . . (p. 336).

Concerning envy of dreams and dreaming, Scott reports that

> After working with the concept of self-envy for a few years, eventually (during the summer of 1973) it occurred to me that the waking ego might envy the dreaming ego and break the link, spoil the connexion

and have none of it—or, at the most, only the memory of a token dream. Obviously it was an exciting wait until practice was resumed and I could discover whether or not the concept was useful (p. 336).

He then presents two brief examples from his subsequent analytic practice in which he was able to discern, and successfully interpret, the presence of such envy. Regarding one of the two patients in question, he describes that "In subsequent weeks' analyses [i.e., analytic sessions] many more dreams were remembered [by this analysand who had made relatively little use of dreams earlier in the analysis]. Many of them were long and . . . some were clearly indicative of situations in which envy and ambition played a role" (p. 337).

In his concluding remarks concerning that sub-section of his paper (p. 337), Scott mentions that "I am asking for the reader's indulgence since the clinical data presented is not copious. . . ."

For good surveys of the standard literature concerning envy and jealousy (surveys which essentially do not deal with that aspect of jealousy about which I am writing here), I particularly recommend the papers by Pao (1969), Joffe (1969), and Spielman (1971).

It is my hope and belief that this present chapter adds a fundamentally clarifying dimension to over-all portrayals, such as those by Kernberg (1975) and Volkan (1976), of primitive internalized object relations.

Summary

Jealousy which is related to an internal object within either oneself or the other person in an ostensibly two-person situation is at the heart of much severe and pervasive psychopathology and accounts, in psychoanalytic treatment, for much of the unconscious resistance, on the part of both patient and analyst, to the analytic process. These jealousy-phenomena, derived basically from inordinately powerful ego-splitting processes in the original infant–mother relationship wherein the infant's earliest ego-formation was taking place, comprise a much more powerful source of severe psychopathology than do those jealousy-phenomena referable to the oedipal phase of development.

These primitive jealousy-phenomena are among the most powerful determinants of, for example, ego-fragmentation, depersonalization, castration anxiety and, in the transference relationship, negative therapeutic reaction. These phenomena, being referable to the earliest infantile phases of ego-development when no clear differentiation between human and nonhuman, or between animate and inanimate, ingredients of the experienced self-and-world had yet been achieved, often are found in the transference-relationship to involve nonhuman objects which have the jealousy-engendering connotation of actual human beings.

Such jealousy-phenomena may become detectable only after prolonged analytic work has occurred, by which time the analyst and patient have come to possess a degree of emotional significance for one another approximately equal to that which the internal object—or ego fragment—in question has for its possessor.

Melanie Klein's concepts concerning the infant's primary envy of the mother's breast, his resultant feeling that a good and a bad breast exist, and the consequences of these experiences for later ego-development, are of fundamental relevance for the formulations which I have presented here.

References

Breuer, J. and Freud, S. (1893–1895). Studies on hysteria. *Standard Edition*, 2. London: Hogarth Press, 1955. See Chapter 3.

Fairbairn, W. R. D. (1952). *Psycho-Analytic Studies of the Person-ality.* London: Tavistock. Published in the U. S. under the title, *An Object-Relations Theory of the Personality*; New York: Basic Books, 1954.

Farber, L. M. (1961). Faces of envy. *Review of Existential Psychol-ogy and Psychiatry,* Vol. 1, No. 2. Reprinted on pp. 118–130 in *The Ways of the Will.* New York and London: Basic Books, 1966. See p. 125 in that volume.

Greenson, R. R. (1965). The working alliance and the transference neurosis. *Psychoanalytic Quarterly* 34:155–181.

Greenson, R. R. and Wexler, M. (1969). The non-transference rela-tionship in the psychoanalytic situation. *International Jour-nal of Psycho-Analysis* 50:27–39.

Herner, T. (1965). Significance of the body image in schizophrenic thinking. *American Journal of Psychotherapy* 19:455–466.

James, M. (1960). Premature ego development: some observations on disturbances in the first three months of life. *International Journal of Psycho-Analysis* 41:288–294.

Joffe, W. G. (1969). A critical review of the status of the envy concept. *International Journal of Psycho-Analysis* 50:533–545.

Kernberg, O. (1975). *Borderline Conditions and Pathological Nar-cissism.* New York: Jason Aronson.

Klein, M. (1932). *The Psycho-Analysis of Children.* London: Ho-garth. See Chapter 8.

―――― (1957). *Envy and Gratitude—A Study of Unconscious Sources.* New York: Basic Books. Republished in 1975 in England by the Hogarth Press and the Institute of Psycho-Analysis, and in the United States by Delacorte Press/Sey-mour Lawrence, under the title, *Envy and Gratitude & Other Works* 1946–1963.

Pao, P-N. (1969). Pathological jealousy. *Psychoanalytic Quarterly* 38:616–638. See p. 633.

Rivière, J. (1932). Jealousy as a mechanism of defence. *Interna-tional Journal of Psycho-Analysis* 13:414–424.

Ross, N. (1967). The "as-if" concept. *Journal of the American Psy-choanalytic Association* 15:59–82.

Scott, W. C. M. (1975). Remembering sleep and dreams. *Interna-tional Review of Psycho-Analysis* 2:333–338.

Searles, H. F. (1960). *The Nonhuman Environment in Normal Development and in Schizophrenia.* New York: International Universities Press.

―――― (1962). Scorn, disillusionment and adoration in the psychotherapy of schizophrenia. *Psychoanalysis and the Psychoanalytic Review* 49:39–60. Reprinted in Searles (1965), pp. 605–625.

—— (1964). The contributions of family treatment to the psychotherapy of schizophrenia. In *Family Treatment of Schizophrenia: Theoretical and Practical Aspects*, ed. I. Boszormenyi-Nagy and J. L. Framo. New York: Harper & Row. Reprinted in Searles (1965), pp. 717–751. See especially pp. 721–722.

—— (1965). *Collected Papers on Schizophrenia and Related Subjects*. London: Hogarth. New York: International Universities Press.

—— (1971). Pathologic symbiosis and autism. In *In the Name of Life—Essays in Honor of Erich Fromm*, ed. B. Landis and E. S. Tauber, pp. 69–83. New York: Holt, Rinehart and Winston. See especially pp. 73–74 and 82–83.

—— (1972). The function of the patient's realistic perceptions of the analyst in delusional transference. *British Journal of Medical Psychology* 45:1–18.

—— (1973). Concerning therapeutic symbiosis. *Annual of Psychoanalysis* 1:247–262. See pp. 256–257.

—— (1977). Dual- and multiple-identity processes in borderline ego-functioning. In *Borderline Personality Disorders: The Concept, the Patient, the Syndrome*, ed. P. Hartocollis, pp. 441–455. New York: International Universities Press. Paper presented March 19, 1976 at International Conference on Borderline Disorders, Topeka, KS. This paper also appears as Chapter 4 in this volume.

Spielman, P. M. (1971). Envy and jealousy—an attempt at classification. *Psychoanalytic Quarterly* 40:59–82. See p. 78.

Stone, L. (1967). The psychoanalytic situation and transference. *Journal of the American Psychoanalytic Association* 15:3–58.

Sullivan, H. S. (1953). *The Interpersonal Theory of Psychiatry*. New York: W. W. Norton. See p. 348.

Volkan, V. D. (1976). *Primitive Internalized Object Relations—A Clinical Study of Schizophrenic, Borderline, and Narcissistic Patients*. New York: International Universities Press.

Winnicott, D. W. (1945). Primitive emotional development. *International Journal of Psycho-Analysis* 26:137–143. Reprinted in Winnicott (1958), pp. 145–156.

—— (1958). *Through Paediatrics to Psycho-Analysis*. New York: Basic Books.

Chapter 6

Borderline Thought Disorder: A Case Report

Background Material

Mr. Bennett, an economist in his early 30s, who was working for a Federal agency, stated in his initial interview that he had come for analysis in dissatisfaction with himself for "not wanting to face the reality of things—wanting to postpone things, not face up to them. I keep myself busy so as not to face up to them." This rather small, slight, erect, and precise person *seemed* confident and outgoing—seemed a comfort-

This chapter, previously entitled "A Case of Borderline Thought Disorder," originally appeared in the *International Journal of Psycho-Analysis,* 50:655-664, 1969, and was reprinted under that title on pp. 109-131 in my *Countertransference and Related Subjects—Selected Papers;* New York: International Universities Press, 1979.

able man of action. But I felt him to be, behind this appearance, a markedly passive-dependent person who sat silent much of the time waiting for me to initiate conversation.

His wife, who unlike him had already had some years of analysis and who suffered from a variety of psychosomatic ailments, had called me some several weeks previously, wanting analysis and tearfully indicating that she despaired of being able to endure her husband much longer. I referred her to a colleague. This added to an early impression of mine that Mr. Bennett had felt coerced by her into seeking analysis, an impression which he soon confirmed. I privately noted the broad, sadistic smile with which he spoke of his wife's migraine headaches, and of the fact that while they had been living in Chicago he had made 31 business trips away, totaling 19 weeks, in one year—after his having made clear to me that such trips always caused her much distress. At the end of the initial interview, one of the notes I made said, "Inquiry as to what he was experiencing during the silences suggests that he may have considerable difficulty with his thinking processes."

I confess that during the early months of my work with this man, I felt a degree of embarrassment at the thought of my colleagues', in neighboring offices, seeing him come to my office. Used to a stream of either intellectually-and-culturally-well-honed training analysands, or wealthy urban-reared chronically schizophrenic patients coming to my office, I found myself, to my shame, feeling snobbish toward this gray, expressionless man who would come in looking like a farmer uncomfortable in his first suit of clothes, and even faintly reminiscent of an immigrant still more ill at ease in the apparel and environment of this, to him, new and foreign land. Always he wore a white shirt, a dark, uncolorful tie, a black or near-black suit, and black shoes.

He lay stiffly on his back on the couch, feet crossed at the ankles. His torso and the lower half of his body rarely, if ever, shifted position throughout the hour. When his eyes were not closed, he was staring straight up at the ceiling. Often, for long periods, his right hand was holding the top of his left shoulder, and his left forearm was crossed over the right one, with the heel of the left hand pressed motionlessly upon the middle of his forehead, as though concentrating intensely in an effort to make contact with the Infinite. This often reminded me, ironically, of the magazine ads of the Rosicrucian Order. His whole demeanor was one of agonized concentration, and I soon came to see, and repeatedly pointed out to him, that he was endeavoring to think his way through psychoanalysis.

This man grew up as the youngest among seven children of an Alabama farmer and part-time carpenter, in a family which eked out a bare subsistence in a generally poor area of the country. All the patient's three brothers were now men several inches taller than he, and all, as well as more than one of his sisters, had been valedictorian in the local high school before him. He grew up heavily burdened by the feeling that in the eyes of both his parents he could not possibly match the achievements, physical or intellectual, of his siblings. His father, the only other physically small male in the family, while widely respected as the best carpenter in the area and included as an equal among the cracker-barrel philosophers and amateur politicians of the nearby village, was generally held in the family to be a lazy and weak man. The home was run by the patient's mother, a physically large and loud-voiced woman. An event of dramatic and pervasive import upon the patient's upbringing was the death of the family's oldest child, a girl, on Good Friday one month before her graduation from high school, by lightning; the same bolt had killed a Negro hired hand

and knocked unconscious, for some few hours, both the patient's mother and another sister. This had occurred when the patient was 6 or 7 months old.

His Thought Disorder as Expressive of Unconsciously Tantalizing, Sadistic Motives

Among the earliest-apparent determinants of the patient's thought disorder were *tantalizing, sadistic* motives. He dwelt much upon his having dreamt during the previous night, having remembered the dream upon awakening, but having gone back to sleep and having found that, by now, he remembered nothing of it. For example (month 7), "I know that the dreams gave me feelings of insecurity—or—it's not really insecurity—something unpleasant or—it was an uneasy sort of position or feeling that I had—I *try* to remember these things and I lose *all traces* of it." He indicated, lying there in his usual agonized stance on the couch, that he was finding all this to be tantalizing. But there was sufficient of apology in his demeanor so that, coupled with my memory of his sadistic smiles on various previous occasions, it left me in no doubt that he was deriving sadistic gratification from the presumed tantalizing effect of all this upon me. Still more directly and with more telling effect—for I had long been used to much more silent and communicatively tantalizing patients than he—he would express amazement that, day after day as the date for bringing in his monthly check came and went, he would have had it in mind just before leaving the house, and would then remember on the way to my office that he had forgotten to bring it along.

In month 8, he mentioned, ". . . *sadist* . . . I had a mental block on this word—I had the damnedest time thinking of this word." I took this as a sign of his guilty and fearful unreadiness to explore his own sadistic feelings. But it was early evident, too, that fear lest he be sadistically teased and derided comprised another determinant of his thought disorder, in this man who evidently had had more than his share of such treatment from his many siblings.

> (month 6) "In the Bennett family . . . there was always somebody in the family who was kidding me about some insignificant thing that could have a double meaning . . . I was conditioned to try to be perfect—to avoid any vulnerability on any kind of issue. The reward for not making slips of the tongue was to not be kidded or teased about something." He went on to say that, when he was about 5 or 6, he had seen at church a little girl his age whom he knew, whose mother had her all dressed up, "and I made a comment to somebody about what a pretty bonnet she had, and for a good 6 or 8 years after, I was kidded about this girl—Ruth Ann Jones—bein' my girl friend . . . and as a result I halfway hated the girl, shied away from her—she was in my class—I was afraid to have anything to do with her for fear the wrath of the whole family would fall on me. . . ."

His Unconscious Fear of
Revealing His Aliveness

As the analysis went on, it appeared that his lack of freedom in thinking and feeling was due in part, further, to his *feeling unloved, unwanted, his consequent fear of his family's death wishes, and his fear of revealing aliveness.* In month 4 he remembered "one time when the subject came up, of whether Edgar [his next older sibling] and I had been wanted. I seem to recall my mother saying that she thought Edgar was a change of life baby—that when he was born he was just skin and bones, and that she had no idea that he would live—and I'm thinking that if she thought Edgar was a change of life baby, that if [N. B. "if"] two-and-one-half years later I was born, I must've been a hell of a surprise!"

In the previous month (month 3), he had reminisced that one time he had made a cigarette out of coffee (which may well have been expressive of an effort to integrate his identifications with father and with mother, as I shall subsequently discuss) "and I got a pretty good [N. B. "good"] beating for that . . . most of the time, when I got a whippin', my mother would make me go out and get a limb off a tree, or off of a bush, and then would use that to whip me with— it's double punishment to me." I commented, "They sometimes seemed like limbs off a tree?" to which he replied, "Right, and I'm sure many of the whippin's I got did feel that way. It seems to me I have been sent back a few times because the one I brought wasn't satisfactory—I must've learned pretty early that it would only prolong the agony to bring back a limb that was smaller than her specifications, let's say." All this was said in a tone that conveyed to me how much despair and fear and helpless hatred he must have felt. "I can remember, too, times when I was told that I'd been bad and the only thing I could expect from Santy Claus was a stocking full of switches." That comment still makes me feel like weeping as I read it. "I don't recall all of [i.e., any of] the beatings I got—I have a feeling I just wiped 'em right out of my mind, . . ." he added, in a comment particularly relevant to the blockage of his thought-processes.

Four months later (month 7), he reflected, "It seems that I grew up with a negative attitude toward life in general—it seemed that there were no rewards; there was only punishment . . . I was good because I was told that I would get the livin' hell beat out of me if I was bad [startling violence in tone]. . . ." Later in the same session, he made a significant slip of the tongue: an intended statement, "Let me recall," came out, "Let me crawl"—a clue to his transference to me as a brutally domineering mother whose beatings he evidently felt ambivalently as both evidence that she did not love him, and yet as acts of love.

During the next session (month 7), he said, "Another problem I have [is] in expressing emotions—for some reason I have great difficulty in expressing emotions—one thought I have is that I wasn't allowed to express emotions—when I was punished by my mother, I wasn't allowed to cry or make too much noise, or else I'd be punished more, or perhaps sent out of earshot." All this was said matter-of-factly, with only a kind of gentle interest in his tone.

His Competitiveness and His Impatience

Two more among the relatively easily discernible determinants of his thought disorder were his *competitiveness* and his at times lightninglike *impatience*. For example, in month 6, he said, "I've noticed that my thoughts occur much faster than I can express 'em—I have thoughts and then I stop to express 'em and then my thoughts are off on some other—they're fragments, I guess—I'm impatient at the pace I move—in other words, I don't wanta be slowed down to the talkin' pace when I can think ten times faster, or whatever it is—I think this has to do with not sayin' everything that I think. . . ." Later in this session, during which there were many silences of a few minutes' length, he said, "I'm anxious to progress as fast as I can—maybe without realizing it, I'm trying subconsciously to analyze my own thoughts to determine what is significant . . . the more significant the things are I say, the faster we can move."

Two months later (month 9), he mentioned that one can "dump memory" in a computer and "desk check" the printed-out results of such dumping, and said he guesses that one doesn't have access to the human memory the way one does to the memory of a computer. This last was said with undertones of not only exasperation and disappointment, but also of competitive triumph over me—in the implication that he could cause a computer to work so much more easily and efficiently than I was proving able to cause him to work. Later in this same month 9, he commented, "My thinking processes are clearer now than they were a few months ago—I think I learn more now from experience than I did—I know that two people can go through the—can start off equal, and have the same experience for a period of time and at the end of that time one has benefited from that experience more than the other. . . . I think now that I'm more aware of the significance of events that I experience than I was before I started analysis. . . ." I asked, "Who would the other person be?" to which he replied, "I think I was thinking of Wilson [another man at his agency] for instance. . . ." I felt this to be a hint of his competitive transference toward me, most probably as a representative of his next older sibling, Edgar, who, like himself, was also an economist and who was the only other college-educated member of the family.

Further concerning impatience, he said,

(month 6) ". . . there is a relationship between a child and waiting in my thoughts—it was an accepted custom or procedure for children to wait in my family . . ." (to wait, for example, their turn to eat when older family-members and guests filled the table, or to wait to play dominoes after the more expert, older family-members had had their fill of playing).

(month 7—an item which touches upon his identification with his mother, a subject to be discussed later—) "My mother was extremely impatient with my father and it seems to me she was also impatient with the rest of us—with me and my brothers and sisters—'When are you gonna get this job done?'—I get a picture of her yellin' at somebody because a job wasn't done, or because it wasn't done right—'right' meaning the way she thought it should be done. (month 9) ". . . I suffer from impatience—and when I say I suffer, I think I use the word correctly. . . ."

During the last month (month 17) of our work, I experienced at first hand what he may have meant by such suffering: in one session I suddenly felt, with panicky anxiety, that I was going crazy from impatience—that I couldn't stand this working as an analyst. This was a feeling of a type, and an intensity, which I had experienced only a very few times in the preceding fifteen years of such work.

His Unconscious Conflict Between His Father-Identifications and His Mother-Identifications

Early in the analysis, data began emerging which indicated that his thought disorder was due, in major part, to *conflictual identifications with his father on the one hand and with his mother on the other hand*. In his tenth session (month 2), he said that for two years now, he often blocks and is unable to think of a word. Later in the same session, he mentioned that two years ago, his father showed much grief over the death of a friend. "He'd start to talk to you, and all of a sudden he'd start to cry. . . . He was incoherent quite a bit in his speech—all of a sudden would start talking about an entirely different subject, or would mumble inaudibly," and for some weeks the father felt that he, too, was near death. Such an outpouring of incoherent thoughts evidently represented a marked change in the patient's image of his father, and his own unconscious guilt about his father's actually-long-standing depression evidently had much to do with the emergence of his own thought disorder.

In month 7, after describing, as he often had by now, his mother's ordering him and the other family members about, he said, ". . . occurs to me that maybe I *hated* her being this way. Somehow, because of this I have inherited habits from my father that I never ever wanted . . . like not talking to my wife, for instance . . . the inactivity and losin' myself in television programs rather than family participation. . . . I was the youngest of seven children—the pattern that all my brothers and sisters followed was the same: they were always loyal and loving and devoted to my mother, and a little estranged or removed from my father . . . so it seems to me such a set pattern preceded me that I had no choice—that's what I had to be; I had to follow the pattern of my brothers and sisters, my predecessors." His unconscious defiance of his mother's, and his siblings', pressure to follow that pattern evidently had acccentuated, as had his unconscious guilt, his identifications with consciously-disapproved-of aspects of his father.

> (month 3) "My mother always had a lotta things to rake my father over the coals about, and as I recall he *never* had anything to say—he wouldn't say yes, no—wouldn't even seem to hear— . . . pretty well took it and tried to ignore what she said. . . ."

In month 9, he expressed his conviction that some of the other employees at his agency were "out to get" a certain one of their number whom the patient felt to be unaware of this intention, and whom he considered innocent. He went on, "There's something in me that says, 'Ya can't stand by and see a guy crucified when he's done nothing wrong. . . .'"

Being reminded of his typically agonized, immobile posture on the couch, I felt that this remark was of transference significance: it was as if he were the silent, crucified father lying there, a reproach to the son who was failing to rescue him from his suffering and his isolation. In month 3, he had said, "I surmise that my hesitance in talking comes from the fact that my father didn't talk very much . . . and it's confusing that my [talkative] son hasn't followed the same pattern as I did. . . ." It seemed to me that the patient, during his own upbringing, had been sufficiently more vocal than his father (being regarded in the family as always ready to argue, even with a signpost), that he may have felt guilty for following so relatively little the father's pattern—may have felt responsible for the father's confusion, confusion because the son had not followed more closely the pattern of his father.

The patient's own deprivation, as regards any sense of contact with his father's thoughts and feelings, presumably was an important factor in his presently being so out of touch with his own thoughts and emotions, and clearly had fostered a sadistic attitude toward his father:

(month 6) "I don't think my father was ever very much concerned about anything—I get a blank impression of his reactions to just about everything."

(month 7) "My father always controlled his feelings so well that I guess it was difficult to know what his feelings really were—I've told you that my mother could yell at him loudly enough [example from month 3: "Alvin, get off your ass and go cut some wood!"] to shake the foundations of a stone building, and he'd give the appearance of not even hearing her . . . I know my father used to complain of having a weak ear. . . ." [But he said that at seemingly unrelated times the father,

regarded in the family as not only lazy but a hypochondriacal cry-baby, would cry out, and] It was a groaning,
sorta weird feeling I got from it. I think [said the patient with vindictive relish] that was one of his better
attempts to express himself. He was pretty good at
blocking out the things my mother used to say; but he
wasn't so good at blocking out the pain."

(month 10) "Bruce is 8 years old today [said with
great fondness and pleasure; then, after a brief si-
lence]—the thing that I think about most, the thing that
concerns me most, is my lack of communication, or lack
of expression, of my feelings to my wife and children—I
think I have adopted a distant attitude, an attitude of
'don't get too close'—I don't know why—I don't think my
father was very close to any of us children, and I know
he wasn't close to my mother . . . [and he went on, later
in the session, to reminisce about how] as a boy, I used to
wear bought overalls and homemade shirts and homemade underclothes, and during the summer I went
barefoot all summer—my mother used to clip my hair
. . . and sometimes shave my head—we didn't spend any
money on haircuts—we had a nice garden and cattle
and hogs and chickens [the care of which was all, he had
made clear in earlier hours, under his mother's domin-
ion]—we always had plenty of meat to eat—I guess
there were months when our grocery bill was as much
as $8 or $10—that seemed like an awful lot to be spending—we didn't buy much from the grocery store. . . . I'll
say this about the depression years, though: I wasn't
aware that there was a depression at that time. . . ."

He evidently had been unaware of the fact of his much-
vilified-and-scorned father's depression throughout that
era; but his own deep-lying compassion and concern and

guilt about this apparently had fostered his introjection of the depressed father. Two months later, (month 12) he began bringing out, with much feelings of love and grief, treasured memories of walking with his father, in an earlier era of his childhood, on Sundays over to a farm some distance away, where the father's mother and sister were living. Father and son had walked together in intimate silence and pleasureful contentment on these occasions.

In a session during the next-to-the-last month (month 16) of our work together, there emerged the following material which expressed not only his oft-voiced concern at finding in himself qualities which he had disliked in his father, but a new and poignant concern to maintain some sense of identification with his father in face of his mother's "brainwashing":

"And this silence is something else that reminds me of my father's habit pattern—the—uh—what I would classify emotional problem, or inability to express full affection for my children and wife, is another characteristic, I believe, of—that reminds me a great deal of my father—the thing that's extremely confusing is that I—I can recall—uh—disliking these—uh—characteristics of my father—and I'm certain that there was a conscious effort and desire on my part to avoid following this pattern, yet somehow through evolution I have found that I have adopted the same habits, same characteristics—I find that I ask myself the question, 'What else—what else about me is like my father?—uh—Is the only thing about me that's like my father things that displease me? [tone of concern]'—I think I ask myself this question because it occurs to me that there was a desire to somehow identify with my father, or somehow recognize the fact that he was [N.B.] my father."

(I'm struck right there with your use of the past

tense.)* "Yeah, I guess—uh—the thought strikes me and I guess pretty much in the same vein—there was a helluva lotta brainwashing going on, and the remarks my mother would make about my father were derogatory, and an attitude like this has a cumulative effect, and it seems to me there was an effort, whether it was conscious or otherwise, on the part of my mother to— I'm lost for expression—to somehow discredit—I don't know if 'discredit' is the word I'm looking for—in— other words to—uh—wash out the words of my father— if this went far enough it would be as if I had no father whatsoever—in other words, you know, 'A father doesn't do things like this' and 'A father shouldn't do things like this'—eventually ya begin to doubt whether this man is your father . . . an effort to discredit, or completely wash out the recollections of my father really being a father—the thought occurred to me that—uh—that through spite or—or otherwise, I might have—uh—adopted some of the habits of my father, just to perhaps convince myself or others that I recognize that he was my father—I accepted him as my father— seems to me kinda a ridiculous thing to do to adopt habits I dislike; but I have to face that possibility."

A month earlier (month 15), after having described his father's appearing absolutely unmoved by the mother's yelling demands, he had said, "I felt that men were the unemotional types who just stayed silent." As I shall elaborate more fully later, it was apparent that the new-found freedom to feel and to express emotion, which developed as the analysis proceeded, undermined the patient's sense of masculinity—masculinity as defined in the just-mentioned idiosyncratic terms ("I felt that men were the unemotional types

*The analyst's comments, in excerpts from the material of the sessions, are shown in parentheses.

who just stayed silent")—and I clearly felt, although I could not help him to see, that his fear of "homosexuality" was one of the major motives in his coming eventually to find it expedient to move away from further analysis.

His Unconscious Defiance

The role of repressed *defiance* in his thought disorder—defiance of the domineering mother-figure (i.e., mother, wife, analyst, and so on) became quite clear early in my work with him.

(month 2) [It suddenly occurred to him that] "Maybe I resent it when a new thought comes into my mind—maybe I feel pushed by a new thought—maybe I suffer from the same thing in my mental processes as I do in everyday routine test aspects. . . ."

(month 4) "I'm confident that as a child I received a great many whippings [from mother]; but I can't remember any of those whippings and I can't remember what I got any of them for."

(month 11) [Late in an hour in which a reported dream, and his associations to it, indicated that his father's elusive emotionality was being portrayed by fish in a lake in his home area] "It seems strange to me [voice now strained for the first time in the session]; but I don't recall ever going hunting or fishing with any of these people [i.e., various home-town persons he had been mentioning] . . . I remember people used to throw dynamite in the water to get the fish, and they also poisoned the water with buckeye—to explain buckeye: it's a kind of fruit with a nut and this nut is poisonous—I don't know if it's deadly poisonous; but it would make the fish come to the top for air and when they'd come to

the top they'd catch 'em [silence of several minutes] I
was trying to think of some situation now or in the past
where I felt I was being pushed into something or
forced into something—my wife exerted a lot of pressure for me to go into analysis, is one thing that comes to
mind [silence of several minutes] I was thinking of
playing golf again [silence] (I notice you don't say what
you were thinking about playing golf; but I also notice I
don't feel like asking you for fear you'll feel pushed.)
[He then went on to speak of a tournament in which he
had participated on the preceding Saturday]"

Through such silences, and the reporting of only tantalizing glimpses of what was going on in his mind, he put
intense pressure upon me to resort to some form of dynamite
or buckeye, as his mother evidently had done incessantly
with his inscrutable father.

His Unconscious Denial as Expressive of His Struggle for Autonomy; His Confusion Concerning His Own Identity

For several years I have become increasingly impressed with the evidence, in one patient after another—
whether neurotic, borderline like this man, or frankly psychotic—that unconscious denial can be best understood as
a part of the individual's *autonomy-struggle*. Considerable data in this man's treatment, for example, suggested
that both thought and emotion were subjected to massive
denial, or repression, for the reason that in his experience
both were felt to be primarily the manifestations of enslave-
ment imposed from without. Such data are of a piece with
his earlier-discussed defiance. Almost incessantly, with his
inscrutability and his conveying of subtle or only fleetingly-

glimpsed areas of feeling, he would invite me to try to coerce him to express thoughts and feelings. From the very beginning, I rarely succumbed to this pressure; from time to time, I endeavored to help him to see that he was inviting me to try to coerce him; generally, my verbal responses were of a neutral, non-committal sort; and the vast proportion of the time, I said nothing.

Frequently, in the early months of our work, in saying anything he would emphasize, in introducing it, that, "The thought occurs to me that . . ."

> (month 15) [Speaking of his father] ". . . takin' care of his family was always secondary to takin' care of his mother—I was always aware of that . . . this particular thing was a source of irritation to me—I don't know if it was a source of irritation to me because I felt my father should pay more attention to me, or because I heard my mother and brothers and sisters talk about the deficiencies and inadequacies of my father—I don't know if it was something I felt myself or something I was brainwashed with—I have a feeling that part of my struggle is to separate my own thoughts from what I was brainwashed with—I have a feeling that some of what I was brainwashed with is still present, but I don't know what the hell it is."

At this juncture I was reminded of his having expressed earlier in the analysis his feelings of exasperation, in his struggle to rid himself of psychological difficulties, by saying that it was as if there were a spring of clear water into which muddy water was recurrently flowing—that one might get the spring cleaned out, only to have it dirtied again with the influx of muddy water. I commented, "Sounds like that analogy between clear and muddy water." He replied,

"Yeah—two springs, one which puts out water that, say, is colored, and the other puts out water that's clear, and the mixture of these two sources gets something that isn't any strong, vibrant color, but that certainly isn't clear—the brainwashing that entered into my particular philosophy is, I'm sure, deep seated, and when I have independent or individual thoughts, or develop some particular philosophy on something, goes back and conflicts with this stored philosophy; I'm sure there's a great deal of internal struggle to decide which of these internal philosophies to follow, and as a result I probably don't follow either one of 'em . . . but perhaps something in between, and perhaps not . . . there's a—I suspect—feeling on my part that letting the emotions play too great a part in directing thought processes will cause me to make mistakes, following the direction of emotions rather than the directions of logic, for instance—I guess there's a fear of letting the emotions play too great a part in—uh—in—my—uh—thought processes. . . ."

It was in the following hour that, in a similar state of confusion, he said,

"I don't know what my attitudes were, separated from the brainwashings that I received."

These passages not only reflect this man's intense struggle for individuality, but show his deep confusion as to wherein does his own true self lie: is it to be considered the clear spring, and is the "brainwashing" that muddy water which contaminates it? But this other spring which was once seen as comprised of muddy water, is now seen as being water of a vibrant color—strongly suggestive of emotion. Is, then, this vibrantly-colored spring to be considered the well-spring of his individuality—of his own true self? On the other hand, so he seems to feel, emotions are contaminants, imposed upon him from the outside and not a part of his essential self, which cause flaws in the purity of his thought-processes. What he evidently does not realize, at this juncture, is that conflict is inescapable, and that an individual self can be born only out of such conflict.

His Unconscious Non-Differentiation Between Inner and Outer Reality

This man's thought-disorder, at perhaps its deepest level, included a *lack of qualitative differentiation between inner and outer reality*—between mental images and verbal thoughts, on the one hand, and the corresponding objects in outer reality. This reification of his thoughts greatly complicated his ability to think freely, for he feared the tangible power of thoughts to do harm either to him or—since, as I shall shortly describe, he greatly feared his own hostility—to others.

I have already quoted his speculation that "maybe I feel pushed by new thoughts" much as though these were equivalent to the persons whose pushing he rebelled against, and his reacting as though the destruction of his father-identification, by the mother's brainwashing, would be equivalent to the destruction of the father in outer reality. In one session, he came in looking at his most gray and cheerless, and after a brief silence, began,

(month 7) "There've been a lotta thoughts running through my mind—I see a fragment—of one thought—and then I see another—the first thought I've been able to hold together is that I just live from one day to the next without purpose, really—without enjoying the day."

The word "fragment" was said with a startling concreteness, as if it were a rock fragment. I was reminded of his having begun a session earlier in the same month with,

> (month 7) "Did you ever see anyone tease an animal . . . till it became frustrated? I have a feeling that as a kid, my brothers and sisters older than me did this to me—and then when I could stand it no longer, I have an image of pickin' up a rock and throwin' it at one of 'em—if I did somethin' like this I would be punished—I should think somethin' like this would affect the control of emotions . . . I get the feeling that I was boiling, so to speak, all the time; I was being annoyed or teased, or whatever it might be called."

He reacted much of the time, indeed, as though the free experiencing and expression of thoughts were potentially as destructive as would be his throwing rocks at me. In a session two months later, after speaking sympathetically of a Negro man at work whom he felt to be discriminated against by the other employees, and after mentioning recent news reports of rock-throwing at Negro students in the South, he said that he knows his father is a member of the Ku Klux Klan, "because one time I found an old sheet with the eyes cut out in the trunk," and added,

> (month 9) "I could get a picture of him out there throwing rocks at these colored people."

One could find, in the manifestations of this man's thought disorder, evidence of its representing a struggle against identification with various aspects of both the father, as is hinted at in the above material, and the mother, whose domineering verbosity he had so greatly resented during his upbringing. There was much evidence that, during his upbringing, words—and hence at a deeper level the thoughts which gave rise to the words—were used as weapons to inflict hurt.

His Unconscious Rage

From the very beginning of the analysis, there were many indications that this man was afraid that his *rage* might get out of control, and there were times, during his rigid silences, when I felt a nagging uneasiness lest he suddenly get up and hit me. These fantasies on my part gained substance from such material as the following:

> (month 3) [He was speaking of his wife's childhood] ". . . when she was a kill—when she was a kid, her parents yelled at her a great deal . . . I know that my wife had an extremely rough time as a kid— . . . [Then, in response to my suggestion that he see what his slip of the tongue, 'when she was a kill,' brought to mind—] When I was 14-15 years old I hit my father for some reason—glasses—around one eye a spot bleeding—some blood on his glasses—I don't know why I can't recall what caused this—it was in the house—it was in his bedroom—I don't remember who else was there; but I remember his reaction: he didn't say anything or do anything—he just got busy with something else and seemed to ignore the fact that anything had happened. . . . I know there was some strong talk, heated talk, before we had this conflict—I don't remember what the argument was about— . . . I told him I wouldn't stand

for his touchin' me, or somethin' [a hint of the unconscious fear of homosexuality which contributed greatly
to his eventual flight from the analysis]—I don't remember what the conversation was about—but I do
remember takin' a poke at him, and I still remember
there was some bleedin' around one of his eyes—that
was the only time I can think of when I mighta been so
mad that I coulda killed him . . . (One gets the impression, from your description, that if you had gone on, he
would not have defended himself.) I think that's true
[calmly]—I think the sight of blood shocked me back
into the reality of what was happening."

His Unconscious Striving for Omnipotence

Another major theme which ran through this man's analysis
and contributed greatly to his thought-disorder was his *striving to rid himself of his so-conflict-ridden human status by
becoming an omnipotent and immortal machine.* This striving evidenced itself very early in our work; within the first
two months I gained the ironic impression that prior to the
analysis he had nearly succeeded in becoming an IBM machine, and had come grudgingly to the analysis primarily in
an effort to divest himself of his few remaining contaminants of human emotion.

(month 2) [A session which began with 10–15 minutes of silence] "If I could control my thought processes
so that I could control my thoughts when I'm angry, I'd
be very happy."

(month 2) "I have a feeling that when your emotions start takin' effect in a discussion, that's when it

changes from a discussion to an argument. . . . This is what I would like to be able to control."

(month 3) ". . . the communications problem I have with my wife . . ."

(month 3) ". . . I have a feeling that I should be keen mentally all the time."

(month 4) "When I have a memory block, it's as if something inside me says, 'I'm afraid you're going to mess up.'"

(month 4) [Mentions that, for over a year now, he has been working with a special type of IBM machine of which only a few have been built, specifically for the particular Government agency where he works, and that] ". . . without a doubt, I know more than anybody else about this equipment. Yesterday I was away for just one-and-one-half hours, and while I was away, three of the six machines broke down. Sanderson made the remark that every time I leave there, the place crumbles. I have a feeling that I withhold some of the knowledge and keep it to myself so that I'll be needed more."

His despising of himself for his human limitations was at times shocking in its intensity:

(month 3) "When I was a kid I was small, underdeveloped, or weak . . . [went on to say that he had had a great deal of trouble with muscle-cramps in his calves, but that this had not alarmed him] because I would have expected it to go along with a general sickly condition . . . I know that I was a sickly individual [tone of hissing scorn] and I guess I expected to be ill and have pain—these sort of things."

(month 4) "To realize I made a mistake kinda shatters me . . . I get the impression I've had lots of fights with my conscience . . . [says that after an exchange with another economist, he used to think to himself] 'That wasn't right. You're not an economist. If you were an economist you wouldn't have done this!'—I don't tell myself what I would have done, . . ." and he went on with a rather staggering account of how typically critical he is toward himself. "My confidence is shattered when I criticize myself for doing something wrong . . . I seem to remember, as a kid growing up, feeling *extremely* limited in my activities—the boundaries of activities for me were extremely limited by evil—I had extremely strong images of what was right and wrong—I don't feel I have that strong images of what is right and wrong [i.e., any more] . . . I'm afraid that I've got the categories of superior, good, average . . . mixed up with good and evil—as far as judging myself is concerned, I think of myself as evil if I don't achieve what I could achieve. . . ."

All this was really quite shaking in its latent intensity, and reminded me how uncomfortable it is for the analyst to occupy the role of such a superego; I understood better, now, why I had been uncharacteristically lenient toward him about a late check recently.

(month 7) [He described a premarital affair with a girl in Mexico, and said,] "There's a feeling of *guilt*. I don't even recognize it; but I'm sure there's a feeling of guilt, [and added that the feeling of guilt] probably contributes to my emotional block. [He then went into detail about his having been taught, by his mother, that many things are bad] As a kid I was taught saint-like behavior, [said with a deliberateness born of suppressed fury]. . . . I didn't dance as a kid—this was one of the things that was considered bad—I didn't drink wine or any alcoholic beverage . . . But it concerns me that there's perhaps still something within me that tells me these things are bad . . . I wonder if it's become a permanent standard . . . It—the standards would be mad at me [N.B.] for . . ." [He associated the premarital affair with his going upstairs at night as a kid and stealing a nickel or dime from his father's pocket]

(month 8) "There's still a great deal of me that's child, I guess—and I suspect that there's a desire to hide this phase of me. . . . Bruce, instead of saying, 'When I get old enough' to do something, will say, 'When I get young enough to get a BB rifle and go out in the woods and hunt' . . ."

(month 15) He referred to his childhood situation as regards his mother's yelling and his father's silence, as "choosing between those two evils [N.B.], those two extremes . . ." in such a tone as forcibly to convey with what godlike superiority and condemnation something in him had reacted to both his parents.

He often likened himself to a machine, at times consciously and figuratively, but often unconsciously and with a startling concreteness:

(month 6) He expressed the feeling that, at work, in their present methods of logging production by the IBM machine, "They're being unfair to the machine. . . . I told Sanderson we were logging the performance of a machine, not of an operator," he said, conveying a feeling of closer kinship with the machine than with his human co-workers.

(month 7) He began, "I was running this rewards and punishments thought through my mind at various ages, the various stages of my life, and nothing comes . . .", for all the world as if he were speaking of running cards through an IBM machine.

In a session in month 12, while speaking of a current work-project, he described it in what he called "our language," namely, "machine language." I found it striking how congenial he seemed to regard "machine language" as applied to himself.

The Unconscious Conflict Between His Striving for Omnipotence and His Infantile Needs

There early appeared evidence that one of his deepest conflicts was that between *his striving, on the one hand, to become fully an omnipotent machine and, on the other hand, to retain an image of himself as being a mentally and physically retarded child who had been beloved and pitied as such by his mother.* In month 3, he mentioned that until he went into the Army, at 17,

". . . my mother used to call me 'Baby'—maybe she'd still be calling me that; but I haven't been around much since I was 17—When I was a kid, I was the Charles Atlas when he was a 97-pound weaklin'."

He said that until age 11 or 12 he had been "very sickly," with tonsillitis, adenoids, hay fever, and nosebleeds, but added that he had been ill only a couple of times since age 13 or 14. He described a scene which occurred frequently in his boyhood, when his mother and sister would be working together out on the lawn, doing the washing, while the patient lay on a "pallet" under a nearby tree. It was evident to me that these experiences had been among the most peaceful, contented times in his life. But it was not until month 8 that he said, ". . . question arises in my mind whether I miss bein' ill myself. . . ." It was becoming evident now how greatly he was threatened lest his own omnipotent strivings be fulfilled and thus disqualify him from sharing human love.

That is, presumably one of the determinants of his thought-disorder consisted in his experience-based conviction that, if only he showed me what an agonizingly difficult time he had in trying to think, then I would give him motherly solicitude and protection. But his own conflict-born sense of helplessness and futility was very real. In month 3, for example, he was saying, "It occurs to me that I got the impression somewhere along the way, as a kid, that I was retarded both mentally and physically, . . . mentally, especially as far as maturity is concerned. The forces I feel are 'You're retarded in this area' and 'I want to be mature.'" Each of these forces was expressed by him with great intensity. I asked, "Where are *you* in all that?", to which he replied with one of the most moving communications from a conflict-ridden self that I have ever heard: "Where *I* am is the battleground."

In these closing months of my work with him, it became evident that what the analysis was exploring (with specific regard to his thought-disorder) was not his thinking per se, but his thinking as expressed in vocalization. With the considerable derepression of his oral desires which occurred during these months—expressed in dreams about touching a girl's breast, about drinking a Coke, and so on—I saw in retrospect something of how greatly the *repression of his sucking- and biting-impulses* had been hindering the free flow of his speech and, since thought and speech are so much wedded, presumably had been hindering the differentiation and free exercise of his thought processes as a still deeper consequence. During these final months, an impressive liberation of thought and speech went hand in hand with the emergence from repression of his oral desires. As part of this liberative process he became more freely able to experience an intuitive, "one grand swoop" (as he called it) kind of thinking, formerly reacted against as womanly, for it was characteristic of an incisively quick-witted aspect of his mother (whose letters, so it now became revealed, were full of playfully darting innuendoes aimed at his wife), and unlike his relatively inarticulate father.

His Unconscious Grief; The Closing Months of the Analysis

During the last several months there emerged many nostalgic, grief-laden memories of his boyhood, with considerable working-through of *feelings of loss* in relation to each parent, and, in month 12, a dream provided a clue to the heavy childhood burden he had borne in trying to cope with his father's depression:

> "My Uncle Luther had died and it was a sudden and unexpected death. . . . Some very small kids, 4- or 5-year-olds, were acting as pallbearers. Seemed like the casket was too heavy for them and some men around them raised the casket and put it up [for the funeral service]. . . . Aunt Cora, Uncle Luther's wife, most significant thing about her was her expression: she seemed

very calm and solemn but not crying. I remember saying to somebody that she must still be in shock."

Upon hearing this I was reminded of the patient's characteristic demeanor and I sensed, in retrospect, to what an
extent such shocking and overwhelming loss (the casket too
heavy for the children), at a level more deeply unconscious
than his previously-revealed sadism and defiance and other
negative feelings, had been contributing to his thought disorder.

A dream reported during this same month (12) reflected his newly-liberated identification with his mother's
liveliness, and his ability to cope more freely with grief:

"My brother Edgar and our cousin John and I were
cleaning out a pool which was divided into little sections. . . . In the area where we hadn't specifically
worked, Edgar told me there wouldn't be any fish in
those sections. I didn't believe this, and went and got a
pole, to catch a fish and show him. I remember seein' a
fish, a little bitty one, and saying to him there *was* fish
there. At this point the water was clear—kind of a
school of fish like porpoise that were leaping in and out
of the water, going all over the pool [slightly awed
tone]—all sections of the pool . . . As I was thinking
about the dream this morning, it seemed to me the pool
and the contents of the pool might represent me . . . To
me it was significant when Edgar said there won't be
any fish in that part of the pool, and then seeing a fish—
of course it was a little bitty one; but it represented a
school of fish, then seeing this school of porpoise swim-
ming through all the sections of the pool [rising tide of
energy in his tone] represents to me that all sections of
the pool were filled as far as schools of fish are con-

cerned. This comment of Edgar, that there won't be any fish in that section of the pool, represents the environment we grew up in, which was a negative environment [covered with prohibitions]. . . ."

His whole tone in describing the dream was expressive of the growth and liberation which the dream-content portrayed.

The final hour (month 17) was one marked by both grief and relief for both of us—for him, grief at losing me, admixed with relief at his becoming free of an analyst who was still viewed, to a significant degree, as his domineering, brainwashing and infantilizing early mother; and for me, grief at losing a person with whom I had been through a great deal and with whom much had been accomplished together, but relief, too, that I would not have to come to grips with his most deeply paranoid proclivities, which were still menacing in their intensity.

Discussion

In a paper in 1962 concerning the thought disorder in schizophrenia I reviewed the relevant literature in this field.* During the subsequent years I have not encountered additional writings which are necessary to be mentioned in this brief paper. In this sketchy account of one among the main themes of a highly incomplete psychoanalysis I have endeavored to show how multidetermined, and how essentially reversible, this man's thought disorder proved to be.

*The differentiation between concrete and metaphorical thinking in the recovering schizophrenic patient. *Journal of the American Psychoanalytic Association* 10:22–49, 1962. Also on pp. 560–583 of *Collected Papers on Schizophrenia and Related Subjects*. London: The Hogarth Press; New York: International Universities Press, 1965.

Part III

Countertransference

Chapter 7

Countertransference as a Path to Understanding and Helping the Patient

A working definition of what I mean by "countertransference" is provided by the first sentence of a lengthy definition in *A Glossary of Psychoanalytic Terms and Concepts*, edited by Moore and Fine, and published by the American Psychoanalytic Association in 1967: "Countertransference: Refers to the attitudes and feelings, only partly conscious, of the analyst towards the patient . . ." (p. 29). The rest of their lengthy definition is one with which I largely concur, but is unnecessary to reproduce here.

This chapter was published, under the title "The Countertransference in Psychoanalytic Therapy with Borderline Patients," on pp. 309–346 in *Advances in Psychotherapy of the Borderline Patient*, edited by J. LeBoit and A. Capponi; New York: Jason Aronson, 1979.

For many years, I have found that the countertransference gives one one's most reliable approach to the understanding of patients of whatever diagnosis. My monograph (Searles 1960) on the nonhuman environment and many of my previous papers have contained detailed data and discussions of the countertransference in my work with frankly psychotic patients, and this chapter will not attempt to condense those earlier writings.

As an example of the usefulness of the countertransference, as regards the question of whether it is advisable for the borderline patient to use the couch, for nearly 30 years now it has seemed to me that the patient is unlikely to be panicked by this experience if the analyst himself, sitting behind the couch, does not give way to panic.

Comparably, in my work with an ambulatorily schizophrenic woman who had moved from sitting in a chair to sitting on the couch, I found that the next analytic-developmental step, of her becoming able to lie down on the couch, involved a question not merely of *her* being able to adapt to the isolation attendant upon her no longer being able to see *my* face. I came to realize, after she had started lying down upon it but sitting up from time to time to get a look at my face, that my relief at those "interruptions" of her lying on the couch was fully comparable with her own. I had been repressing the feelings of deprivation attendant upon *my* own no longer being able, while she was lying on the couch, to watch *her* fascinatingly mobile facial expressions.

When a borderline patient who had been sitting in a chair for some months began lying on the couch, I found that during the first session of my sitting behind it I was speaking to her much more than had been my custom. Upon noticing this, my first thought was that I was supplying, empathically, sufficient verbal feedback to her to help her to become accustomed to this new and, for her, much more emotionally-isolated situation. Only some time later in this session did I realize that, again, I myself evidently was repressing abandonment-anxiety, and struggling to keep such anxiety repressed and projected upon her.

In the work with the borderline patient, there are several readily-apparent reasons why the realm of the countertransference is so important. I intend to discuss additional, less obvious reasons; but first I shall make brief mention of some of the more obvious ones.

The intensity of the borderline patient's repressed emotions is so great as to make unusual demands upon the emotionality of the analyst. These demands are greatly accentuated by the patient's wide gamut of ego-developmental levels at work in his mode of relating with the analyst, such that the latter finds himself called upon to relate with the patient upon unpredictably shifting levels which vary from relatively mature, healthy-neurotic modes to extremely primitive modes essentially akin to those found in the transference psychoses of frankly schizophrenic patients. Not uncommonly, the analyst feels related with the patient upon two or more of such levels simultaneously.

So much of the borderline patient's ego-functioning is at a symbiotic, pre-individuation level that, very frequently, it is the analyst who, through his own relatively ready access to his own unconscious experiences, is first able to feel in awareness, and conceptualize and verbally articulate, the patient's still-unconscious conflicts. Though these conflicts inherently "belong" to the patient, they can come to be known to and integrated by him only through his identification with the analyst into whom they have been able to flow, as it were, through the liquidly symbiotic transference.

Because the *borderline* patient does indeed seem, during much if not most of our work with him, to be walking a tightrope between neurosis and psychosis, he requires us to face our fear lest he become psychotic, our envy of him for his having this avenue so widely open to him, our hateful

desire for him to become psychotic, as well as our ambivalent fear and wish to become psychotic, ourselves.

Because the normal phase of mother–infant symbiosis
in him never has been resolved into predominantly individuated ego-functioning, we find that in the transference-sym-
biosis which naturally ensues over the course of the analysis,
we are cast not only as the symbiotic mother in the transference but, equally often and by the same token, as the symbiotic infant. We must accustom ourselves, therefore, to the
experiencing of symbiotic-dependency feelings toward the
mother-patient such as are only relatively subtly present in
our work with neurotic patients.

The Impact upon the Analyst of the Patient's Split Ego-Functioning

Gunderson and Singer (1975) in an article entitled, "Defining Borderline Patients: An Overview," provide a helpful
survey of the large literature of descriptive accounts of borderline patients. Among several features which they found
that most authors believe to characterize most borderline
patients, the foremost is the presence of intense affect. In
entering, now, into my more detailed discussion, I want first
to highlight the impact upon the analyst of the patient's
unintegrated ambivalence—or, perhaps better expressed,
the impact upon him of the unintegrated affects which the
patient expresses toward him referable to the splits in the
patient's ego-functioning, such that intensely hateful affects
are not integrated with (and thus modified by) intensely
loving affects, and vice versa.

I cannot fully convey here these impacts, for the reason
that I cannot achieve, at will, such a complete splitting of
intense emotions as prevailed at the level of ego-functioning
in these patients on these occasions; I must elaborate upon

the quoted comments, therefore, with some brief description. One woman patient said, "I can't tell you how much I love you or how much of a shit I think you are." In saying, "how much I love you," her affective tone was one of glowingly unambivalent love; but in saying only moments later, "how much of a shit I think you are," her affect was unambivalently one of hostile contempt. Another woman, in reminiscing that her mother used to address her as "my darling rat," conveyed by her tone that the words "darling" and "rat" had been expressive of forcefully contrasting emotions without any acknowledgment, in the mother's ego-functioning, of any conscious conflict between these two images of her daughter. A chronically schizophrenic woman once said to me, "You should have the Congressional Medal of Spit." The first seven words of that eight-word sentence conveyed heartfelt admiration; but the last one, said with no break at all in the rhythm of her speech, was uttered in unalloyed contempt.

The examples of patients' affective expressions which I have just cited are of expressions which switch instantaneously from loving to hateful ones. Even more unsettling, oftentimes, is a patient's expression of highly incongruous emotions simultaneously. Such phenomena comprise a part of what is not only difficult but also fascinating in the work with borderline patients, for one discovers that there are combinations of intense emotions which one had never encountered before within one's conscious memory.

For example, I have come to realize that two of the part-aspects of one of the patients with whom I am working comprise what I experience as an irresistibly funny homicidal maniac. I had long been aware of his quick-tempered fury at any perceived insult, and of his underlying murderousness; but as the work has gone on it has become evident that he possesses also an enormous ability to be funny, giving me at times to feel overwhelmed with the urge to laugh at some of his raging comments, and yet to feel, simultaneously, that it is of life-and-death importance not to let him detect my amusement. On rare occasions with him and comparable patients, I have been seized with a strangled, epileptic-seizure-like laughter, and on some of these occasions have managed successfully, apparently, to disguise it as a cough or somatically-based fit of choking. My underlying terror of detection in some of these instances is lest I be murderously attacked physically or—hardly less frightening—be subjected to a demolishing verbal attack. In a greater number of instances, the terror is lest the outraged patient sever, instantly and irrevocably, the treatment relationship which he and I have built up so slowly and arduously.

In my work with one such patient after another, it becomes evident that the patient's largely-unconscious sadism has had much to do with my finding myself in so tortured a position. Only somewhat milder forms of this same phenomenon are to be found in one's work with a supervisee who, simultaneous with a hawklike sensitivity to any increment of somnolence on one's part, is reporting the clinical material in a soothing tone, or a boring one, or some other tone which drives one almost irresistibly toward sleep.

To return to borderline patients, a woman was reporting a dream in her usual overly-modulated tone which was thoroughly enigmatic as regards emotions, saying, ". . . We were all under some kinda interstellar influence, some kinda unseen force that was controlling things. . . . kinda malevolent force hovering around. . . ." Meanwhile, as I was writing down the dream, I noticed that each time I wrote the word "force," I had a momentary thought either that it was written "farce" or else that I had to be careful not to write "farce." I sensed there to be an unusual theme, here, of a murderous farce, or a sinister farce. The patient gave a brief chuckle at the beginning of her description of the parts of the dream which I have quoted; but in the main she sounded to be fending off an awed, whistling-in-the-graveyard feeling. Later in this session she commented, without identifiable emotion of any sort, that her former room-mate, years ago in law school, had been electrocuted in a strange "accident." During the years of her analysis, her fear lest she possess an omnipotent destructiveness proved to be one of the major themes of our work together.

To simply mention other unusual affective combinations, I have been struck by the diabolical naîveté of one of my male patients, and by this same patient's ferocious idealizing of me—his idealizing me with ferocity. I have felt one patient to give me a slashing smile upon her walking in from the waiting room, and another (this one far more ill than borderline) to give me a decapitatingly saccharine verbal greeting when I walked into the seclusion room for my usual session with her. Another female patient has often provided me gratification with the caustic warmth of her so-ambivalent responses to me.

I have found this same phenomenon (of strange-seeming combinations of affects) at work in many teaching-interviews I have had with patients who were manifesting pathologic grief-reactions. That is, I have found myself experiencing sadistic urges toward depressed patients who clearly were repressing intense grief; only gradually did my initial shock at finding these sadistic urges in myself, in that setting, give way to an understanding that I was experiencing something of the sadistic feelings which were at work at an unconscious level in the patients themselves, and which thus far had been preventing the further accomplishment of their work of grieving.

Surely some of these instances of patients' giving expression, simultaneously, to so intensely incongruous emotions are manifestations of incongruously non-fitting introjects, within the patient, derived from the two parents; the disharmoniously-wedded parents have counterparts (how-

ever much exaggerated or otherwise distorted) in comparably poorly-married parental introjects largely unintegrated
in the patient's ego-functioning. But even more pathogeni-
cally, neither parent was well-integrated within himself or
herself. Thus the mother alone, or the father alone (or both)
presumably presented to the child, as a model for identification, the embodiment of intensely incongruent emotionality
such as we find in the patient himself. Hence either parent,
taken alone, can have been the source (so to speak) of an
abundance of non-fitting parental introjects within the patient.

Amusement

In relation to those occasions, which I mentioned earlier,
when the analyst finds himself in the grip of amusement
which he experiences as crazily incongruous with the more
predominant and explicit aspects of his interaction with the
patient, I wish to emphasize that, during the childhood of
such a patient, some of the most traumatic effects of his
family-relatedness derived from his having to maintain
under dissociation his essentially healthy laughter. It is this
healthy laughter which, more often than not, in the patient–
therapist interaction is experienced first by the analyst, and
then only after much resistance on the latter's part. Laughter is, after all, one of the precisely most appropriate, most
healthy, kinds of response to the crazy things that have gone
on in the childhood-families of borderline patients, and that
transpire not infrequently during their analytic sessions in
adult life.

   In the many teaching-interviews I have done, it is usual
for there to emerge some occasion, during the interview, for
the patient and I to laugh at least briefly together. Not
rarely, this is the first time the therapist and other hospital

staff-members, for example, have seen such a capacity for humor in the patient. It is rare indeed for me to encounter a patient in whom I am unable, during a single interview, to perceive a sense of humor, no matter how straight-faced or laden with lugubriousness it may be, or manifested in however sadistic or psychotically-distorted a means of expression.

Our traditional training, as well as the mores of our culture, have so schooled us with the rigorous taboo against laughing *at* the poor victim of psychosis that it is difficult for us to realize that some of his most grievous warp, in childhood, derived from the family-wide taboo against healthy laughter, lest such laughter do violence to the so vulnerable sensibilities of the other family members. If we can dare to let our "own" healthy laughter come into the patient–therapist interaction, we can help him to find access to his "own" long-repressed healthy capacities in this regard. Parenthetically, in my many-years-long work with a chronically schizophrenic woman, there are many sessions in which I feel that the only solidly healthy responses she manifests consist in her occasional belly-laughs, unaccompanied by any verbal communications. It is amusement which I share, at such times, however uncomprehendingly in any secondary-process terms.

The Analyst's Experience of Transference-Roles Which Are Both Strange in Nature and Inimical to His Sense of Reality and to His Sense of Personal Identity

Turning from the subject of the impact upon the analyst of the patient's emotions *per se*, I want briefly to delineate the integrally-related topic of the analyst's experiencing of the strange transference-roles in which he finds himself by reason of the patient's developing transference, at times psychotic or near-psychotic in its reality-value for the patient.

The major roots of the patient's transference reactions are traceable to a stage in ego development prior to any clear differentiation between inner and outer world, and prior to the child's coming to function as a whole person involved in interpersonal relationships with other persons experienced as whole objects. Hence the analyst finds these transference-reactions and -attitudes of the adult borderline patient to be casting him, the analyst, in roles strangely different from those he commonly encounters in working with the neurotic patient whose transference casts him as, say, a domineering father or as a sexually seductive, masochistic mother. Now, instead, the analyst finds the patient reacting to him as being non-existent, or a corpse, or a pervasive and sinister supernatural force, or as God, or as being the patient's mind, or some anatomical part-aspect of his mother (her vagina, for example, or her fantasied penis). My monograph concerning the nonhuman environment (Searles 1960) contains many examples of schizophrenic patients' transference-reactions to the therapist as being one or another of a wide variety of nonhuman entities, and one finds an equally wide range in the work with borderline patients.

Not only the bizarre content or structure of the patient's transference-images of him, but also their near-psychotic reality value for the patient, come at times formidably to threaten the analyst's own sense of reality and his own sense of identity. For example, I found that one of the sources for my persistent hatred of one such patient was that his intense transference to me as being his highly obsessive mother exerted such a powerful pull upon me toward going back to my earlier, much more obsessive, only partially outgrown self, that I hated him for this. A woman reported, several years along in our work together, that the thought had just occurred to her, for the first time, that perhaps I am *not* crazy. She went on to associate the craziness which, she now realized, she had previously been attributing all along to me, with that which she had perceived in her father since the patient's early childhood. All along I had had to cope, alone, with the patient's persistent but unconscious transference-image of me as being crazy. Another woman, whose childhood had been lived in remarkable isolation from both parents, and who had used to talk with insects and birds, manifested transference-reactions to me as being one or another of these creatures, and I never became able fully to determine whether, even in childhood, the conversations she had had were with real creatures of this sort, or with fantasied ones.

The omnipotent creativity, for good or evil but predominantly for evil, which frankly psychotic patients attribute to their own and the therapist's thought-processes, is to only a somewhat lesser degree true of the borderline patient also. Unlike the frankly psychotic patient, the borderline individual possesses, most of the time, sufficient of observing ego so that he does not fully misidentify the therapist as being someone (or a part-aspect of someone or something) from the patient's real past. But the borderline patient comes, nonetheless, close to doing this. Therefore, the therapist may feel submergedly threatened lest this transference role become, indeed, his—the therapist's—only subjective reality.

A middle-aged woman said in a session several years along in her analysis, during a brief interchange between us as to whom various persons in a just-reported dream were personifying or representing, "People are never to me who *they* think they are. They are who *I* think they are." She said this in a tone of small-child-like grandiosity and without appearing consciously disturbed or threatened. She said it in terms of pointing out to me, or reminding me of, an obvious fact. The charming-little-child quality of this expressed recognition on her part was in marked contrast to the genuinely threatening effects upon me, many times in earlier years when her negative transference had been much more intense and her ability to differentiate between mental images and flesh-and-blood outer reality had been much less well established. During those years I had felt anything but charmed by her reacting to me with the full conviction that I was (to give but one example) a literally stone-hearted witch.

To the extent that a patient is unable to distinguish between the analyst as, say, a mother in the transference-situation, and the actual mother in the patient's early childhood, he is likewise unable to differentiate between *mental images of persons* (i.e., images within his own head) and the corresponding *persons in outer reality*. This is another way of understanding why the analyst reacts to the borderline patient's transference-images of him as being such a threat to the latter's sense of personal identity—that is, as to why the patient's transference-*image* of him, an image which the patient experiences as being so fully and incontestably real, carries with it the threat, to the analyst, that it will indeed fully create or transform him into conformity with that image.

I shall turn again to my work with frankly and chronically schizophrenic patients for relatively unambiguous examples of this point. Each of the following two instances occurred relatively early in my work with such patients, at a time when more areas of my own identity were existing at a repressed or dissocated level than I find to be the case these days in my work with patients. One chronically and severely assaultive woman asked me, at a time when I was conscious of feeling toward her only a wish to help her and a physical fear of her, "Dr. Searles, *why* do you hate me?" She asked me this in a tone of assuming it to be an incontrovertible fact that I hated her, that hatred was the predominant—if not only—feeling I was experiencing toward her, and that all this was something we both had known all along. In response to her question I felt thoroughly disconcerted and at a loss to know what, if anything, to say. I thought that theoretically I must hate her, but was entirely unaware of hating her and—most pertinent for the point I am making here—I felt completely alone, without any ally in her, as regards any attempt on my part to question, with her, whether her view of me was not at all exaggerated, oversimplified, or otherwise distorted.

Another chronically ill woman, who for several years in our work perceived me most of the time as being, in flesh-and-blood reality, a woman, and who was herself the mother of several children, once said to me in very much the same tone as that used by the woman I have just mentioned, "*You*'re a reasonable woman; what do *you* do with a daughter who . . ." She was speaking for all the world in terms of our being two women comparing notes, companionably, about the problems of rearing daughters.

In the neurotic patient it may be that an unconscious *personality-aspect*, such as hostile domineeringness, based upon an unconscious identification with the domineeringness of, say, the father, is projected during the course of the analysis upon the analyst, who is perceived by the patient, meanwhile, as being essentially the same person as before but with, so the patient now perceives him, a hatefully and perhaps intimidatingly domineering aspect. The analyst may sense himself, in response to these developments, to have an uncomfortably domineering personality-aspect, but does not feel his basic sense of his own identity to be appreciably disturbed.

Although such a state of things may be true in psychoanalytic work between a neurotic patient and the analyst, in the borderline patient there is insufficient of ego-integration for the unconscious domineeringness to exist as merely a repressed component of the patient's ego-identity. It exists, instead, in a dissociated, split-off state as a largely uninte- grated introject derived from experiences with the parent in question. It exists as a separate self, as it were—a compo- nent with its own separate identity. Now, when the analyst becomes involved in psychoanalytic psychotherapy with such a patient, he finds that the patient, through projecting this introject upon the analyst, comes not merely to perceive the analyst as being the analyst with a newly-revealed hate- ful domineeringness. The analyst finds, instead, that the patient becomes more or less fully convinced that the ana- lyst has been replaced by the hatefully and intimidatingly domineering father.

That is, in the work with the borderline or schizo- phrenic patient, the unconscious affect is encapsulated in, or pervades, an introject-structure which has an identity-value all its own. This affect-laden structure which the patient, to the extent that he is schizophrenic, is convinced *is* the real identity of the analyst has, through its being projected forci- bly and persistently upon the latter for many months or even years, at times a formidably shaking effect upon the ana- lyst's own sense of his identity.

But on the positive side, the analyst, through being attentive to the resultant fluctuations in his sense of his "own" personal identity in the course of the sessions with these patients, finds that he possesses a priceless (and, more often than not, previously unrecognized) source of analytic data. In a paper entitled, "The Sense of Identity as a Percep- tual Organ," I (Searles, 1965a) mentioned that somewhere midway through my own analysis, after I had undergone much change, I visualized the core of myself as being, none- theless, like a steel ball bearing, with varicolored sectors on its surface. At least, I told myself, this would not change. But by this time, in 1965, I noted that I had lost, long ago, any such image of the core of my identity. In a succession of papers I have described the process whereby my sense of identity has become sufficiently alive to change so that it is now my most reliable source of data as to what is transpiring between the patient and myself, and within the patient. I have described the "use" of such fluctuations in one's sense of identity as being a prime source of discovering, in work with the patient, not only countertransference processes but also transference processes, newly-developing facets of the patient's own self-image and so on; and in supervision, of discovering processes at work not only between the supervisee and oneself, but also between the supervisee and the patient.

For a number of years during the analysis of a young woman I felt, more often than not during the session, somnolent and much of the time indeed, sensed that her transference to me was, even more, as being comatose, moribund. Many of the sessions felt endless to me. After several years, her transference to me began to emerge into her own awareness through such dreams as this:

> "I was at a dinner party. This woman seated across the table from me seemed to fluctuate between being dead and being alive. I was conversing with her and it was almost as though the more involved I became with her, the more dead she would become. That kind of thing went back and forth several times. From a distance she seemed vigorously alive, but up close she seemed lifeless and dull."

Associative connections between that woman in the dream, and myself as a representative of a number of personality-aspects of various persons from the patient's childhood, as well as connections to components of herself which were identified with those emotionally-dead figures from her past, emerged in the subsequent analytic work.

A childless woman, after detailing how moved she had

felt at the aliveness of a pair of twin babies she had seen the day before, became somberly philosophical and said, with an undertone of fear and awe in her voice, "There's always the death in the background." I heard this as a clear but unconscious reference to me, behind her, as being death; I said nothing. She went on, ". . . I do have a lot more thoughts about the finiteness of my own life."

More than one patient, of various diagnostic categories, have associated me—partly by reason of their not feeling free to look at me during the session—with those parts of a parent's body at which they had not been permitted to look, during their childhood—with, most frequently, the parent's genital.

Parenthetically, it seems to me not coincidental that in those so-frequent instances when such transference-responses as those I am citing are prevailing in work with borderline patients for years, the analyst seldom indeed finds it feasible to make effective transference-interpretations. The patient is largely deaf, unconsciously, to verbalized intelligence from an analyst who is powerfully assumed, again at an unconscious level in the patient, to be something quite other than a whole human being.

Further, in a number of patients of varying degrees of illness, I have found that *words*—words from either patient or analyst—are equivalent to *father*, intruding unwantedly into a nonverbal mother–infant symbiosis. This transference-"father" is most significantly traceable to components of the biological mother herself, in these instances of split mother-transference, wherein intense jealousy permeates both the transference and the countertransference. Such jealousy-phenomena are detailed in Chapters 5 and 8 in this volume.

The borderline patient's impaired sense of reality is another typical factor which makes the development, and work of resolution, of the transference-psychosis stressful for both participants. Helene Deutsch's classic paper on "as-if" personalities (Deutsch 1942) is highly relevant here. One woman emphasized to me that "I am very different in person from the way I am here." This curious phrase, "in person," seemed to indicate that the analytic sessions possessed for her the reality-value merely of a TV show or a movie, for example. Later in the session she commented that her relationship with her father is so stormy that she sometimes feels an urge to write a novel about it; my own private impression was that, in that relationship, she was indeed living a novel. I have found it commonplace for these patients to emphasize that "in my *life*" or "in my *real* life" they are quite different persons from the way they are in the analysis. Admittedly, an analytic relationship commonly can be seen to be in many ways different from other areas of a patient's life; but these patients refer persistently to the analytic relationship and setting as being not really part of their lives at all. Many times, while reminiscing about events earlier in their lives, they will recall that, "In my *life*, ..." saying this as though from the vantage point of a very old person whose life is essentially *all* past now or—very often, in my experience—from the vantage point of one who has already died and can therefore look back upon his own life in its totality, as something now behind and quite apart from him.

The Analyst's Reactions to the Development of the Transference-Borderline-Psychosis in the Patient

Next I shall discuss various emotions which the therapist comes to experience in consequence of the development of the transference-borderline-psychosis in the patient, and some of the sources of those emotions. While the literature is not in full and explicit agreement that a transference psychosis typically develops in psychoanalytic therapy with the borderline patient, it seems generally agreed that he brings into the treatment-relationship a vulnerability to (or, one might say, a treatment-need for) this development, and that the emergence of so intense and primitive a constellation of transference-reactions is at the least a standard hazard in the therapist's work with these patients. I think it fair and accurate to say that the borderline patient needs to develop, and if treatment proceeds well will develop, a transference-borderline-psychosis in the course of the work.

Certainly in my own work with borderline patients, and in my supervision of analytic candidates and psychiatric residents concerning their work with such patients, as well as in my study of the literature regarding psychoanalytic therapy with borderline patients, I find that a transference-borderline-psychosis commonly develops over the course of the work and needs, of course, to become resolved in order for the treatment to end relatively successfully.

My own clinical and supervisory experience strongly indicates to me that there are certain intense, and intensely difficult, feelings which the therapist can be expected to develop in response to the patient's development of the transference-borderline-psychosis. It may well be that, as the years go on, we shall become able to do psychoanalytic therapy with borderline and schizophrenic patients with increasing success in proportion as we become able to accept that, just as it is to be assumed, as an inherent part of the work, that the *patient* will develop a transference-borderline-psychosis or transference-psychosis, it is also to be assumed, as a no less integral part of the work, that the *therapist* will develop—to, of course, an attemptedly limited, self-analytically explorable, and appreciably sharable-with-the-patient degree—an area of countertransference-borderline-psychosis or even countertransference-psychosis in his work with such a patient. It should be unnecessary to emphasize that going crazy, whole hog, along with the patient will do no good and great harm. But I believe that we psychoanalytic therapists collectively will become, as the years go on, less readily scared off from this work, and better able to take it up and pursue it as a job of work to be done relatively successfully, in proportion as we become able to take the measure, forthrightly and unashamedly, of the feelings we can *expect* ourselves to come to experience, naturally, in the course of working with these patients.

Pao (1975) reports his project concerning a schema, devised at Chestnut Lodge by himself, Fort (1973) and presumably others on the staff there, for dividing schizophrenia into four subgroups. Pao, the Director of Psychotherapy at the Lodge, describes that in the course of this project he interviewed each new patient shortly after admission. It is of much interest to me that, evidently without having encountered my (Searles 1965a) paper concerning the sense of identity as a perceptual organ, his experience led him in what seems to me the same general direction:

> My emphasis is that the diagnosis should begin with the study of the interviewer's own emotional reactions in the interaction between the patient and himself. . . . Such personal experience must be supplemented by a careful scrutiny of the patient's background, the course of illness, the patient's ability to tolerate anxiety, etc.

I can believe that the time will come, in our work with neurotic patients, when, just as we now use, as a criterion of analyzability, the patient's capability for developing a transference neurosis, we may use as an additional criterion, of earlier predictive significance in our work with the patient, his capability in fostering a countertransference neurosis, so to speak, in the analyst.

Having said that by way of preface, I shall detail some

of the therapist's expectable feeling-experiences in the course of his work with the borderline patient.

The therapist comes to feel guilty and personally responsible for the initially-relatively-well-appearing patient's becoming, over the months or years of the transference-evolution, appreciably psychotic or borderline-psychotic in the context of the treatment-sessions. It is only in relatively recent years, after many years of tormented countertransference experiences of this sort, that I have come to realize how largely referable is the therapist's guilt and remorse, in this regard, to unconscious empathy with the patient's own child-self. That is, the patient in childhood tended to feel that only he possessed the guilty awareness of how deeply disturbed the mother is and that, moreover, he personally was totally responsible for driving her to the edge of, or even into, madness. The father may have been the more central parent in this regard; but much more often it was, from what I have seen, the mother.

It is garden-variety experience for children in our culture to hear reproaches from a parent, "You're driving me crazy!", and of course I do not mean that such words alone, even with more than a modicum of appropriately maddened demeanor, cause the child any serious and lasting trauma. But the parents of borderline patients have, themselves, more than a mere garden-variety, neurotic-degree of psychopathology; hence it is a formidably serious degree of parental psychopathology for which the child is being assigned, day after day, a totally causative personal responsibility.

The therapist's guilt in this same regard stems partly from his finding, over the course of the work, that the patient's crazier aspects provide him (the therapist) covertly with much more of lively interest, and even fascination, than do the patient's relatively dull areas of neurotic ego-functioning. Although the therapist's conscientious goal is to help the patient to become free from the borderline-schizophrenic modes of experience, privately and guiltily he feels fascinated by these very sickest aspects of the patient, and fears that his fascination with them has led him to foster, to deepen, these most grievously afflicted components of the patient's personality-functioning.

Typically the treatment-process itself, in the work with these patients, becomes highly sexualized, such that the patient reveals newly-experienced and fascinating border-line symptoms in a basically coquettish, seductive manner, while the enthralled therapist struggles to match this price-less material with brilliantly penetrating interpretations. Typically, too, the treatment-process becomes laden with acted-in aggression. For instance, as I have mentioned in a paper written some years ago (Searles 1976a) the therapist, who develops formidable quantities of hatred toward the patient, comes to feel for a time that the only effective "out-let" for his hatred is to be found in seeing the patient suffer from the latter's persistent symptoms.

All these details of the therapist's countertransference have had, so my clinical experience indicates to me, proto-types in the patient's childhood experience with the parent in question. As one simple example, the child could not help deriving gratification, no matter how guilty a gratification, from feeling himself capable of bringing mother out of her depressive deadness into a highly animated and vocal state verging upon madness.

My work with a patient far more ill than borderline has shown me another point relevant for this discussion. She is a chronically schizophrenic woman with whom I have worked for many years. After the first few years of our work she refused to acknowledge her name as her own and, although she has improved in many regards over the subsequent years, it has become rare for her to be conscious of bits of her own real, personal childhood-history such as were rela-tively abundantly available to her, despite her many al-ready-present delusions, at the beginning of our work. For many years now, one of the harshest of my countertransference burdens is a guilty and remorseful feeling that I personally have destroyed, long since, her only real and sane identity—destroyed it out of, more than anything else, my hateful envy of her for her many and extraordinary capabilities, and for her childhood lived in a setting far different from my own small-town, middle-class one.

It is only as she has been improving, recently, to such an extent that some of her psychotic-transference reactions have become clearly linked with newly-remembered childhood experiences, that I have felt largely relieved of this burden of guilt and remorse. Specifically, I have come to see that my long-chafing, and often intensely threatening to the point of engendering in me fantasies of suicide, feeling of having destroyed her sense of identity has a precise counterpart in *her* having been given to feel, by her mother, that the child had destroyed the mother's so-called real and true identity—an identity based, in actuality, in the mother's ego-ideal as a woman of myriad magnificent accomplishments, above all in the field of dramatics. The mother had been much given to manic flights of fancy, and her fantasied accomplishments were not, to her, so much ambitions thwarted by the patient as a child; she reacted, rather, to the daughter as having destroyed these supposedly actualized accomplishments of hers and, in the process, destroyed the mother's supposedly real, true identity.

The Analyst as Unwanted Child

To return to the discussion of borderline patients *per se*, I have indicated that the therapist is given to feel that he has had, and is having, a diabolically, malevolently, all-powerful influence in the development and maintenance of the patient's transference-borderline-psychosis. But I have found, in my work with a reliably long succession of patients now, that such an experience of myself, in the work, comes in course of time to reveal, at its core, the experience of myself as being an unwanted little child in relation to the patient. It gradually dawns on me that this is who I am, in the patient's transference-relationship with me, as I listen month after month and year after year to the patient's reproaches that all the rest of his or her life is going relatively well these days, with my being the only fly in the ointment. If only he were rid of me, he says more and more explicitly, his life would be a breeze. In case after case, I become impressed, inevitably, with how much the patient is sounding like a mother who is reproaching and blaming her small child, giving him to feel that, had he only not been born, her life would be a paradise of personal fulfillment.

In the instance of my work with one patient after another, the awareness of my unwanted-child countertransference comes to me as an excitingly meaningful revelation and, although its appearance has been made possible only by my having come to realize, more fully than before, how deeply hurt and rejected I am feeling in response to the patient, this phase comes as a relief from my ertswhile grandiosity-and-guilt-ridden countertransference identity as the diabolical inflictor of psychosis. In some instances, more specifically, I no longer hear the patient as reproaching me with diabolically *spoiling* his otherwise satisfactory life, but hear him saying, as the stronger, parental one of the two of us, that I as the smaller, child-one am not, and never was, loved or wanted.

All these processes in the patient's childhood regularly involved his becoming the object, beginning in early childhood or infancy or even before birth, of transference-reactions on the mother's (and/or father's) part from her own mother and/or father (or sibling, or whomever) to the patient. Typically, the more ill the adult patient is, the more sure we can be that such transference-responses on the parent's part were powerfully at work remarkably early in the patient's childhood. I have written a number of times of the schizophrenic patient's childhood in this regard, and I am aware that a number of other writers have done so. But I feel that we are only beginning to mine this rich lode of psychodynamics.

Here is, I believe, a prevailing atmosphere in the background of many borderline patients. Beginning when the patient was, say, two years of age (or even younger; I do not know just when), his mother had an unconscious transference-image of him as being, all over again, her own mother and/or father, in relationship to whom she had felt herself to be an unwanted child, and whose love she had despaired of evoking. Now she blames and reproaches her little son (or daughter) for all sorts of events and situations which are far beyond his realistic powers to control, as if he were God Almighty, just as later on, in psychotherapy, the adult patient who was once this child comes to vituperate against his therapist as being a diabolical God. During the patient's childhood the mother does this basically because she unconsciously experiences herself as being an unwanted child to this transference-"parent" of hers, who is actually her little child. I sense that as we come to understand more fully the poignancy of such mother–child relationships, we will discard the crude and cruel "schizophrenogenic mother" concept (to which I, among many others, devoted much attention in my early papers) once and for all.

The Analyst's Guilty Sense of Less-than-Full Commitment to His Therapeutic Role

A countertransference-experience which has been long-lasting in my work with one patient after another is a guilty sense of not being fully committed, inwardly, to my functional role of the patient's therapist, despite my maintenance of all the outward trappings of therapeutic devotion. Any thoroughgoing discussion of this aspect of the countertransference would require a chapter in itself, since it has, undoubtedly, so many connections to the patient's primitive defenses of fantasied omnipotence and of splitting, with powerfully idealized or diabolized transference-images of the therapist. It is my impression, in essence, that it is only in proportion as there is a deflation of grandiosity, in the transference and the countertransference, that the therapist can come to feel fully committed to his now human-sized functional role as the patient's therapist. My treatment-records abound with data from earlier phases in the work with, for example, schizophrenic patients who would talk adoringly and loyally of a delusional construct hallucinatorily conversed with as "my doctor," while shutting me out of any functional relatedness with them; but at those rare moments when I would feel he or she was giving me an opportunity, supposedly long sought by me, to step into the shoes of "my doctor," I would quail at doing so.

In this same vein, but in my work with a much less ill female patient, she developed a headache during the course of a session, and in association to this headache reported conjectures about "rage at myself—*at you, maybe my mother* [my italics]. . . ." I sensed that she was manifesting an unconscious transference to me as being her mother who was only "*maybe* my mother," which fit not only with my frequent countertransference reaction to her, but also with her childhood experience of a mother who persistently remained tangential to the mother-role, rather than more fully committed to it. It fit also, needless to say, with her own yet-unresolved, fantasied omnipotence, which allowed her to acknowledge only grudgingly, at best, any mother-figure as being "*maybe* my mother."

The Analyst's "Own" Feelings as Comprising Layer Under Layer of Countertransference-Elements

I cannot overemphasize the enormously treatment-facilitating value, as well as the comforting and liberating value for the therapist personally, of his locating where this or that tormenting or otherwise upsetting countertransference reaction links up with the patient's heretofore-unconscious and unclarified *transference*-reactions to him. In other words, the analyst's "own" personal torment needs to become translated into a fuller understanding of the patient's childhood-family events and daily atmosphere. I find it particularly helpful when a "personal," "private" feeling-response within myself, a feeling which I have been experiencing as fully or at least predominantly my "own," becomes revealed as being a still deeper layer of reaction to a newly-revealed aspect of the patient's transference to me.

For a case in point here, I shall turn briefly to my very long work with a previously mentioned chronically schizophrenic woman. I felt on many occasions over the years how seriously disadvantaged I, as her therapist, was in trying to function, since my role in her life precluded my responding to her in the only manner appropriate to her behavior toward me, by administering a brutal physical beating of her such as her mother frequently had given her. Only after many years did I come to realize that, in so reacting, I was being her transference-father; she had come by now to clearly portray me, in the transference, as a diabolical, omnipotent father who controlled from a distance both her and her mother, and who delegated to the mother the physical punishment of the child. His Godlike-aloof role forebade, by the same token, that he dirty his hands with such matters.

A borderline man expressed, during a session after a number of years of work, the realization, at an unprecedentedly deep level, that "You are not my father." What I found fascinating about this were the attendant evidences of still-unresolved transference which revealed to me that, in saying this, although he was consciously expressing the realization that I was in actuality his therapist rather than his father, unconsciously he was expressing the realization that I was his uncle, who had provided most of his fathering to him following the death, early in the patient's boyhood, of the actual father. Experiences such as this have led me, incidentally, to assume that any presumed "therapeutic alliance," supposedly involving relatively transference-free components of the patient's ego-functioning in a workmanlike bond with the analyst, needs constantly to be scrutinized for subtle but pervasively powerful elements of unconscious transference.

Suspense; Choice Between Illness and Health; The Patient's Acting-Out on Basis of Identifications with the Analyst

Suspense is prominent among the feelings of the analyst who is working with the borderline patient—suspense as to whether the patient will become frankly psychotic or will suicide or both; or as to whether he will leave treatment suddenly and irrevocably; or even, at times when the transference is particularly intense and disturbing to analyst as well as patient, as to whether the analyst himself will fall victim to one or another of such outcomes.

In the writings of Kernberg concerning borderline conditions I find much to admire and from which to learn. But one of the major differences between his views (as contained in those writings of his which I have read) and mine is that he does not portray the suspenseful aspect which seems to me so highly characteristic of the analyst's feelings in working with the borderline patient. Kernberg (1975) says, for example, that patients with "borderline personality organization . . . have in common a rather specific and remarkably stable form of pathological ego structure. . . . their personality organization is not a transitory state fluctuating between neurosis and psychosis" (p. 3). In a similar vein, he (Kernberg, 1972) comments that "Under severe stress or under the effect of alcohol or drugs, transient psychotic episodes may develop in these patients; these psychotic episodes usually improve with relatively brief but well-structured treatment approaches" (p. 255).

Kernberg's writings on borderline states are in part the product of his work in the Psychotherapy Research Project of the Menninger Foundation, and I do not doubt that his experience in that project helps to account for the widely-admired soundness, both theoretically and clinically, of his writings. But in those passages which I have quoted, passages which in their tone are typical of a recurrent emphasis in his work (and, incidentally, passages which I am not contesting here, *per se*, as regards their validity insofar as they go), Kernberg fails to convey how very far removed, indeed, does the analyst feel, in this work, from any such statistician's or theoretician's coolly Olympian view. All too often, for example, the analyst feels desperately threatened lest his patient become frankly psychotic, and the analyst finds little or no reason for confidence that, in such an event, the psychosis will prove transitory.

Any discussion-in-depth of this area of the countertransference would include an exploration of the analyst's envy of the patient for the latter's psychopathology; his hateful wishes to be rid of the patient by the latter's becoming frankly psychotic and hospitalized off somewhere; and his fears of becoming, and wishes to become, psychotic himself. I (Searles 1965) have discussed various among these countertransference phenomena, as regards the work with frankly psychotic patients, in a number of papers.

In my several-years-long work with a woman who showed a borderline personality organization at the outset, I found that she recurrently held over my head, mockingly, year after year, the threat that she would become frankly and chronically schizophrenic. She did not say this in so many words; but her behavior conveyed, innumerable times, that implicit, sadomasochistic threat. In many of the sessions during those years, I felt a strong impulse to tell her ironically that I had felt for years, and still did, that she could become chronically schizophrenic if she would just try a little harder. Essentially, I was wanting at such times somehow to convey to her that this was a *choice* she had. I suppressed this urge each time; but had I given way to it, this would have been an attempt to deal with her infuriating, year-after-year expressions of defiance and mockery and of, above all, the highly sadistic, implicit threat of her becoming chronically psychotic.

The following comments of mine in a paper (Searles 1976) concerning psychoanalytic therapy with schizophrenic patients are in my opinion fully applicable, in principle, to such work with borderline patients also. I wrote there of the crucial issue of *choice*—of the patient's coming to feel *in a position to choose* between continued insanity on the one hand, or healthy interpersonal and intrapersonal relatedness on the other hand. In order for the analyst to help the patient to become able to choose, the former must be able not only to experience, indeed, a passionately tenacious devotion to helping the latter to become free from psychosis, but also become able to tolerate, to clearly envision, the alternative "choice"—namely, that of psychosis for the remainder of the patient's life. I do not see how the patient's individuation can ever occur if the analyst dare not envision this latter possibility. The patient's previous life-experience presumably has proceeded in such a manner and his therapy at the hands of a too-compulsively "dedicated" analyst may proceed in such a manner likewise, that chronic psychosis may be the only subjectively *autonomous* mode of existence available to the patient.

I described further, in that same paper, that an analyst who, for whatever unconscious reasons, cannot become able to live comfortably with the possibility that his patient may never become free from psychosis cannot, by the same token, foster the necessary emotional atmosphere in the sessions for the development of the contented, unthreatened emotional oneness to which I refer by the term therapeutic symbiosis (Searles 1961), a form of relatedness which is of the same quality as that which imbues the mother–infant relatedness in normal infancy and very early childhood. Any so-called individuation which occurs in the patient which is not founded upon a relatively clear phase of therapeutic symbiosis in the treatment is a pseudo-individuation, and only a seeming choice of sanity, with the urge toward psychosis, the yearning for psychosis, subjected to repression rather than faced at all fully in the light of conscious choice. Essentially, at the unconscious level, the patient chooses to remain psychotic.

Although these just-paraphrased passages may be reminiscent of what I have termed the Olympian quality of the passages from Kernberg, most of my writings have emphasized—as I emphasized in the bulk of this recent paper—the struggles which even the experienced analyst must go through, as an inherent part of his countertransference-work with one patient after another, to come to any such harmony with his own formerly so-ambivalent feelings which have been at the basis of his experiencing so much of a threatened suspensefulness.

Along the way, it is especially threatening to the analyst to feel kept in suspense as to whether the patient is headed toward destruction precisely by reason of the latter's functioning loyally as being a chip off the old block— namely, the analyst as perceived by the patient in the transference. That is, the analyst is finding much reason to fear that it is exactly the patient's identification with one of the analyst's qualities, no matter how exaggeratedly perceived by reason of the patient's mother- or father-transference to him, which is carrying the patient toward destruction. Thus the analyst feels responsible, in an essentially omnipotent fashion, for the patient's self-destructive acting-out behavior outside the office. The analyst feels that the patient's behavior vicariously manifests his—the analyst's—own acting-out proclivities.

For example, although I seldom feel inordinately threatened lest any one of my psychiatrist-analysands act out his or her sexual fantasies toward one or another of his or her own patients, I had a more threatened time of it in my work with one analysand. This man was convinced, for years, that I had sexual intercourse with an occasional patient, casually and without subsequent remorse or other disturbed feelings. When, then, he became strongly tempted to give way to his sexual impulses toward one or another of his own current patients, he reported these impulses, during his analytic sessions with me, as being in the spirit of his over-all wishes to emulate me as an admired, virile father in the transference. Not to leave the reader in any unnecessary suspense here, I can report that this aspect of his transference became analyzed successfully.

Another example of this same principle is to be found in another paper of mine, "Violence in Schizophrenia" (Searles, Bisco, Coutu, and Scibetta 1975), in which I describe my single teaching-interviews with a number of schizophrenic patients whose histories included seriously violent behavior. In the instance of one particularly frightening man, with whose therapist I worked subsequently in supervision, the role of a threatened suspensefulness, in both the therapist and me, was especially prominent. My paper describes as follows the end of the therapy with this man, who had run away from the sanitarium previously:

"... he again ran away, was found and taken by his parents to another sanitarium, and ran away from there and joined the Marines without divulging his psychiatric background. Our last bit of information about him was a telephone call to the therapist from an official at an Army prison, stating that this man had stabbed a fellow Marine three times, that his victim was barely surviving, and that an investigation was under way to determine whether Delaney was mentally competent to stand trial. The therapist and I agreed that he had finally committed the violent act which we both had known he eventually would. . . . I want to emphasize the aspect of relief, of certainty, which this clearly afforded me and, I felt, the therapist also. It was as though the distinction between the patient's actualized murderousness and our own murderous fantasies and feelings was now clear beyond anyone's questioning it. . . .

"Both the therapist and I, in relating to him, evidently had mobilized in ourselves such intensely conflicting feelings of love and murderous hatred that a regressive de-differentiation occurred in our respective ego-functioning, such that we attributed to the patient our own murderous hatred, and unconsciously hoped that he would give vicarious expression to our own violence, so as to restore the wall between him and us. More broadly put, such a patient evokes in one such intensely conflicting feelings that, at an unconscious level, one's ego-functioning undergoes a pervasive de-differentiation: one loses the ability deeply to distinguish between one's self and the patient, and between the whole realms of fantasy and reality. Thus the patient's committing of a violent act serves not only to distinguish between one's own 'fantasied' violence and his 'real' violence but, more generally, serves to restore, in one, the distinction between the whole realms of fantasy and outer reality" (pp. 14–16).

Still concerning the matter of the analyst's experiencing suspense, to think of this less globally now (as regards, say, the question of whether the patient will become psychotic or suicide), and more particularly as regards any symptom or personality-trait or current transference-reaction, I find pertinent the following note I made half a dozen years ago concerning my work with a man who manifested a predominantly narcissistic form of ego-functioning.

"Regarding the therapist's experiencing *suspense*. Thinking back on the hour yesterday with Cooper, it occurs to me that, in reacting to his projection upon me of his own sadistic unfeelingness, I tend to function as distinctly *more* so than I actually feel—partly for the reason, as I see it now, of trying to make this issue become clear enough so that he can see it and we can thrash it out, analyze it, resolve it.

"In other words, one of the major reasons why it is so difficult to maintain a genuinely neutral position, not reacting in tune with the patient's transference, is because it is so very difficult to endure the tantalizing ambiguity, the suspense, of the unworked-through transference reactions which one can see in the patient, and to which one *does* react genuinely. That is, I do experience myself as uncomfortably sadistic, unfeeling, unlikable and unadmirable to myself in reaction to Cooper's transference."

In a paper subsequently, "The Function of the Patient's Realistic Perceptions of the Analyst in Delusional Transference" (Searles 1972), I describe some aspects of my work with a far more ill patient, in terms both of her delusional-transference perceptions of me, and of my own subjective experience of what I was "really" feeling, and communicating to her, in the therapeutic sessions. That paper mainly emphasizes my discovery, over the course of years, that again and again and again, seemingly purely-delusional perceptions of me on her part proved to be well rooted in accurate and realistic perceptions of aspects of myself which heretofore had been out of my own awareness.

What was mentioned above, concerning my work with the narcissistic man, suggests something of why the analyst may introject (unconsciously, of course, for the most part) some of the patient's psychopathology, in an attempt to hasten its resolution and thereby end the feelings of suspense which permeate the treatment-atmosphere in one's work with so tantalizingly ambiguous a patient.

It has seemed to me that some of these same psychodynamics have applied in a considerable number of instances of my work with patients who have been involved in chronically troubled marital situations wherein there is a chronic, suspense-laden threat of divorce hanging over the marriage. In the course of my work with each of these patients, it has appeared to me no coincidence that, concurrent with especially stressful phases of the analytic work, my own marriage has felt uncharacteristically in jeopardy. My strong impression is that the analyst under these circumstances tends to regress to a level of primitively magical thinking, whereby if his own marriage were to dissolve, this would end the years-long suspenseful question as to whether the patient's verge-of-divorce marriage will, or will not, endure. Whether the analyst were thereby to bring about, vicariously, the disruption of the patient's marriage, or on the other hand to preserve the patient's marriage by sacrificing his own, in either eventuality the tormenting element of suspense in the analytic situation would—so, in my speculation, the analyst's primitively magical reasoning goes—be brought to a merciful end.

Differing Kinds (Repressive versus Non-Repressive) of the Analyst's Sense of Identity as an Analyst

Lastly, I want explicitly to discuss a point which has been implied throughout this chapter—namely, that the analyst's sense-of-identity-as-an-analyst must be founded in a *kind* of analyst-identity which in major ways is different from the traditionally-striven-for analyst-identity consonant with classical analysis. For the sake of this discussion, at least, it is not an oversimplification to say that classical analysis enjoins the analyst to develop, and strive to maintain, a sense-of-identity-as-an-analyst which constrains him to evenly hovering attentiveness to the analysand's productions, and to participating actively in the analytic session only to the extent of offering verbal interpretations of the material which the analysand has been conveying to him. Such a traditional analyst-identity is neither tenable for the analyst who is analyzing a borderline patient, nor adequate to meet the analytic needs of the patient.

Knight (1953) described that in a relatively highly structured interview, the borderline patient's basic difficulties in ego-functioning tend not to become available for either the patient or the psychiatrist to see and work upon:

> During the psychiatric interview the neurotic defenses and the relatively intact ego functions may en-

able the borderline patient to present a deceptive, superficially conventional, although neurotic, front, depending on how thoroughgoing and comprehensive the psychiatric investigation is with respect to the patient's *total* ego functioning. The face-to-face psychiatric interview provides a relatively structured situation in which the conventional protective devices of avoidance, evasion, denial, minimization, changing the subject, and other cover-up methods can be used—even by patients who are genuinely seeking help but who dare not yet communicate their awareness of lost affect, reality misinterpretations, autistic preoccupations, and the like (pp. 102–103).

To be sure, Knight's comments suggest that a relatively free form of analytic-interview participation on the part of the patient is most facilitating of the emergence of the latter's borderline difficulties, and with this I am in full agreement. But his comments suggest, too, that such a patient is unlikely to be helped much by an analyst who himself is clinging, in a threatened fashion, to some rigidly-constructed analyst-identity. I hope that this chapter, when taken along with my previous writings concerning countertransference matters, will serve forcefully to convey my conviction that the analyst must far outgrow the traditional classical-analyst identity in order to be able to work with a reasonable degree of success with the borderline patient—to be able, as examples, to utilize his sense of identity as a perceptual organ in the manner I have described here; to enter to the requisite degree into (while maintaining under analytic scrutiny) the so-necessary therapeutic symbiosis; and to be able to preserve his analyst-identity in face of the extremely intense, persistent, and oftentimes strange transference-images which, coming from the (largely unconscious) processes at work in the patient, tend so powerfully to dominate the analyst's sense of his actual identity.

I have seen that various psychiatric residents and analytic candidates who, partly because of a relative lack of accumulated experience, have not yet established a strong sense-of-identity-as-therapist, are particularly threatened by the intense and tenacious negative-transference-images wherein the patient is endeavoring, as it were, to impose upon the therapist a highly unpalatable sense of identity. By the same token, it should be seen that an analyst who is struggling to maintain, in his work with such a patient, a professional identity untainted by such emotions as jealousy, infantile-dependent feelings, sexual lust, and so on, is undoubtedly imposing, by projection, such largely-unconscious personality-components upon the already-overburdened patient. In essence, I am suggesting here that, in the analyst's work with the borderline patient, he needs to have, or insofar as possible to develop, a kind of professional identity which will not be working on the side of the forces of repression but will, rather, be facilitating of the emergence from repression of those feelings, fantasies, and so on which the borderline patient needs for his analyst to be able to experience, on the way to his own becoming able, partly through identification with his analyst, to integrate comparable experiences within his—the patient's—own ego-functioning.

Summary

The countertransference provides the analyst with his most reliable approach to the understanding of borderline (as well as other) patients. The impact upon him of the patient's split ego-functioning is discussed. His experience of transference-roles which are both strange in nature, and inimical to his sense of reality and to his sense of personal identity, are explored; in the latter regard, the value of his sense of identity as a perceptual organ is highlighted.

There are detailed some of the analyst's reactions—his

guilt, his envy, and so on—to the development of the transference-borderline-psychosis in the patient. The analyst
finds that, underneath the patient's transference to him as
being an omnipotent, diabolical inflictor of psychosis, is the
patient's transference to him as being an unwanted child.

The analyst's guilty sense of less-than-full commitment
to his therapeutic role is described briefly, as is the general
principle of his finding, time and again, that what have felt
to be his "own" feelings toward the patient include layer
under layer of responses which are natural and inherent
counterparts to the patient's transference-responses and
-attitudes toward him.

The prominent role of suspense is discussed at relative
length, and the related issue of choice between illness and
health. The phenomenon of the patient's acting-out on the
(partial) basis of unconscious identifications with the analyst, and the impact of this phenomenon upon the countertransference, are mentioned.

Lastly, the significant role, in the countertransference,
of the analyst's sense of identity as an analyst is discussed,
and it is suggested that the borderline patient needs for the
analyst to have, or insofar as possible to develop, a sense-of-
identity-as-analyst which will be enhancing predominantly
of derepression, rather than repression, of countertransference attitudes and feelings.

References

Deutsch, H. (1942). Some forms of emotional disturbance and
    their relationship to schizophrenia. *Psychoanalytic Quarterly*
    11:301–321.
Fort, J. (1973). The importance of being diagnostic. Read at the
    annual Chestnut Lodge Symposium, October 5, 1973.
Gunderson, J. G., and Singer, M. T. (1975). Defining borderline

patients: an overview. *American Journal of Psychiatry*, 132:1–10.

Kernberg, O. (1972). Treatment of borderline patients. In *Tactics and Techniques in Psychoanalytic Therapy*, ed. P. L. Giovacchini, pp. 254–290. New York: Science House.

—— (1975). *Borderline Conditions and Pathological Narcissism*. New York: Jason Aronson.

Knight, R. P. (1953). Borderline states. *Bulletin of the Menninger Clinic* 17:1–12. Reprinted in *Psychoanalytic Psychiatry and Psychology*, ed. R. P. Knight and C. R. Friedman, pp. 97–109. New York: International Universities Press.

Moore, B. E., and Fine, B. D., Eds. (1967). *A Glossary of Psychoanalytic Terms and Concepts*. New York: American Psychoanalytic Association.

Pao, P-N. (1975). On the diagnostic term, "schizophrenia." *Annual of Psychoanalysis* 3:221–238.

Searles, H. F. (1960). *The Nonhuman Environment in Normal Development and in Schizophrenia*. New York: International Universities Press.

—— (1965). *Collected Papers on Schizophrenia and Related Subjects*. London: Hogarth Press. New York: International Universities Press.

—— (1965a). The sense of identity as a perceptual organ. Presented at Sheppard and Enoch Pratt Hospital Scientific Day Program, Towson, MD, May 29, 1965. Reprinted in Concerning the development of an identity. *Psychoanalytic Review* 53:507–530. Winter 1966–1967.

—— (1972). The function of the patient's realistic perceptions of the analyst in delusional transference. *British Journal of Medical Psychology* 45:1–18.

—— (1976). Psychoanalytic therapy with schizophrenic patients in a private-practice context. *Contemporary Psychoanalysis* 12:387–406. Reprinted in *Countertransference and Related Subjects—Selected Papers*, pp. 582–602. New York: International Universities Press, 1979. Paraphrased passages are from pp. 597–598 in latter volume.

—— (1976a). Transitional phenomena and therapeutic symbiosis. *International Journal of Psychoanalytic Psychotherapy* 5:145–204.

Searles, H. F., Bisco, J. M., Coutu, G., and Scibetta, R. C. (1975). Violence in schizophrenia. *Psychoanalytic Forum* 5:1–89.

Chapter 8

Countertransference-
Experiences with
Jealousy Involving
an Internal Object

In Chapter 5, I stated in summary that jealousy which is related to an internal object within either oneself or the other person in an ostensibly two-person situation is at the heart of much severe and pervasive psychopathology and accounts, in psychoanalytic treatment, for much of the unconscious resistance, on the part of both patient and analyst, to the analytic process. These jealousy-phenomena, derived basically from inordinately powerful ego-splitting processes in the original infant–mother relationship wherein the infant's earliest ego-formation was tak-

This chapter was published originally, under the title, "The Analyst's Experience with Jealousy," on pp. 305–327 in *Countertransference*, edited by L. Epstein and A. H. Feiner; New York and London: Jason Aronson, 1979.

ing place, comprise a much more powerful source of severe psychopathology than do those jealousy-phenomena referable to the oedipal phase of development.

These primitive jealousy-phenomena are, I emphasized, among the most powerful determinants of, for example, ego-fragmentation, depersonalization, castration anxiety and, in the transference relationship, negative therapeutic reaction. These jealousy-phenomena, being referable to the earliest infantile phases of ego-development when no clear differentiation between human and nonhuman, animate and inanimate, ingredients of the experienced self-and-world had yet been achieved, often are found in the transference-relationship to involve nonhuman objects which have the jealousy-engendering connotation of actual human beings.

Such jealousy-phenomena may become detectable, I reported, only after prolonged analytic work has occurred, by which time the analyst and patient have come to possess a degree of emotional significance for one another approximately equal to that which the internal object—or ego-fragment—in question has for its possessor.

I noted that Melanie Klein's (1957) concepts concerning the infant's primary envy of the mother's breast, and the effects of this envy upon his later ego-development, were of fundamental relevance for the formulations which I was presenting there.

Introductory Comments

This chapter largely comprises descriptions of my psychoanalytic therapy with each of two chronically schizophrenic patients, descriptions which highlight the role, in their therapy, of such "internal-object jealousy." The countertransference-aspects of my work with these patients will be described time and again, although not focused upon exclusively.

These two clinical narratives were written in 1974, as part of an intended monograph concerning internal-object jealousy. In the interim since that time, each of these patients has continued in psychoanalytic therapy with me, and each has continued to improve. The first of them, Miss Herman (a pseudonym), had to be rehospitalized at Chestnut Lodge for about six months, but has resumed recently her full out-patient status, and is now better integrated than she has ever been before in my experience with her. The second of these patients, Mrs. Douglas (a pseudonym), continues to be an in-patient at Chestnut Lodge, but shows during her sessions with me a degree of ego-functioning which is appreciably better than was characteristic of her in 1974, and is due soon to start making visits to her relatively distantly-located relatives. There is considerable reason to hope that she will be able to move to out-patientcy within a couple of more years.

At the present writing, Miss Herman and I began working together, in her psychoanalytic therapy, 25 years ago last month, and Mrs. Douglas and I shall have been working together, in her psychoanalytic therapy, for 25 years within another six months. Mrs. Douglas' treatment has been at a frequency of four hours per week throughout. Miss Herman's treatment was on a basis of four hours per week until one-and-one-half years ago, when we agreed to reduce the number of hours to three per week. Neither of these patients has had drug therapy, in all this time, beyond occasional night-time sedation. A detailed history of Mrs. Douglas' illness, and of some other aspects of the earlier years of my work with her, is included in another of my published papers (Searles 1972). For more than 12 years I have sound-recorded (with her knowledge) all her sessions, and have preserved all these tapes for research purposes. This present communication is presented in my belief that not only the title-subject itself, but also the more general countertransference-experience with such staggeringly long-range treatment endeavors as these two, are of inherent interest to my colleagues.

Miss Esther Herman

Miss Esther Herman, a 41-year-old woman with paranoid schizophrenia, was transferred to Chestnut Lodge after a year of unsuccessful treatment at another hospital. After many years of living an increasingly reclusive life, as a kind of maid-and-companion to her elderly, widowed mother, she had become acutely psychotic, and her psychosis had settled into chronicity by the time of her arrival at the Lodge. Our work together brought to light a very severe impoverishment of her personal identity as a human being, and a corresponding predominance of identity-kinship with various nonhuman ingredients of her surroundings. Having become troubled, evidently, about the depth of her emotional involvement with her pet cat, she had said—among the uncharacteristic philosophical utterances which emerged from her in her acute psychosis, as reported by her older siblings—"People should love people, not cats." In my work with her—a small, slight woman—I found her to express anxiety lest the wind blow her away like a piece of tissue paper; it required a number of years of treatment before her feeling of corporeal insubstantiality gave way to the delighted and relieved realization that "I have weight!" Meanwhile, she had circled despondently, oftentimes, on the lawn of the hospital, like a bird with a broken wing, or had sat crumpled for long periods on the grass there. A private patient of mine in that era came to my office looking shaken, and reported that he had just passed, on the lawn, what he had thought to be a pile of clothing, and had seen a woman uncannily materialize, moving slowly but unmistakably, from it.

This woman's few friends and acquaintances, over the earlier years, had overtly been pitying and condescending toward her because of the constricted life she was leading; but there developed much evidence that, behind their pity, they had intense envy of her for her apartness from the many frustrations of their more ordinarily-human lives— their marital problems, their career-concerns, and so on. In my own work with her, her underlying fears lest she be exposed to envy caused her to cling tenaciously to images of herself as being far more impoverished than was, on the over-all, her actual state. For example, before very long she had improved sufficiently to be exercising various "privileges" which many of her fellow-patients, more incapacitated even than she, had not attained; but she clung tenaciously to a view of herself as having nothing, and chronically expressed bitter envy and resentment of people around her, whose lives in general she perceived as relatively trouble-free.

Her mother, who died of a coronary occlusion about two years after Miss Herman's admission to Chestnut Lodge, had held, according to the social worker who interviewed her, a remarkably rigid and constricted image of the daughter as being, essentially, a nice little girl. The older siblings were much concerned to protect the mother from the impact of the daughter's illness, and the mother clearly could not imagine that the daughter, when once again out of the hospital, would be anyone at all different from the nice little girl the mother had always known her to be. During the first several months of my work with the patient, I heard on endless occasions, during the otherwise predominantly silent sessions, "I was always a nice little girl—I went to the corner grocery store," repeated such a maddeningly great number of times as to indicate that this was all the life she had been allowed to have, either in her own eyes or in those of her mother. The two had functioned without any overt dissension over the years, and I thought accurate the social worker's impression that "Esther had lived as just the dim shadow of her mother."

Miss Herman showed, from the beginning of her stay at the Lodge, a severe splitting in the Kleinian sense, as regards her introjects, and a corresponding power in fostering splits in her interpersonal milieu. Her family-members were, in her view, for literally several years, totally good and blameless; her loyalty to them was unbroken, while the staff of the hospital, notably including me, were blamed by her for all her difficulties. During our sessions she clearly strove to maintain an angelic, "nice little girl" self-image—a self-image which could not accommodate at all to any sexual or aggressive feelings—and this involved her reacting to me, much of the time, as correspondingly diabolical, malevolent.

In a context of her paranoid berating of me as essentially having caused her illness, and as causing her incarceration and therefore her separation from her family, she would say, "My family want me well," but this statement of hers acquired, as the months and years went on, an increasingly woeful tone, an increasingly strong hint of her dawning realization that her family wanted no part of her unless she were "well"—unless she were able to become again the constricted caricature of a person she had long been, prior to her acute psychosis.

Her psychotherapeutic sessions came very much to life, after the first several months, in a setting of our having stormy and venomous arguments with one another—probably linked genetically with the "squabbling," as the family called it, which had recurrently occurred between herself and her older sister, who had shared the same room until the patient was in her twenties. I knew at the time that these arguments had a sexual component, for we would go into a kind of orgastic ecstasy of self-righteous vituperation at one another. I now realize, in retrospect, that there was a jealous component in them also; it was very much as though there were one angel in the room, and each of us were self-righteously and vindictively demonstrating that he (or she) was that angel, and the other was now being exposed as a devil. In this dimension of the transference-situation, the jealous competition evidently was for the role of Mother's Angel.

Miss Herman was enormously formidable in her power to mobilize ordinarily-unconscious guilt in the other person. She is the only patient whom I have ever found so very upsetting that I have had to terminate prematurely the treatment-session. This happened twice in my work with her; once, I recall, was on an occasion when the session was being held in her room on a locked ward, and she was confronting me with some imperfectly-laundered item which had come back from the hospital laundry. I felt so stung, so infuriated, by her treating me entirely as though I were the hospital laundress who had done the item, that I stormed out of the room. I can now believe, in retrospect, that I was at the time unconsciously jealous of the hospital laundress, as having, nonetheless, a far simpler job than my task as this difficult woman's attempted psychotherapist.

Only after many years of therapy did it become clear that, from her view, she felt so highly vulnerable to being utterly overwhelmed, crushed, by various superego-figures in her environment, such as me, that the only way she could survive any one of them was by playing them off against one another—pitting them in destructively jealous competition with one another, in relation to her.

These dynamics became clearest in a relatively recent session. She had been living on an out-patient basis for some years now, in her own apartment, handling her own finances,

and had received word from the Internal Revenue Service that her tax return for the previous year was being
subject to audit. She seemed, from my view, to be responding to this information in a relatively mature and capable
manner; but it was evident that this problem was being
enormously complicated, for her, by her feeling—as she had
phrased it bitterly and helplessly for years—"under analysis," a feeling she customarily experienced not only during
her sessions with me, but in relation to the many superego
figures in which her daily life abounded, some real and
many, particularly in the past, largely figments of her paranoid-delusional projections. She was feeling in this instance,
that is, under *very* critical scrutiny—a meticulously critical
evaluation as to how she was setting about meeting this
practical problem—from not only me, but also from her
older sister, her administrative psychiatrist, her social
worker, and a number of other persons in her life. It was
very striking to me to see that all these several persons
(including myself), to whom she might realistically turn for
help of one sort or another, were being reacted to by her not
as being potential helpers, but rather as, collectively, a vast
additional hindrance and burden to her (in her already-
burdened life-situation), in light of the destructively critical
orientation she attributed to each of us. That is, the repression of her dependency-needs, behind this paranoid defense,
was quite apparent.

In the first five minutes of the particular session in
question, it became evident to me that she tended to feel
overwhelmingly criticized and condemned, in this regard,
by her social worker (whom the patient sees regularly once
each week, and who in my opinion gives the patient relatively little cause, in actuality, for feeling so threatened),
and clearly was invoking her sister's support against the
social worker. The sister herself was a social worker, and it
was apparent to me that the patient was playing very skill-

fully (although apparently largely unconsciously and certainly not in a consciously powerful, dominant position) upon the latently jealous rivalries between the two other women, in regard to her. She evidently gave each of them to feel protective of her, and angry at the supposed bullying callousness and condemnation, toward her, on the part of the other woman in the threesome. Never before had she functioned, during the session, in such a manner as to enable me to empathize so fully with her—to see that, from her view, such Machiavellian behavior on her part was her only means of staving off her being crushed by these superego-behemoths (which included, as was clear enough, myself during the session in question). It was clear to me, but still not to her after all these years, to what a degree her feeling "under analysis" involved her projecting of her own repressed feelings of a perfectionistically critical, inhumanly condemnatory sort—feelings which she had vented upon me, with disturbing and unrelenting harshness, innumerable times.

The projectional aspect of her feeling scrutinized in so critically-evaluative a manner reminded me of my reaction to my fellow staff-members at Chestnut Lodge, twenty years ago, following our learning, at the Lodge, of the death of my training analyst, with whom my analysis had ended about a year or two before. For perhaps two or three days thereafter, I felt an uneasy self-consciousness among my colleagues at staff conferences and elsewhere, feeling that they were watching me with a critical eye as to what, if any, feelings I was experiencing in this setting. My uneasiness on this score vanished with my realization that, in actuality, *I* had been evaluating *them*, critically, as to how *they* were responding to me—whether, for example, in an overly- or underly-sympathetic manner—in this situation.

I have mentioned a few of the manifestations of Miss Herman's incomplete differentiation between human and

nonhuman realms. This was a factor in the jealousy-phenomena which, from very early in the work with her, permeated her treatment. She formed such intense and intimate and "personal" attachments to various nonhuman
things as to give one to feel jealously left out, as from a
relationship between two other persons. In equipping her
apartment for out-patient living she came to say, for instance, "I love my little vacuum cleaner," with all the adoration a woman usually reserves for a husband or a child. In
one of her sessions, for instance, she spoke in such a tone,
"My darling vacuum cleaner . . . That vacuum cleaner is
just wonderful." She said that she had told her sister this
(about the vacuum cleaner) also, on the telephone. It seemed
clear to me that she was making a formidable effort to evoke
jealousy, toward her vacuum cleaner, in both her sister and
in me. During this session she expressed dissatisfaction toward me, for the nth time, for not "turning off" the hallucinatory voices which continued to plague her—for not, as it
were, cleaning them up, as her vacuum cleaner so beautifully cleaned up her apartment. Later on in the same session, she reported, "The voices just say, 'How come every-
body's so sweet and nice to ya?'" I suggested, "The voices
sound a bit jealous of you?," at which she promptly said,
"*Yes*," in emphatic confirmation.

There was a prolonged era in our work, coinciding approximately with that during which she was very slowly
—almost imperceptibly, in fact, over years of time—ventur-
ing bit by bit into out-patient living and then becoming
more and more firmly established in it—during which I
(having left the Chestnut Lodge staff and established a full-
time private practice in Washington) felt jealously pitted
against Chestnut Lodge as to whom, or which, were more
important to her. Here was involved, again, her incomplete
differentiation from the nonhuman realm, for "Chestnut
Lodge" evidently meant something different from, or cer-

tainly far more than, a collection of persons (a large collection indeed) who had been significant to her during the many years of her treatment there. She spoke of it in such a way as to conjure up more, in my mind, the grounds of the sanitarium, the physical settings of the several successive units in which she had lived there, and so on. By now I had been off the Lodge staff for several years, and she evidently felt in the middle of a tug-of-war as to whether to cling to— or gravitate further back into—her old ways of living at Chestnut Lodge, or to relinquish those increasingly and gravitate more into the extra-institutional life which I personified.

For me, this phase of her treatment involved on occasion experiences of jealousy which made me feel a peculiarly painful sense of division within myself. I had my own separation-reactions to deal with, in consequence of my having left the staff of Chestnut Lodge, and it felt to me strange indeed, after having worked for so many years there and feeling myself to be part of the institution still as regards her treatment, to now find myself pitted, in the work with her, in jealous competition with Chestnut Lodge. I know that, working alone with her in the earlier years—without the aid of the vast number of personnel-members (and fellow patients) her improvement to her present level of functioning had required—I could not possibly have met with this even partial success. I felt a deep sense of respect for what "Chestnut Lodge" had done, and was continuing to do, for her and, here again—as in my work with other patients in other contexts—I felt a sense of awe at the prospect of becoming sufficiently acknowledged by her, in terms of her dependency upon me, so that she and I would be able to continue the psychotherapeutic work without her needing to resort at all to the help of any administrator, social worker, nurse or aide at Chestnut Lodge. This weaning process (on, obviously, both our parts *vis-à-vis* the Lodge) is not yet complete, if it ever in her or my life-time will be complete. But it is progressing steadily, and it progresses to the degree that she and I can deal with, among other matters, the kind of jealousy-phenomena upon which this paper is focusing.

Any full-length book comprised of my reporting of a necessarily tiny sample of the events of this woman's astronomically long treatment would inevitably pursue, as the major one among many themes, the analytic exploration of her hallucinatory phenomena, for it is that theme which gives greatest continuity and coherency to her treatment and to the ego-growth she has manifested during her treatment.

In the early months of our work she made clear that she was subject to the hearing of voices, and later on made clear that she had experienced these at the previous hospital, also, from which she had been transferred to the Lodge. During perhaps the first year or two of my work with her, whenever she spoke of these she clearly indicated that she found them to be a highly weird, uncanny, nonhuman phenomenon—an "electric voice," as she called them. But increasingly after that first year or two, she made clear that the voices were increasingly human in quality; they spoke to her much as a companionable other human being would, saying to her teasing things, witty things, amusing things, consoling and reassuring and explanatory things, and even, on at least one occasion, telling her accurately and helpfully where she had left her glasses which she had misplaced absent-mindedly. She continued to reproach me for not "turning off" the voices; she is, to this day, predominantly sure that they are caused by some sort of electronic device which, she is more than half sure, I could turn off if I only would. But it was clear, nonetheless, that they represented nothing like the weirdly nonhuman threat they once did, for otherwise she could by no means have moved at the Lodge into units occupied by less and less ill patients, and, by now, into relatively firm out-patient living. Parenthetically, after about three years of our work together, her parental family-members conveyed to the Lodge staff their finding her to be (at what proved to be this relatively early stage of the treatment, already) a far more healthy person than they had ever known her to be. She came to be, as the years of her treatment went on, still far more strong in her ego-functioning than she had been at that early juncture.

I well remember the time, several years along in our work when, for the first time, as she was reporting some between-sessions hallucinatory experience, I found myself feeling jealous of the described relatedness between herself and the hallucinatory voice. Specifically, she described having heard, while in a local drug store, a man's voice saying something of an intimate and clearly sexually-interested sort to her. The jealousy I experienced on hearing this was reminiscent to me of that which I had come to feel, years before, in working with a hebephrenic man who was much involved, during our sessions, with hallucinatory presences; my experience with him is detailed in Chapter 5, which is also on the subject of jealousy involving an internal object.

Although Miss Herman reports, on innumerable occasions, her hearing of voices during our sessions, it is rare for me to experience jealousy in this regard, for usually I can see clearly that the folksy comforting (or advice, or what-not) which the voices are providing her are a poor-second best, in terms of her unconscious yearnings, to the wished-for identical words in my voice. Generally, she hears them at times when I have been silent, and when I do speak, rarely if ever do I express the kind of companionable, or supportive-psychotherapy, sentiments which the voices generally convey to her.

In one session, she reported, "The voices just said, 'You're about to find out the truth: you've won.'" The voices' tone, as quoted by her, was such as to imply that they were surrendering to her, although I felt sure, from innumerable previous attempts, that she would disclaim any such conno-

tation. She went on, "I don't like it," with relatively decisive
disapproval in her tone, indeed, but then her tone became
unconvincing when she said, in an intendedly emphatic
manner, "I didn't come all the way out here to hear the
voices; I came to see my *doctor*." I felt that, in her saying this
in the tone in which it was said, she was introducing, unconsciously, the possibility that she comes here primarily to
hear the voices. The "my doctor" was said with softness,
fondness, in contrast to a note of relative dislike in her
saying "the voices." Her statement clearly tended, in essence, to portray "the voices" and "my doctor" as rivals for
her interest. Later on in the session—at a time when, again,
I had been silent—she said, "The voices say, 'Why are you so
nervous?' [the voices' tone, as quoted, being polite and solici-
tous]."

My jealousy of the hallucinated male voice she reported
having heard in the drug store, which I mentioned a bit
earlier here, is similar to another unusual jealousy-experience I had in another session with her, likewise after she
had been in treatment for many years. In this instance (also
reported on p. 116), she commented to me before my vacation, "You'll get tanned, won't you, Dr. Searles? . . . attractive . . . bronzed. . . ." As she talked, I could sense she was
visualizing my looking so, and this made me feel jealous of
the attractive image of me which she was visualizing.

This just-described occurrence, which lasted possibly
a minute, and involved my experiencing this peculiar
jealousy, reminded me of her having said innumerable
times, in the early years of her treatment, "My family want
me well," and "My family want to see me well." In retrospect, I saw that in all likelihood her illness had served as a
necessary defense against the family-inspired jealousy, in
Miss Herman, of their image of her as "well." I remembered, too, the shock I had felt, very early indeed in the
work, upon hearing from her that her "family"—probably

more specifically her mother; her perceptions of her family were those more of an undifferentiated unit than of clearly-delineated individuals—used to caution her not to lean her face on her hand too long, for instance, lest she disturb—permanently, supposedly—the contours of her precious little face; she had presented this, in passing, as one more bit of evidence of how cherished she had always been in her family. In essence, one sensed how careful she had had to be, not to disturb their images of her (one recalls her mother's "nice little girl" image of her) by her allowing any flesh-and-blood human being, with sexual and aggressive feelings and all the rest, to emerge from within her—as indeed emerged when she finally became overtly psychotic.

In all my long work with her, perhaps the most frustrating aspect—maddeningly so, oftentimes—of the work is that she gives me clearly to visualize a much more capably-functioning person in her than, in her daily life as well as in her treatment sessions, she is presently being; but then, when I endeavor to help her to become cognizant of these larger capacities of hers, she manifests increased fearfulness and paranoid suspicion. I can well believe, from my previously-mentioned isolated experience of feeling jealousy of the attractively bronzed man she was evidently visualizing as she looked at my face, that similar jealousy is mobilized within her on occasions when she senses that I am visualizing her as being a person capable, for instance, of driving a car, of being married, and so on.

Mrs. Joan Douglas

Mrs. Joan Douglas is a chronically schizophrenic woman whose illness has been, in the main, much more severe, even, than that of Miss Herman. The work with her has shown that jealousy (and related envy) has been among the major emotions against which her awesomely severe psychosis has been serving as an unconscious defense. I by no means wish to imply that this is all that her tremendously severe and complex illness is about; but it is among the several most prominent aspects of her illness.

When I became her therapist, she was 37 years of age, and had been psychotic for some four years. She was functioning in a paranoid-schizophrenic manner, extremely resistant to psychotherapy, and manifesting an ever-changing, endless series of delusions. After the first few years of my work with her, she became much less dangerously homicidal than she had been initially and much more collaborative in many ways (not only with me but with others about her in the sanitarium); but then she began manifesting predominantly an enormous confusion about her personal identity. For many years now, she had disavowed steadfastly her real name—reacting to her whole pre-psychotic life experience as being thoroughly alien and unacceptable to her. Her sense of identity, in its stead, has consisted over the past approximately 15 years in an endless series of identity-components. Any one component may persist for a few weeks; but, much more often, it is replaced by another within days or even hours. Many times during psychotherapy sessions she has experienced herself as being, now, a totally different person from the one who had been there a moment before. Her perceptions of me, as well as her experiences of her own body-image, are incredibly distorted. She perceives me, more often than not, as multiple and frequently changing totally. She is convinced that she has been murdered many times (each shift in her identity seems to be felt by her as her having been killed), and often feels, and perceives me as being, dead—always with great concreteness and literalness.

When I began working with her, it quickly became evident that her profuse delusions were serving to defend her against being conscious of feelings of envy and jealousy (there were many other determinants of her delusions, which are beyond the scope of this chapter). For example, she would describe ballet dancers she had seen in a concert hall in Washington, or one or another prominent and successful and widely-envied person (such as in a movie or on television), and would describe the horrible tortures or deaths they had suffered, unbeknownst to them. She was delusionally convinced, in other words, that they were not really to be envied—far from it—despite their superficial appearance of success, and so forth.

Throughout my experience with her, she has had only "splashes of memory"—disconnected fragments of memories—of her pre-psychotic past. These memory-fragments, taken with historical data provided by her siblings, have made clear, from very early in our work, that her upbringing was permeated with intense envy and jealousy from a variety of sources. The sibling-rivalry in her large and outstandingly-accomplished parental family was evidently fierce. She seems to have become for many years an adored favorite of her father, to a degree that evidently made her positive oedipal complex greatly complicated. Our work together, over the years, has made abundantly clear that, behind this, has been a much more tenacious and powerful, unresolved negative oedipal complex. From the very beginning of our work it was clear that she was manifesting enormous penis envy, and her castrativeness toward males, including myself, has seemed at times limitless, although in actuality she is in this regard, as in various others, now a much more kindly person than she once was.

All these envy-and-jealousy phenomena seem to represent not unusual clinical findings, except for their unusual intensity. But there are several additional findings, having to do with envy-and-jealousy phenomena involving introjects, which indicate that psychotically-defended-against jealousy is among the major determinants of her remark-ably severe identity-disturbance.

It is not irrelevant, I am sure, that over the years I have experienced envious and jealous feelings toward her to a more personally-troublesome degree than with any other patient. Such feelings are long-accustomed to me in my work with any one of my patients, at one time or another. But never before in my work have I found cause to feel so troubled, literally for years, lest the tenacity of this woman's severe illness be due, more than anything else, to my envy and jealousy of various of her attributes, and of various of her relationships with "others"—no matter to what a degree these "others" be projected aspects of herself. This counter-transference problem is by now sufficiently non-interfering, in my work with her, that I feel reasonably sure, in retro-spect, that this envy and jealousy, and attendant guilt about such feelings, have been in the nature predominantly of my experiencing within myself such feelings which were being psychotically-defended against in her, as by projection upon me. There is certainly every reason to believe, from both her pre-psychotic history as well as her course in treatment, that such feelings in her are enormously intense, and vastly less admissible to awareness than are such feelings in me. At any rate, to detail some of the regards in which I have envied her in the past: her being a woman, able to possess sexually a man, as a woman does; her having had for many years a husband; her having borne four children, children some of whom, at least, seemed to be more successful and accom-plished than my own three children; her possessing a fabu-lously creative imagination (even though it is more accurate to say that she is possessed by it), a rare wit, and a kind of indomitable strength which I could well use in my life; her having come (as I have not) from a socially prominent and wealthy family in which various of the members are individ-uals of outstanding accomplishment; and so on.

Now, as for the jealousy-phenomena she has manifested, I want first to mention that, after several years, I began seeing that the Mrs. Joan Douglas component of her identity was so alien to her that it could best be dealt with as being in the nature of a paranoid projection, with respect to her conscious ego-functioning. She said, for example, "That Joan Douglas! Why, if I were a cat, the hairs on my back would rise!" Moreover, and more specifically relevant to this chapter, I came later to see that she clearly reacted with jealousy to this Mrs. Joan Douglas whom everyone—the ward-staff as well as myself—kept trying, whether gently and indirectly, or bluntly and furiously, to help her to realize, or make her realize, is herself. From her view, everyone kept bringing up this Mrs. Joan Douglas, who was evidently so important to them, and whom she was firmly convinced was not at all related, even, to herself—herself, who seemed to be so much less important, to the person talking with her, than was this Mrs. Joan Douglas.

Furthermore, as the years went on it became evident that prominent among the determinants of her endlessly-changing series of personal-identity components was a fear of her projected jealousy. She felt unfree to inhabit any one identity-component more than a matter of hours or days or weeks, because of a feeling that she must vacate it and relinquish it to the "real" possessor of that identity who was experienced by her as murderously jealous of the patient for having stolen it, as it were. Parenthetically, most of these identity-components were given names, by her, which I have not been able to link up with any real persons, present or past.

Thus she will come into a session feeling only the most tenuous, if any, sense of relatedness with the person who was present in the preceding session—with, that is, the different identity-component which had held sway in her during that previous session. Moreover, when I remind her of some of the things she had said during that previous session (a day or two before, usually), she quickly manifests jealousy of that supposedly other person, evidently feeling that that person—whom she feels to be not at all herself, and only most distantly, if at all, related to her—means more to me than does she, who is sitting before me in this session.

Although she is verbal more often than not, there have been many predominantly silent sessions, and more than a few in which she has been mute throughout. It is common-place for her to be hallucinating auditorially, to all appearances (she has many times reported visual and olfactory hallucinations as well), and showing every evidence of responding obediently to an hallucinatory prompter, often identified as her mother. Particularly during the sessions when she has been either mute, or verbally very highly oppositional to me, I have felt jealousy on many occasions in response to the so-much-more-intimate relationship which is prevailing between her and the hallucinatory figure in whose communications she is attentively and obediently immersed. She often nods obediently and understandingly, as she listens.

After many years, the sessions developed at times a distinctly *group* interpersonal atmosphere (a phenomenon which I have experienced with other highly ego-fragmented patients). This came about through her responding to various nonhuman items in my office—the several plants, the lamps, the wicker basket in which I keep napkins for the couch-pillow, and a modernistic wooden sculpture, and so on—as being persons. This had far more of an interpersonal impact than a child's play would have upon a bystander, and was an indubitably real experience to her. For many months she was convinced that the wicker basket was her sister, with whom she was clearly on far more lovingly intimate terms than she ever was with me; and she indicated on many occasions that she was experiencing more of a sense of human kinship with one or another of the plants, for example, than she ever felt with me. In this setting, I many times experienced jealousy in response to her relatedness with one or another of these items—which, remember, to her was quite evidently a person. She often pleaded to me the cause of this or that innocent person who had been turned (as by Circe), she was sure, into this form (the plant, or the wooden sculpture, or what not), and was yearning to be restored again to her or his rightful human form.

Her own jealousy of my perceived relatedness with one or another item in the office, in actuality nonhuman but perceived by her as essentially human, has emerged on many occasions. After many sessions in which I found her to be reprimanding me, in one way or another, for being so informal and unprofessional as to be leaning casually against my nearby desk as we talked, it dawned on me that she was speaking in an identifiably jealous way of my desk. She evidently was jealous of the intimate casually-touching relationship it enjoyed with me. She has many distorted perceptions of my tape-recorder (which is in full view); throughout the several years of my using it in our sessions, she has been convinced—and remains so—that it contains whole but miniaturized people; she often reminds me, in this regard, of the way an aborigine might react to a photograph of a person, as being the person himself. For the purpose of this paper, however, I want to mention particularly her referring a number of times to the recorder as "your daughter," in a jealous tone. After several such incidents it dawned on me that I do indeed treat my tape recorder in a lovingly-attentive, cherishing manner—very much as, for a time at least, her father treated her, and as her former husband had treated their daughter.

The "group-relatedness" atmosphere of the sessions first became apparent to me during the 17th year of the work, about four years ago and lasted, as I recall, not more than a few months.

With some temerity—because the material from the

sessions is so multideterminedly psychotic and confusing—I shall now present a few passages, from sample sessions, to show the raw material of the kind of envy-and-jealousy manifestations, in the work with her, of which I have been writing.

In the session on March 16, 1972 emerged a highly typical example of her daily-life experience of a perceivedly other person (in actuality an hallucinatory figure) "who" has suffered violence as a result of the patient's own unconscious, murderous jealousy:

> ". . . one of my baby daughters, who was a *perfect* little lady, and *never* did anything wrong, who was just an exquisite little character [her tone is one of effusive saccharinity throughout]. . . I don't see how my perfect gem should die at the Lodge [as she was convinced this baby had]—the baby—she's never done anything wrong!" [tone of wonderment and protest]

Mrs. Douglas has had in reality one daughter and three sons, all of whom are now adults. But she is delusionally convinced that she has had innumerable babies, many of whom, she is anguishedly sure, have suffered all imaginable forms of destruction or torture; she has told me many times of hearing them crying at night in the walls of the building where she lives. Her unconscious sadism, and murderous hatred, toward babies is clearly enormous.

In the session of December 12, 1972, she was mute for about the first 25 minutes, meanwhile appearing to be immersed in listening obediently to an hallucinatory voice. I spoke only seldom and briefly during this time. After about 15 minutes of her silence, I suggested (guessing, here, on the basis of my past experiences with her which, however, had been so varied that I was feeling much less than sure), "Your mother won't let you talk, huh?—to me?" She nodded in convincing confirmation of the accuracy of this surmise, but remained silent.

Then, about 10 minutes later she suddenly broke her silence by announcing, decisively, "Barbara Batchelder murdered at Chestnut Lodge 48 times." That name I had seldom, if ever, heard before; she utters almost innumerable names in our sessions. She said "murdered" in a tone such that I assumed she meant "committed murder," rather than "was murdered"; but in listening to the playback of the session, I was unsure whether she had meant the latter. In any event, her communication had a faintly shocking effect upon me; I have heard innumerable far more shocking communications from this woman, however.

In response to what she had said, I replied, "Rather shocking thing to hear, or not?" She said bitterly and caustically, "Well, not for a *psychiatrist* that was the psychiatrist during the time when 997 quaduary trillion women from Europe *died* at Chestnut Lodge." I said, "I—psychiatrist at Chestnut Lodge?" She agreed, "Yeah." I went on, " So that a little thing like *that* wouldn't shock *me*?" She agreed, "No."

She was being unusually realistic in speaking of me as having been a psychiatrist at Chestnut Lodge; much more often in our work over the years, she has identified herself as being the doctor, or the psychiatrist; later in this same session, she asserted that she is the psychiatrist. This particular distortion in her sense of identity clearly is linked to an intense and unresolved power struggle in her relationship with her mother, beginning very early indeed in the patient's childhood, as to who had the status of mother, and who, that of child.

About 15 minutes later in the session she began explaining, here using one of her many odd vernaculars, "See, uh—Queen of Egypt, she come to Chestnut Lodge; she fix all women so they in contact with *nothing*, for the rest of their lives." I responded, in a kind of semi-playful tone, "Really?—

Why would she hate women that much?" She said, "I don't
know. She jealous—stupid—" I interjected, "Sounds jealous,
yeah, she sounds jealous," agreeing with her. She went on
"—and—anyway, there's some confusion there about—uh—a
man named—uh—Ken Wainwright [a name I'd never heard
before] and the Shebas [she had spoken for years of Sheba,
in apparent reference to certain of my own qualities, and to
God only knows what, or whom, else]. He was supposed to be
her electricity [meaning, so I gathered, her sexual stimulus,
her inspiration, her *raison d'être*]. Steada being *her* electricity, he went running around *raping all* the *women* he *con-
tacted* everywhere and turning them into radium, daylight,
so forth—" I suggested, "*She* felt ignored by him or abandoned by him?" She agreed, "I guess *so*. So then she proceeded to destroy all the women. . . ."

There is abundant data, from my work with her over
the years, to indicate that such a murderously, possessively,
jealous woman was an aspect of her mother's personality,
and an aspect of her own personality during the dozen or so
years of her own married life, and later on in this session
there were clear hints that she was seeing such a woman in
me; she usually perceives me as comprised of more than one
person, and many of the constituent persons she has perceived in me, over the years, have been women—not infrequently homicidally-inclined women, as she herself has been
many times in reality. I assume that it had been such a
possessively jealous hallucinatory-mother-figure who had
made her afraid, during much of the session, to share verbally with me anything of what she was experiencing.

What was unusual, and encouraging, to me about this
session was that she was proving able to explore, with me,
the meaning of someone's murderous jealousy. She had
acted out such jealousy innumerable times, from the very
beginning of our work; but we had not been able, before, to

work together in exploring it as a dimension of the psychotherapeutic investigation.

In the session of June 7, 1973, some 10 or 15 minutes along in it I responded to something she had said a moment before, in my usual attempt to facilitate her developing this further. She responded, in a rather self-effacing tone, "I—I think Mrs. Brooks (a pseudonym) [her older sister, toward whom the patient had accepted, long since, the status of a kind of feeble-minded one, unworthy of being considered really a sister] is in here and *she* was talking to you." I inquired, "You think she was in—that head?," referring to her head. Since very early in our work she had experienced both her head and mine as being replaced unpredictably by an endless series of heads; I was long accustomed to her referring, for example, to her own head as being an alien object. She replied, in a confirming tone, "Mm." I went on, "That would, I think, make you feel rather left out, if you thought that a conversation was going on between Mrs. Brooks in your—in that head, and me, or us ["us" because she usually perceived me as multiple; so I not infrequently referred to myself as "us"]?" This she did not confirm; but I believe it to be a valid surmise. I believe, that is, that her sense of identity shifts so very frequently, oftentimes during our sessions, that at many junctures she feels she is not at all the person, in her chair, who was conversing with me a moment before; and this, I find much reason to believe, fosters jealousy in her toward that previous aspect of herself—that previous "person." She had pointed out to me quite explicitly, by way of reminder—on some occasion when I was trying to help her remember something which had occurred during the most recent session—that millions of persons "have sat in this chair during these sessions," clearly referring not to other actual patients of mine, but to the innumerable components of her fragmented self.

After some five minutes of conversation about other matters she was saying, "Well, if ya died, you're a chameleon; if you didn't die, you'd be a plant." She then paused for several seconds; I was long used to her frequently experiencing either herself, or me, or both, as being literally dead. I responded, in an ironically polite tone, "You of course have no way of knowing whether I have died?" She was again silent for several seconds, and then said, "Yeah, there's evidence on your face." I replied, in a calmly inquiring, unastonished manner, "Evidence on my face, of my having died?" She nodded in confirmation. I asked, directly and factually, "What's the evidence?" After several more seconds of silence from her I persisted, "Can you describe the evidence?" To this she retorted in a loud, harshly rejecting tone, "I don't have to *tell* you those things; I'm not a teacher any more." Parenthetically, she has never been a teacher in any conventional sense, although surely she has been a teacher in many unofficial ways, both within and without her psychotherapeutic work.

I replied, "No, you don't; that's true. You don't have to. To the extent that you want to remain *largely incomprehensible* to your *fellow human beings*, it would be fine *not* to tell me. See, that way *even I*, who have spent so many *years trying* to fathom your way of experiencing yourself, and the world you live in, *even I* wouldn't be able to fathom it. So that to the *extent* that you wish to be unfathomable, don't bother teaching me." I said all this in a kind of gently sarcastic tone, with a kind of ironic patience, until the last four words, at which my tone switched suddenly to a rapid, brutally-rejecting one.

After this she was silent again for several seconds, and then explained, "Well, the teachers would only come over to me and murder me *again*, so—" I interjected, "If you taught me?" She said, confirmingly, "Mm." I went on, "The jealous teachers would only come over and murder you again?"

She replied, "Yeah. . . . When *she* [apparently referring to a momentarily dominant one among the hallucinatory "teachers"] wants you to know something, she'll *tell* you." I suggested, "They're so jealous of their prerogatives, are they?", and she said, in emphatic confirmation, "Yeah."

In the session of June 30, 1973, within the first few minutes we had spoken, in the course of a lively back-and-forth discussion, of many persons—many of whom she herself had introduced into the conversation. Then, after I had been trying vainly to help her to remember one of her sons, to whom I felt she had alluded indirectly, she said, in a kind of rejected, left-out demeanor, "Well, he's over there in the circle [said very concretely, as usual, as if referring to a circle of people a few feet away, in this very room; she told me in a session a month later that she has to share her room at Chestnut Lodge with 27 other people; actually only one other person, her roommate, lives there, and these 27 people proved, on further inquiry, to be shadowy hallucinatory presences] anyway. So you have 47 persons over there, and I guess they're all your family." I suggested, "So you don't see why *I* don't go *over* there." She said, "Yeah." I went on, "Particularly as I do seem discontent here?—do I?" She replied, "Yeah." I long ago had started to realize something of how easily wounded she was at any indication of my being other than contentedly immersed in being with her, without any thought of anyone else. It was evident that she had found reason to feel once again rejected, not part of my intimate family circle of 47 persons. I cannot say that in this instance she was appearing jealous; rather, I surmise, she felt too insignificant to me to be able to hope, even, to be in such a competition.

Less than five minutes later, however, she was in the midst of one of her long-familiar upbraidings of me for not bestirring myself to the constructive activities which, she felt, urgently needed doing: ". . . You've had a lot of opportunity around here to tell people what to do; but you never seem to think too much about it. You just kinda feel sorry for yourself all the time. . . . You coulda gotten my body started being made, and my mother's, and a few things like that; but you haven't done it." I suggested, "I've let you down, thus far?" She agreed, "Yeah. So I got Victor Immanuel [a fantasy-figure of whom I have long heard. Of course I realize that this is the name of the last king of Italy; but I do not know what more personal significances the name has for her], because he's a real worker, and knows what to do, and knows how to go about it. [I distinctly felt that she was trying—with little if any success—to make me jealous of Victor Immanuel.] Maybe he'll help you—let you help *him*, something like that. But I *asked* you to put up an ice skating rink, and you didn't do *that*, and you—you just let things drift. Day after day, nothing gets done; nobody builds up the gyms anywhere; they all need to be *fixed*. And everything of ours has to be made *giant* size; but you haven't done it yet. We've got big giants standing around all the buildings, and you haven't—you know, raised the ceilings, or *anything*." She spoke in a tone which varied from exhortation, to disgust, to scorn. She was perceiving me, here, entirely as she had often perceived her husband, and as, in her childhood, her mother had often perceived the patient's father.

I replied, "Puzzles you that I could be so—inert?" She readily agreed, "Yeah." I went on, not harshly but persistently, "Yet if I ever seem anything *but* inert, you feel that I'm discontent, and restless, and wanting to be elsewhere?" She said emphatically, "Yeah." Although she did not seem to feel any personal responsibility for modifying these conflicting demands she made upon me, she had here acknowledged, more clearly and simply than ever before, the fact of her making opposing demands upon me.

Some 10 minutes later, minutes filled with verbal communications about many matters, I commented that "I get the impression that whenever I speak of someone other than yourself, you assume that I like that person better than I like you?" She replied, in a tone implying that she had not thought of it this way before, but decisively confirmatory of it, "I guess *so*." By now, I felt that I had gained a memorable series of glimpses into the detailed and pervasive manner in which the heretofore-unseen jealousy among her various identity-components, or introjects, was contributing to the enormous and long-persisting fragmentation of her ego-functioning.

My earlier chapter concerning jealousy involving an internal object, a summary of which was given at the beginning of this one, contains a relatively detailed theoretical discussion of this subject, and a review of the relevant literature.

References

Klein, M. (1957). *Envy and Gratitude–A Study of Unconscious Sources*. New York: Basic Books. Republished in 1975 in England by the Hogarth Press and the Institute of Psycho-Analysis, and in U. S. by Delacorte Press/Seymour Lawrence, under the title, *Envy and Gratitude & Other Works 1946–1963*.

Searles, H. F. (1972). The function of the patient's realistic perceptions of the analyst in delusional transference. *British Journal of Medical Psychology* 45:1–18.

—— (1976). Jealousy involving an internal object. Presented at the New York Conference on Borderline Disorders (under the auspices of Advanced Institute for Analytic Psychotherapy), New York City, Nov. 20, 1976. Expanded version published on pp. 347–403 in *Advances in Psychotherapy of the Borderline Patient*, eds. J. LeBoit and A. Capponi. New York: Jason Aronson, 1979. Reprinted as Chapter 5 in this present volume.

Part IV

Handling
Inevitable Issues

Chapter 9

Psychoanalytic Therapy with Borderline Patients: The Development, in the Patient, of an Internalized Image of the Therapist

I shall discuss here some of the difficulties which the therapist and the borderline patient have in enabling the patient to develop a stable, internalized image of the therapist. A minority of the points which I shall touch upon here have also been dealt with in chapters 1, 3, and 7 of this book.

Earlier versions of this chapter were presented as the Fifth O. Spurgeon English Honor Lecture at Temple University School of Medicine, Philadelphia, April 25, 1980; and at the Fifth Annual Meeting of The Virginia Psychoanalytic Society, Virginia Beach, VA, June 13, 1980. This material also appears in *The Borderline Patient: Emerging Concepts in Diagnosis, Psychodynamics and Treatment*, edited by J. S. Grotstein, M. Solomon, and J. A. Lang; Hillsdale, NJ: The Analytic Press, 1986.

It seems widely agreed that the borderline patient, until he is relatively far along in therapy, has difficulty in maintaining a stable, internalized image of the therapist between sessions. LeBoit (1979) makes a statement which, although perhaps considerably oversimplified, is relevant here:

> A number of authors now hold the position that the process of cure with the borderline patient comes about through the introjection of a healthier object, replacing the pathological parental object. As the patient will not surrender his internal bad objects until the analyst becomes a sufficiently good object for him, the success or failure of the treatment hinges upon this transposition. . . . The analyst . . . serves . . . not only as a transference object, but also as a new parental model for the patient to identify with and to internalize (p. 24).

On the one hand the borderline patient is spared, by his lack of well-established internal images, from normal grieving; as one man was able to say still, after several years of treatment, "I don't miss anybody. . . . I never miss people. . . . I don't feel unhappy when I'm away from anyone." But on the other hand, such a patient's lack of a firmly internalized image of the therapist makes the patient prone to feelings of panic lest the absent therapist has gone out of existence entirely. Such patients tend typically to make between-sessions telephone calls to the therapist, for needed external feedback affirming for the patient that the therapist still exists in the patient's external, if not internal, world. Similarly, when the patient arrives for a session after a brief interruption in the therapy, he has difficulty in shaking off a sense that the situation, and the therapist, are strangers to him.

It is similarly widely agreed that, in the context of the session itself, such a patient needs relatively much visual and auditory feedback to sustain his tenuous internalized image of the therapist. But it is in the context of the sessions that therapist and patient have their best opportunity to explore the largely unconscious internal contents, in both participants, related to the patient's difficulty in this regard.

The Patient's Split-Off Hatred Toward Any Nascent Internalized Image of the Therapist

When one man said, "I hate myself; . . . I feel like chewing myself up and spitting myself out!," I heard this as an expression of unconscious ambivalence toward not only his "self" but toward such internalized images of me as he had so far developed: on the one hand he wanted to chew them up (as if to ingest them), but on the other hand he wanted to spit them out. When, a few days later, he said, literally hissing with intensity, "I look at myself and I can't *stand* it! I just wanta spit myself out!", I felt I was seeing something of the intensity of the hatred still directed at his internalized images of me, such that these images did not survive well the interims between sessions, nor survive reliably during the sessions themselves.

One woman would turn and look at me before leaving, at the end of each session, in a strange fashion which gave me to feel that she was mentally photographing me, as if to hold me, thus, in her mind until the next session. Another woman said, "The only way I know a person is there—that a person exists—is, I have to keep a person in mind, or the person dies, the person disappears."

The Patient's Subtly Autistic Unrelatedness; Unintegrated Oedipal Rivalry as One of the Determinants of This

These patients have learned, long since, to pretend to participate in interpersonal relationships much more fully and
consistently than is actually the case, and have become so
skillful in so doing that it is difficult for the therapist to
discern those times when the patient has taken refuge, unconsciously, once again, in autistic unrelatedness. The patient may manifest his less-than-full relatedness by arriving
late and then referring, significantly, to himself as *being*
late, still many minutes along in the session after his actual
arrival—indicating that, although physically present, he
has not yet arrived fully, in a psychological sense.

In one's work with a borderline patient who has become, at a conscious level, relatively well related with the
therapist during the session, but who experiences the times
between sessions as being stretches of bleak unrelatedness
with anyone, I have found this understandable in terms of
the splitting so characteristic of borderline patients: the
unrelatedness which is being dissociated during the session
itself is displaced into the interims between sessions, and
needs to become discovered by the two participants as being
at work, subtly, during the sessions themselves, sessions in
which both patient and therapist have felt, heretofore, that
they were involved in a relatively strong, and even intense,
interpersonal bond with one another.

In Chapter 1, I mentioned that whereas in some borderline patients, symbiotic processes predominate, in others,
subtle autism is more dominant. Thus, one woman patient is
silent for long stretches of time while lying on the couch, for
the reason, so it becomes evident, that she has become fused
with me in my silence. And on the other hand, a relatively
talkative man is belatedly discovered to be subtly exiling me

upon his assuming the couch, such that throughout the session itself, at an unconscious level he is alone in the room throughout.

In Chapter 5, I have pointed out that the borderline patient's autistic non-relatedness, in the transference, has one of its etiologic roots in his oedipal rivalry: he has fostered, unconsciously, a state of unrelatedness between himself and the therapist such as prevailed—so his oedipal ambitions would have it—between his own two parents whenever those two were alone in a room together. One such patient said, "I just can't picture my parents together; they never seem to be on the same wave-length" (Searles 1979a, p. 362).

The Therapist's Struggle to Develop a Stable, Internalized Image of the Patient

It seems to me unrealistic to expect the patient to develop a stable, internalized image of the therapist unless, and insofar as, the therapist has proved able, first, to have developed such an image of the patient. For a variety of reasons, this is a formidable task for the therapist.

The patient's need to project his own dissociated internal contents into the therapist is so intense as to interfere not only with his own development of a stable, internalized image of the therapist, but also with the therapist's developing a comparable image of the patient. One of the reasons why this need to project is so intense is that much of the patient's dissociated experiences, or introjects, have important roots in his preverbal history. These experiences are so verbally-inarticulable that the patient can communicate them, predominantly, only by projecting them into the therapist and giving the latter, thus, to experience them at first hand. To the extent that this aspect of the therapeutic interaction succeeds, the therapist with his relatively strong ego becomes able to experience these in awareness, and express them in appropriate words, as relevant analytic data for shared work with the patient. Many of these feeling-states are so strange, so complex and paradoxical, that, the therapist finds, even a relatively healthy person can scarcely, if at all, find words to express them. In my work with such a patient, whereas for years I used to be intensely exasperated with her for being able to say only that she felt "nervous," as I came to experience within myself the indescribable feelings she was largely warding off and projecting into me, I came fully to appreciate why she had felt so helpless to articulate what she, on occasion, was experiencing.

I hope to be conveying, here, something of how the patient's need to project into the therapist, as a primitive means of communicating these primitive feeling-experiences, works powerfully against the therapist's being able either to remain steadily available for the patient's developing a durable introject of him, or to develop a stable, realistic, internalized image of the patient. One could surmise, also, that the patient's mode of communicating thus has, as one of its additional determinants, the effort to ensure that the therapist *not* durably exist, in psychological reality, for such introject-formation. We glimpse here, I believe, how *very* ambivalent is each of the two participants concerning the development of an internalized image of the other one.

The unaccustomed, for the therapist, nature of many of the borderline patient's transference-reactions and -attitudes toward him is another major difficulty in the therapist's development of a stable internalized image of the patient. These transference-phenomena are often so threatening to the therapist that he tends unconsciously to flee from the developing transference-role in question or, if he starts to become aware of it, to interpret it prematurely—to put this hot potato, which he himself cannot endure, back into the patient's lap, as it were.

The Patient's Strange Transference-Reactions to the Therapist (as Being Nonhuman, Dead, Crazy, Multiple, and So On)

My (Searles 1960) first book, *The Nonhuman Environment in Normal Development and in Schizophrenia*, describes as a universal human struggle the endeavor to become subjectively human, as distinct from the surrounding nonhuman environment, and to become able to differentiate one's fellows as human, also. The borderline individual, like the frankly psychotic one, is much involved in such an identity-struggle and, in his typical transference-responses to the therapist, invests the latter with various of the patient's own subjectively nonhuman personality components. Thus, in one's work with the borderline patient, one finds that the patient's transference-reactions are not predominantly to one as being a single and whole and alive and human being, but rather to one as something less than, or other than, human. Margaret Little (1966), in her paper, "Transference in Borderline States," says of one of her patients that "in fact to her I *was* her eczema, the source of all her troubles and the prime cause of the general ineffectiveness, loneliness and despair which had brought her into treatment; I was the loneliness itself, and also, as appeared later, her mother's loneliness, anxiety and despair" (p. 476).

One woman reported a dream of a woman who seemed to alternate between being dead and being alive; and in the session, her associations made clear that this woman represented me in the transference. Another woman, whom I interviewed before a group of psychiatric residents, replied, when I asked her something about her mother, "The first thing about my mother is that she's dead," and, although this was literally now the case, several of the residents present had the sense, as did I, that the patient had perceived the mother so even while the latter had been alive. When I asked a man, during one of his analytic sessions, whether he had ever confided in his much-elder sister anything of the area of concern which he was presently exploring, he reacted with a degree and kind of shock which helped me to realize that, for him during his childhood, his sister had been psychologically dead, and that many of our more moribund sessions had to do with his transference to me as being that "dead" sister.

Many borderline patients have had a parent who was frankly psychotic. One such woman reported to me, several years along in her analysis, that the thought had just occurred to her that "Maybe you're *not* crazy, after all." For years, theretofore, I had had to live, alone, with the knowledge of her unconscious transference to me as being crazy; only now did she realize that she had unconsciously so regarded me, all along.

As I described in Chapter 4, the borderline patient's ego-functioning tends to be, at an unconscious level, dual or multiple in nature; hence many of his transference-reactions cast the therapist as being two or more persons simultaneously. I customarily sit in a corner, in analytic or therapeutic sessions, behind the couch, and I found it notable when one woman reported a dream in which she was in a bus station where "over in one corner there was this, uh, man and woman, . . ." A man, while lying on the couch, was reporting a dream in which, ". . . I really thought these two men back of me were going to catch me. . . ."

Another category of borderline transference-phenomena involves the therapist's being one or another of the patient's psychopathologic symptoms. One man said, on the couch, "There's this load on my back [sic] of murkiness about my future years, this cloudiness, this terrible suspense. . . ." Earlier in the session he had reproached me for my sitting silently, back there, while he was having to do all the work. Another man who likewise lay on the couch while I was sitting behind him, was saying of his life at home currently,

"The depression just sort of sits there and sooner or later overwhelms me."

A woman reacts to me, unconsciously, as being the carbuncle which, in childhood, had afflicted the back of her neck and nearly killed her, and which she is afraid will materialize there again.

A man says, consciously referring to his relationship with his eldest son, "I've never seen a father–son relationship like this [N.B.]—it's already dead; it just sits there. . . ."

Another man unconsciously equates me with his electric blanket which, during the night, he can turn up or down; this is in line with Modell's (1968) description of the borderline patient's transference to the analyst as being a transitional object, and is one of many clinical examples, in my experience, in which the therapist is unconsciously equated with, or perceived as fused with, some inanimate object. Such "inanimate" transference-perceptions are referable in part, of course, to the patient's unconscious identity-aspects as being subjectively inanimate. One woman gave a fleeting glimpse of her own subjectively inanimate identity in saying, with a tone of futility, "*I* can't see my way out of this situation at the office; it's up to other things [N.B.; then, as if to obscure what she had revealed, she added hastily]—and other people. . . ."

A man in reporting a dream detailed that "while I was on a bus, it just abruptly switched to you—we were facing each other and you said, 'Now, Bill. . . .'" When he said "it just abruptly switched to you," he clearly meant, consciously, that the focus of the *dream* had switched to me; but what he conveyed, unconsciously, at this moment in the dream-narration was that the *bus* had switched to—that is, turned into—me. His need for me to serve as a firm holding environment (such as a bus) was evident many times over the years of my work with him.

Another man reports, in the present tense, a dream in

which he inadvertently causes some damage to the building in which my office is located, "and I'm in a panic that you're gonna be enraged and *the building is gonna be enraged* [my italics] and everything. . . ." His phrase, "the building," evidently is consciously intended as an abbreviated way of saying, "all the people in the building"; but the affective tone of his italicized statement conjures up, nonetheless, the sense of an erstwhile holding environment (the building) which has become murderously rageful toward him.

I hope that the presentation of these typical examples of borderline transference, presented here in an inevitably relatively glib and superficial manner, something like a stroll through a zoo, will nonetheless serve to convey something of how intensely uncomfortable, for the therapist, are such transference-roles, especially when—as happens more often than not—they are the product of intense and sustained, dissociated emotions on the part of the patient. It is important to realize that, when the nature of the transference eventually emerges with the kind of clarity I am describing in these examples, the therapist has reason to feel much relief that long-subterranean responses on the patient's part have surfaced at last, into a relatively conscious realm where they can at last be seen by both participants, and explored mutually.

A woman says uneasily, at the beginning of a session, "I dunno; as I was lying down, I had some sense of your being like an apparition—spooky, in some sorta way. . . ." She went on to describe that, during the previous night, she had awakened, screaming for help. Another woman, after reporting an unearthly kind of dream, sensed me as being (there behind the couch) an unseen, malevolent deity, bent upon destroying her. A man, lying uncomfortably on the couch, was talking in an attemptedly philosophical, but actually whistling-past-the-graveyard manner, and said, "There's always the death in the background. . . ." I had reason, from many quarters, to hear this as an unconscious reference to me, sitting behind him.

Various patients have conveyed in various ways that I, sitting behind them, personify their past, or attributes of their past. One woman said, "I didn't have the guts to burn the bridges behind me." Another says, "Whenever I feel at all nostalgic, I try to put it completely behind me." A man, long involved in an unhappy marriage, says, "My past has always been a ball and chain I've had to drag along behind me."

Another man is saying, of his troubled relationship with his son, ". . . I don't want my anger at him—[pause]—to get in the way of his developing more self-confidence. . . ." Various clues too numerous to present here indicated to me that, at this juncture in the work, I represented to him, unconsciously, his unwanted anger at his son.

A woman clearly manifested, in one session after several years of analysis, a transference to me as being her feelings—not merely certain of her feelings, not only her unconscious feelings, but all of her feelings. My notes state that "Part of the data was that, without me—I'll be away tomorrow—she has submerged panic lest she lose all feelings, and she reports 'an urge to grab you' in order to be able to feel." This woman and I had accomplished much together, by then, and I felt that she had progressed farther, at this point, than an early borderline patient of mine who had reported happily, one morning upon coming to her session (now many years ago), that she was carrying her feelings with her, in her purse. I do not believe I had dared, at that relatively early time in my psychoanalytic career, to become as important to her, and know that I had become as important to her, as was the case in my work with this much later patient, all of whose feelings I personally had come to embody, for her, in the transference.

Another woman, who had progressed far in her analysis, said, in a light, chatty manner, while I remained silent, "One thing I like about coming here is that it makes my mind work. My mind is inclined to sit back and do nothing— whoops! [brief, amused laugh]—not you—Are you my mind? . . ."

A man, whose language showed many identifications with that of his immigrant father, reported to me, sitting behind him, "I was thinking *in back of myself* [my italics; he clearly meant this, consciously, as equivalent to "in the back of my mind"], 'Why are you having such a hard time getting this [legal] brief written?'"

The Patient's Defensive Splitting Is Opposed to the Two Participants' Developing Stable, Internalized Images of One Another

The splitting which is generally agreed to be among the borderline individual's major defenses is another factor which works against not only the patient's development of a stable, coherent, internalized image of the therapist, but the therapist's development, similarly, of such an image of the patient. The following clinical examples are intended mainly to highlight the impact, upon the therapist, of the splitting in the patient's transference-reactions to him.

One man brought to me a gift of two matched drawings he had done, prior to framing them, and set them up across the room. I commented admiringly about them and, for reasons which I shall not attempt to detail here, chose to accept the intended gift of them. A couple of weeks later he brought in one of them, framed, and put it on view in the same general location as before, across the room, and assumed the couch. The feeling-atmosphere between us seemed genuinely friendly; but I interrupted his reporting, not many minutes along in the session, by commenting,

"You know, I'm sitting here looking at that drawing over there, and I'm thinking, it's very beautiful—but where's the other half of it?" His friendly demeanor immediately vanished: he expostulated, violently, "You son of a bitch!—I *knew* you'd say that!" This led, naturally enough, into a further exploration of some of his less positively-toned transference reactions to me. Seldom have I found the split-off "half" of a patient's transference-reaction to emerge so neatly in response to a technical intervention of mine. Only as I write this do I see that here, now, he gave me a truly worthy psychoanalytic gift.

A patient's split-off negative-transference image of the therapist is assigned, frequently enough, to a spouse to feel in awareness and to vocalize. For example, one woman reported as she turned up for a long-accustomed Saturday morning analytic session—reported in a relatively friendly and reasonably affable tone, as usual with her—that her husband had snarled at her, as she was leaving the house to come to her session, "As you still seeing that bastard?"

A man described his having shown to his wife, with warm pride, a copy of my first book. He reported to me, dutifully, that his wife had glanced at the book and retorted, curtly, "Searles is a charlatan; I can't believe he can write any better than he can analyze people."

Another man achieved, after a number of years of psychoanalytic therapy, sufficient integration of previously-split transference-images of me to be able to say, in one breath, "I can't tell you how much I love you or how much of a shit I think you are." But each of the two affective tones in the two halves of the sentence—the one intensely loving, indeed, and the other equally intensely harsh and rejecting—was undiluted by the other, and the whole statement was jolting in its over-all impact upon me.

A man who split off, for years, his feelings of unrelatedness during the session, displacing these onto situations between the sessions, once put it that "The time I spent here used to feel like the only time I was alive—the rest of my life was kinda dead," and described that still (after years of therapy), "What a let-down it is each time I go to work from here. The Bureau [where he was working] is so empty and meaningless. Relationships go from something to nothing. You talk about having some relationship for the rest of your life; but, for me, it doesn't happen like that. To me, there is no such thing; this relationship [for example] can disappear at any moment, and there would be no trace of it anyone can see. But that's how it *is*: every day I leave here and there's nothing left, and in its place is the Bureau—only it's not in its place; it's [that is, the Bureau is] no good as a replacement. . . ."

The patient who is involved in a split-transference toward the therapist, and who therefore conveys totally opposing demands upon the latter—for example, to be silent and to speak, or to be at one and to be, simultaneously, apart and unrelated—is basically dissatisfied for the reason that he wants the therapist to heal the unconscious split within him, the patient.

The Therapist Feels This *Transference-Role to Be His* Only *Link with the Patient*

The therapist who is working with a borderline patient is given to sense that this transference role, which the patient unconsciously perceives him as occupying, in his—the therapist's—only means of relating to the patient. Another way of thinking of this is to conceive that the patient is projecting one of his introjects into the therapist, and the therapist senses that this introject, which he personifies to the patient, is the only possible person he can be in relationship with the patient. This involves the borderline person's existing in accordance with the *pars pro toto* principle—that is, that this present *part* of his over-all potentially possible ways of relating with the therapist is the *totality*; his experience has not given him to realize, as yet, that this is only part of a many-faceted totality, a totality which contains within it many different, potentially more gratifying, ways of relating.

For example, one woman said, "At work it seems to me that I just *live* in *terror* of being asked to do something that's not in my power to do." The words she emphasized were said in a tone which conveyed that she is *really living* only when she is in terror. When she said this, I was reminded of patients whom I had interviewed (in teaching-interviews) who had given me to know that terror, or even panic, was preferable to their boredom, and of one who agreed when I suggested that he felt alive only when he felt in imminent danger of being murdered. Such patients give the therapist to sense that being in relatedness with the patient requires that the therapist be perceived, by the patient, as terrifying. All this has to do with the patient's inability to experience in awareness, at this point in his ego-development, anything like the full gamut of human feelings. One man phrased it that "I don't feel sadness; sadness isn't really something I feel. I understand devastation, and I understand rage." A woman described that the emotionality of her older sister (who had served as mother-figure for her) had been limited to "shocked and stunned," and hence she—the patient—had become considerable of a daredevil in childhood, in order to get the only available kind of emotional response from her sister.

One sees this same principle, as regards severely limited possibilities for relating, in work with frankly psychotic patients also. In a paper wherein I (Searles 1977a) described some aspects of my work with a chronically schizophrenic man, I reported that "It required some years before I realized, sitting in one of the silences which still predominated during our sessions, that it had now become conceivable to me to be tangibly related to him without my having to either fuck him or kill him" (pp. 18–19).

The Therapist's Unconscious Attempt to Flee from a Transference Role by Interpreting It Prematurely, or by Personal Reminiscences

Therapists, including myself, tend frequently to interpret prematurely a patient's transference-reaction wherein the patient has been projecting into the therapist some introject which has been giving the therapist to sense his own transference-role to be a most uncomfortable one. The therapist endeavors prematurely to highlight, for the patient, the role of projection in the way the latter has been perceiving him— to confront the patient with the possibility that, to paraphrase, "The way you have been perceiving me is little if at all true of me, but is highly true of yourself, as regards one of your less palatable identifications with your father or mother." My belief is that if the therapist has not yet come to find the transference-role in question reasonably tolerable to himself, he cannot realistically expect that the patient, whose sense of identity is less strong and well-integrated than his own, will yet be able to cope with this hot-potato kind of projected introject. When we try prematurely to unburden ourselves by such an interpretation, we usually do so with the implied denial that there is *any* reality basis for the patient's transference-perception of us and this, too, is to my way of thinking not rational. The patient needs to become able *really* to find, over the course of time, a sample of everything in the therapist.

    In my own work, I find that not only do I tend prematurely to make transference-interpretations in such settings as those I have described briefly here, and, similarly, that I tend to make psychotherapeutic (rather than psychoanalytic) interventions precisely at points wherein the patient's long-held, previously unconscious, transference image of me as personifying the sickest aspects of his mother, or father, or whomever, is starting to emerge into better awareness on his part. That is, just when some long-manifested introject, which is at the basis of much of the patient's depression, for example, starts to become seen by him in me, then I experience an urge to make some explanatory, supportive, non-transference interpretation. Further, if I can manage to hold my tongue, I then realize that this urge is based upon my wish to avoid emerging, in the patient's perception of me, as being very sick—as, in his childhood, he had abundant reason to perceive one or another of his mothering or parenting figures.

For many years I have been interested in the question of the degree to which a therapist can permissibly, and even usefully, convey to a patient information about the therapist's own life history. I am aware that this is a complex and difficult question. To my way of thinking, the therapist inevitably does convey much information about himself, much of it non-verbal and conveyed unconsciously—no matter how well analyzed the therapist has been. Further, I doubt that any therapist or analyst, no matter how classical in orientation, abstains totally from conveying consciously bits of his own personal history to the patient. I can well believe that such communications have a permissible and even, in aggregate, essential role in any patient's several-years-long experience with the therapist.

But I wish to call attention, here, to the likelihood that the therapist—and I know this to be true in my own work—will get into reminiscing to the patient about bits of the therapist's own past, in unconscious flight from some emerging transference-role which threatens the therapist's more

cherished views of his own identity. I shall give one example
of this kind of interaction.

In a session during the closing months of my several
years of work with her, a woman made relatively brief
reference to a younger sister who was living the life of a
recluse in New York City. Throughout the patient's therapy,
she had made mention relatively infrequently of this sister,
and had given me much reason to know that she had felt, in
childhood and adolescence, intense jealousy of this then-
beautiful girl. For many years now, she had felt remote
from the sister.

Midway along in this session, quite some time after her
having made some brief mention of that sister which highlighted, again, the latter's reclusiveness, she asked, "Do you
enjoy what you do? Do you get fun out of it? Do you look
forward to it?," and other questions in that vein. She asked
these in a fashion so inviting that I felt a strong urge to
confide in her my feelings at some length about this—including the most depressive among my gamut of feelings
about my work. But I thought privately that by now, after
about six years, she had had sufficient experience with me
to have some fairly clear impressions, herself, as to the
answers to these questions. I felt, nonetheless, in considerable conflict about this, for I was aware that she would be
terminating (as agreed), in another few months, and there
was much to be said on the side of her being given, at long
last, a relatively generous amount of consciously verbalized
information about me.

I replied in approximately these words: "I have a considerable urge to tell you in detail about myself, in response
to what you've asked. But my better judgment is that there
is something to analyze in this. You sound as though you
know me scarcely at all, and I surmise that's about how you
feel toward Hilda [the sister]."

She replied, "I thought you were going to say my

mother," and went into much pertinent transference-detail, then, about her mother and sister, dwelling particularly upon the latter. Her hatred and contempt for Hilda had never been so open and intense, over the years of the therapy, as now—and likewise her feelings of competitive triumph over her sister, whose days of glory had faded.

> "Hilda was kinda one aspect of what Mother wanted to be. . . . Hilda was kinda one segment of that, and maybe I was another segment: not beautiful, but bright. . . . I always had the impression that Mother thought of herself as both bright and beautiful. . . ."
> "The last time I really talked with Hilda was at Mother's funeral [a few years before] . . . and she seemed vacant. . . . It felt like I wasn't really talking to anybody—like there wasn't really anybody there. . . . Hilda was vacant; the inside of her had atrophied or hadn't been permitted to develop, and she was just a beautiful shell—(laughs)—I'll bet I just say that out of wild-eyed jealousy. . . ."

In hearing the last few of the statements she made, I felt shocked at the intensity of her hatred and contempt toward, and of her vindictive triumph over, her sister. The patient's laugh was a relatively light, good-natured, non-malevolent-*seeming* one; but it did not fool me for a moment, for I had long known her to be an expert at carefully-practiced laughter in infinite variety. I heard her light-seeming laugh as a very clear attempt to gloss over the hatred that had become evident, for a few seconds, just before. Parenthetically, the agreed-upon, scheduled termination had been necessitated by factors outside the control of either of us. She had accomplished much in our work together but, as is obvious here, much remained unexplored.

At the end of this session, I did not feel fully confirmed

in the wisdom of the way I had responded to her questions to me. The atmosphere as she left was such that I didn't know what her feelings were; it seemed to me as likely as not that an important opportunity for reality-relatedness between us had not been seized by me. But at least, I felt, this session had pointed up, in a way useful for me, some of the issues involved in the therapist's conflict as to whether to tell the patient something of himself, or not, in response to the patient's inquiry. In any event, I definitely felt that some of the power of my suppressed urge to tell her of myself was, in retrospect, my unconscious way of avoiding the transference-role of Hilda, perceived by the patient as being "vacant; the inside of her had atrophied or hadn't been permitted to develop." Had I told her what I felt so warmly invited to confide to her, of my experience of my daily work, I would have been reassuring myself that I am alive inside, but I would have made it appreciably more difficult for her to explore, in the closing months of our work, her transference to me as being her reclusive sister.

The Patient's Experience of Attempted Transference-Interpretations as Being Paranoid Projections from the Therapist

I have had experiences with a number of patients which have helped me better to understand how difficult it is for a patient to associate at all freely, during the session, if he has a powerful transference to the therapist as being a highly paranoid parent-figure and as tending, therefore, to project, powerfully and tenaciously, repressed or dissociated inner contents upon, or into, the patient. Typically, the patient who is highly resistive to, or otherwise warding off of, attempted transference-interpretations is protecting himself, thus, from the therapist's perceivedly malevolent threat, in the transference, to find in the patient, and to hold the patient totally responsible for, inner contents of the therapist's own, which the therapist cannot consciously recognize, and accept personal responsibility for, as such.

I have come to understand this from my own feelings in being on the receiving end of powerfully-projected material from such patients. I find that, as such a patient walks in from the waiting room for the nth time, I am automatically battening down all my hatches, securing myself as an intendedly impregnable fortress—and I do see, here, the sexual connotation of the word "impregnable." All this helps me to realize that such a patient, projecting into the therapist the patient's own great need to project, must inevitably be highly constricted in the attempt at free association: he dare not reveal more than guarded bits of himself, lest all these projections come home to roose, projections perceived as originating from within the therapist.

In, again, my own experience with such a patient as he walks in from the waiting room, I find that I tend to take refuge in viewing him diagnostically, as predominantly afflicted with a character disorder of one sort or another, for example, for to the extent that I can maintain such a nosological view, I tend not to take *personally* his insulting, arrogant, infuriating, stinging, wounding, and what-not customary reactions to me.

It is of the essence, in psychoanalytic therapy as in psychoanalysis, that the therapist facilitate, insofar as feasible and at such a pace as is appropriate for the patient's current level of functioning, the patient's coming to discover that the problems, conscious and unconscious, which impelled him into therapy are at work in the transference—are being manifested, that is, in his responses and attitudes toward the therapist. But if the therapist endeavors too frequently and too prematurely to call the patient's attention to the likelihood that the patient, here and here again, is responding to the therapist, at times when the patient has not been aware at all of doing so, it is easy for the patient to infer that the therapist is being what we would call essentially paranoid—self-referential, referring everything, or practically everything, to the therapist himself. If the therapist endeavors repeatedly to make plain, however, that much of the significance which he regards himself as possessing, *vis-à-vis* the patient, derives from his personifying, for the patient, significant persons from the patient's childhood, the patient will be somewhat less likely to write off the therapist as being imbued with paranoid suspicion and grandiosity.

In my experience, it develops on rare occasions that the transference-countertransference emotions in my work with borderline patients become so intense that it feels to me all I can do simply to stay in the same room with the patient throughout the session—whether because I am finding him so infuriating, or insufferable, or disturbing in various other ways. Although I cannot report here with confident precision—for I have not kept sufficiently full research-notes upon the matter—I have the distinct impression that it is such patients whom, at the level of their internalized images within me between my actual sessions with the patients themselves, I experience as disturbing presences within myself. When I think back to the most disturbing periods of work I have done, with the most disturbing patients over the past years in my private practice, these typically have been borderline patients. I have found, further, that the work with any one of those most difficult patients has come to feel most unmanageable when I have become unable to know surcease from the patient even between sessions, but have found him or her disturbingly present, in my memory and in my fantasies during sessions with other patients (as well as at home). In what feels to be quite a tangible sense, this so-disturbing patient, present at the level of an internal feeling-image within me while I am in a session with another

patient whom I ordinarily have not found markedly difficult, threatens to overwhelm me, from within, in such a way
that I shall become immersed imminently, here with this
other patient, in essentially the same kind of transference-
countertransference difficulties as those I have been finding
too much for me in my work with the original so-difficult
patient.

Surely, some of this involves my having identified with
that so-difficult patient as an aggressor; hence I would tend
to feel, and behave, like that patient in my work with all my
other current patients. I cannot attempt to discuss these
dynamics—essentially, I suppose, *folie à deux* dynamics—
more fully here; but I hope to have succeeded, at least, in
indicating how difficult it is for the therapist, in working
with these so-trying patients, to develop a stable internalized image, within himself, of the patient. When one goes
through experiences such as these, in the position of the
therapist, one can now know, at first hand, something of
why the patient—who projects into the therapist so much of
his psychopathology—would become able only with great
difficulty, and after many storms, to develop within himself
a stable, internalized image of the therapist.

Summary

I have discussed some of the difficulties which the therapist
and the borderline patient encounter in enabling the patient
to develop a stable, internalized image of the therapist. The
patient's lack of such an image, in the early phases of the
work, is evident both between and during therapy sessions;
but his autism, in this connection, is often subtle and not
easy, therefore, for the therapist to detect. The role of the
patient's split-off hatred toward any nascent internalized
image of the therapist is touched upon here.

It is necessary for the therapist to lead the way, in

developing an internalized image of the patient, before the latter, partly by identification with the therapist here, can do similarly. The bulk of the chapter describes the therapist's own difficulties in this regard.

These difficulties are referable in part to the patient's projecting of his own introjects and other unconscious contents, in great abundance and with great intensity and tenacity, into the therapist. Further, and in consequence of this, the therapist finds himself in strange, oftentimes subjectively nonhuman, transference roles which are referable to very early stages of ego-development, on the patient's part, prior to the latter's individuation and prior, likewise, to his being able to distinguish between human and nonhuman, animate and inanimate, ingredients of the surrounding world. The patient's defensive splitting adds to the complexity and disturbing nature of the transference roles which beset, as it were, the therapist.

The therapist, in unconscious flight from one or another of these transference roles, tends to interpret them prematurely to the patient, or to launch into warmly human reminiscences.

In describing those instances in which the therapist finds particularly persecuting his internalized image of an extraordinarily difficult patient, some of the dynamics of *folies à deux* are touched upon.

References

LeBoit, J. (1979). The technical problem with the borderline patient. In *Advances in Psychotherapy of the Borderline Patient*, ed. J. LeBoit and A. Capponi, pp. 3–62. New York and London: Jason Aronson.

Little, M. (1966). Transference in borderline states. *International Journal of Psycho-Analysis* 47: 476–485.

Modell, A. H. (1968). *Object Love and Reality: An Introduction to a*

Psychoanalytic Theory of Object Relations. New York: International Universities Press.

Searles, H. F. (1960). *The Nonhuman Environment in Normal Development and in Schizophrenia.* New York: International Universities Press.

——— (1977). Dual- and multiple-identity processes in borderline ego functioning. In *Borderline Personality Disorders—The Concept, the Syndrome, the Patient,* ed. P. Hartocollis, pp. 441–455. New York: International Universities Press. Reprinted in Searles (1979), pp. 460–478. Reprinted as Chapter 4 in this volume.

——— (1977a). The development of mature hope in the patient-therapist relationship. In *The Human Dimension in Psychoanalytic Practice,* ed. K. A. Frank, pp. 9–27. New York: Grune and Stratton. Reprinted in Searles (1979), pp. 479–502.

——— (1978). Psychoanalytic therapy with the borderline adult: some principles concerning technique. In *New Perspectives on Psychotherapy of the Borderline Adult,* ed. J. F. Masterson, pp. 43–65. New York: Brunner/Mazel. Reprinted as Chapter 1 in this volume.

——— (1979). *Countertransference and Related Subjects—Selected Papers.* New York: International Universities Press.

——— (1979a). Jealousy involving an internal object. In *Advances in Psychotherapy of the Borderline Patient,* ed. J. LeBoit and A. Capponi, pp. 347–403. New York and London: Jason Aronson. See p. 362. Reprinted as Chapter 5 in this volume.

Chapter 10

Some Aspects of Separation and Loss in Psychoanalytic Therapy with Borderline Patients

For various reasons, some of which I shall touch upon, the borderline individual has inordinate difficulty in integrating the experiences of separation and loss which are inherent in human living generally, and in the course of psychoanalytic therapy more specifically. But more than that, his borderline personality-organization

This chapter was presented as a paper at a conference on The Borderline Syndrome: Differential Diagnosis and Psychodynamic Treatment, at UCLA Extension Department of Human Development, Los Angeles, CA, March 14, 1981. It was published on pp. 131–160 in *Technical Factors in the Treatment of the Severely Disturbed Patient*, edited by P. L. Giovacchini and L. B. Boyer; New York and London: Jason Aronson, 1982.

287

itself renders ever-present, for him, the danger of separation and loss. If we accept (as do I) the finding of Mahler
(1968) that the borderline patient's personality-structure is
developmentally traceable to difficulties in the phase of separation and individuation, we see that his tenuously established individual ego faces continually the threat, on the one
hand, lest his fear of his separateness impel him into regression into symbiosis with the other person (equivalent, for
him, to a symbiotic mother), with consequent total loss of
individuality; and the threat, on the other hand, that his fear
of such symbiotic fusion will impel him into autism (that is,
psychosis) of such degree that he will suffer a loss of any
human relatedness.

The Analyst's Projecting Unconscious
Loss-Reactions into the Patient

In beginning, now, a much less than comprehensive discussion of this large subject, I shall mention some aspects of the
reactions, on the parts of both the analyst and the patient, to
their separation from one another between sessions.

The analyst typically ends each session in a manner
that, while intended to be minimally upsetting to the patient, minimizes any feeling of loss which the analyst himself tends to have, at this imminent separation from the
patient. Even more, when the analyst announces that he will
be away for a day or a week, say, he tends to do this in a
calm, matter-of-fact manner—consciously designed, again,
to minimize separation-anxiety on the patient's part—
which, again, is easy for the patient to perceive as indicating
that the analyst himself feels no loss whatever at the prospect of the forthcoming separation from him. One could
surmise, here, that the patient perceives little, if any, evi-

dence that the analyst will miss him at all, or have any thought of him at all, during the forthcoming separation.

Commonly, not only in my own work but in that of supervisees (and other colleagues) about which I hear, this kind of analytic stance tends to represent an appreciable repression of feelings of separation-anxiety and loss on the analyst's part, as regards such separations. Thus the patient who manifests persistent difficulty in gaining access to such feelings on his own part, during the analyst's vacations (for example), may well be identifying with the analyst's own manner of defending against such feelings within himself. Obviously, the analyst tends to project such feelings into the patient, and look unconsciously to the latter to recognize and express such feelings for both participants.

A woman who had been in analysis with me for several years started speaking, at the beginning of a Monday session, of "My attachment to you—it's horrendous—You know why Mondays are so blah?—for me?" I inquired, "Why?," and she replied, "At the beginning of the weekend, you go away and leave, and then it's as though when you come back on Monday I've forgotten you—I've dismissed you. I *have* to, because it's too painful [to do otherwise]. . . ."

In hearing this, I found interesting what I sensed to be an aspect of her identifying with me, in the transference, for when she said, ". . . I've forgotten you—I've dismissed you," it sounded entirely that she was doing to me what she felt I had done to her. This in itself was nothing new or surprising. But then when she went on, "I have to, because it's too painful [to do otherwise]," it sounded to me that she unconsciously fantasied that I had to dismiss and forget her, for otherwise it would be too painful for me. Immediately, while attributing to her an unconscious fantasy of this sort, I sensed there to be an element of reality in her unconscious perception of my defensive dismissing of my own dependency upon her.

The Role, in the Patient's Acting-Out, of His Unconscious Identifications with Largely Unconscious Attributes of the Analyst

In the instance of patients who tend to become involved, persistently, in self-destructive acting-out between sessions (and especially during the analyst's prolonged absences), I have found, time and again, that such behavior has, as one of its major determinants, the patient's introjection of some internal psychological contents of my own (contents which are, as always, partly indeed here in me, but partly attributed to me, unconsciously, by the patient in terms of whom, or what, I represent to him in the transference).

That is, much "self"-destructive behavior, on the patient's part, during my absences, proves on further analysis to have been behavior directed, unconsciously, against the patient's introjected image of me. Typically, such behavior tends to seem to me maddeningly ego-syntonic for the patient, who comes into the session and reports it in a spirit of vindictive relish, as though he has injured the analyst rather than, or in any case more than, himself.

In Chapter 9, I discussed some of the difficulties involved in the borderline patient's development of an internalized image of the therapist. It may be, indeed, that we are working with a patient who has not yet developed an enduring internalized image of the analyst. But, much more often, the patient has introjected various aspects of our largely-unconscious personality-attributes, and is manifesting, between sessions, various identifications with us, identifications which, from our vantage-point, are so disguised as to be unrecognizable as such for prolonged periods of time, all the more so insofar as these consist in identifications with attributes of ourself not merely distortedly perceived by the patient who is in the grip of powerful transference-reactions to us, but also highly unpalatable to our conscious sense of our own identity. The more ill the patient is, the more does he tend to identify, earliest, with the analyst's own sickest, least fully conscious introjects.

Brief Critique of the "Bad Mother" Concept; The Patient's Illness is Continually Being Interpersonally-Maintained in Current Living

Much has been written, by many writers—including myself, years ago (Searles 1965)—concerning the Bad Mothers of schizophrenic or borderline patients. I have gradually learned that such villainizing of these mothers underestimates (1) the importance of the patient's identifications with the Bad-Mother components of his mother; (2) his own holding himself primarily responsible for her emerging as a Bad Mother, with his guilt and grief (as well as rage) about this being unconsciously defended against, in him, by his identification with those Bad-Mother components in her which he has been unable to cure; and, (3) the simplistic villainizing of these mothers glosses over the analyst's own ever-alive Bad-Mother components. As I have come to see these things more clearly, there has come about a profound shift in my once-held, relatively static view of the schizophrenic, or borderline, patient as tending to be more or less crippled by traumatic events which occurred many years ago, in his infancy or early childhood. There is some truth in that, I still believe. But as I have found over and over, with borderline patients for example, how able the patient is to reproduce—largely unconsciously, of course—his early mother-child relatedness with me in the transference, as well as with persons round about in his adult living, and evoke the most lively Bad-Mother responses from me, or small-child feeling-reactions in me to the Bad-Mother components in him, I get a much livelier sense than I once had as to the extent to which this adult patient's illness is continually being fed and maintained through the unconscious complicity of the persons, including the analyst, round about him in his current living.

To put it simply, the crazy (or borderline-crazy) patient succeeds in evoking really crazy (but largely unconscious) responses from other persons, day in and day out, year after year. He forms increments of *folies à deux* with many people in daily life, such that his psychosis, or borderline psychosis, receives, day after day, a great deal of verification from his external reality. A paper of mine (Searles 1972) in 1972, for example, detailed something of the extent to which a chronically schizophrenic woman's delusional experience, during the sessions, was founded upon real components in my own personality-functioning during our sessions—components which I tended to maintain out of my awareness as being alien to my own sense of identity.

In line with some of these concepts, I have found very often, if not regularly, that the borderline patient has deep-seated feelings of guilt and grief at having failed to enable his mother to be alive and responsive to him. His own long-time, large-scale inability to feel fully alive, and to feel imbued with a full gamut of human emotions, consists in large part in identification with such an aspect—a schizoid or chronically depressed aspect—of his mother, a crippledness on her part from which he had been able to rescue her only briefly and infrequently.

The Patient's Inability to Experience a Full Range of Human Emotions; His Defenses Against Recognition of the Full Extent of This Inability

The borderline individual's inability, at the beginning of treatment, to experience a full range of human emotions has been reported by many therapists. These patients often show a proclivity for complexity in their lives, as an unconscious defense against the realization of the emotional shallowness of their interpersonal relationships. They are reminiscent to me, here and in various other respects, of chronically schizophrenic patients. Shortly after going to work at Chestnut Lodge, in 1949, I saw how commonplace it is for schizophrenic patients to present a loftily supercilious demeanor, to the effect that oneself and the other common swine, roundabout, could not possibly grasp the complexity of the world in which the patient is living. This kind of demeanor, I early felt, is one of the major factors keeping alive the well-known prejudice, in society as a whole, against schizophrenic patients.

My first Chestnut Lodge psychotherapy-patient, a chronically paranoid-schizophrenic young man who had made an extremely serious suicide-attempt during one of his two previous admissions there, perceived me as being (like other persons round about) a "cipher." It became evident, in the course of our work, that he was projecting into me (and others, generally) his own subjective emptiness, deadness, impoverishment as regards emotions. But what makes this so difficult to deal with is—as I have seen innumerable times since then—the fact that such a patient is not *only* projecting; he attunes himself to those areas in oneself which really do tend to qualify one for the designation of cipher. Society as a whole tends to hate schizophrenic patients because the latter are attuned, with such hawklike accuracy, to the felt-deficiencies in society.

To return to borderline patients, not only an investment in complexity, but also (and by the same token) an investment in the gratifications of subjective omniscience are commonplace features. Time and again, there is an implied, "I told you so; I foresaw this and tried to prepare you for it" message from the patient, as his only identifiable emotional response to an event which, for a person with the usual range of human emotions, would be the focus for diverse and intense feelings.

Typically these patients are largely enigmatic—sometimes maddeningly so, over the years—as regards any feelings identifiable to the listener (the analyst), even when (or, probably more accurately, especially when) speaking of some event or situation which the listener feels *must* be the focus of all sorts of emotional reactions on the patient's part. One such woman began a session by saying, in a submergedly somewhat awed, frightened, but mainly—as usual—affectively enigmatic voice, "Feel like I'm in a whirl of activity, like being on a merry-go-round—going out every evening, . . . the Clinic [where she is working as a nurse] is frantically busy. . . ." She spoke, in the next few minutes, of many, many activities, largely professional but also social ones, and, in the notes I was making behind the couch, I summarized my best impression that "It is predominantly impossible to know what patient's feeling tone is, about all this."

Some borderline patients are able to experience a certain few emotional bands, as it were, on the spectrum of human emotionality. One woman, for example, said,

"I don't feel sadness; sadness isn't really something I feel. . . . I understand devastation and I understand rage and I understand terror; but I don't know the milder forms [she had referred to sadness as being a mild form of devastation]. . . . When I feel irritated or annoyed, I don't really feel those feelings; what I feel is rage. . . . I can either feel complete devastation or nothing. I don't have those in-between states; they just never had a chance to develop. The others were too strong. So it's either those strong states or nothing, and most of the time it's been nothing. . . ."

In a session six months later this same woman was saying, "At work, it seems to me that I just *live* in *terror* of being asked to do something that's not in my power to do. . . ." The words she emphasized were said in a tone which conveyed that she is *really living* only when she is in *terror*. Upon hearing her say this, I was reminded of various teaching-interviews I had done, at various hospitals, with chronically schizophrenic patients to whom terror or panic, even, felt preferable to their customary boredom, and of one such patient to whom I suggested that he felt alive only when he felt he might imminently be murdered, and he agreed convincingly. A borderline woman remembered, relatively early in her analysis, having been scared, innumerable times throughout her childhood, by her older sister; she would report these memories in her usual affectively-enigmatic tone. Gradually, it became clear that any hatred she tended to feel toward her sister, about this, was at least balanced, if not somewhat overbalanced, by appreciation for the relief the sister had thus afforded her, relief from the chronic boredom which more basically permeated the patient's upbringing.

One borderline woman's emotionality was limited, during a phase of her analysis, to being, as she put it, "shocked and stunned." I found evidence that this reaction involved an identification with the mother's only accessible (to the child) emotionality, and it helped me to understand the origin of a certain daredevil quality on the patient's part: she had learned, in childhood, that through various daredevil-activities she could evoke an emotional response from her mother—a "shocked and stunned" kind of response. I have seen essentially this same phenomenon in a chronically schizophrenic woman with whom I have worked for many years. This latter woman's mother's only consistently evocable emotional response, from the child's vantage point, was a shocked, deeply insulted kind of reaction; otherwise, the mother dwelt inaccessibly in her own world of fantasies. It is surely no coincidence that the patient herself developed really remarkable capacities for being both shocking and insulting in her subsequent interpersonal relationships.

The Patient's Inability to Accomplish Grief-Work

The borderline individual's inability (without therapy) to accomplish grief-work is both one of the major diagnostic criteria for the borderline state, and is, necessarily, one of the major tasks of the therapy. The Mitscherlichs' (1975) volume, *The Inability to Mourn*, and Volkan's (1976) *Primitive Internalized Object Relations* are relevant to this general topic, as is Volkan's (1981) *Linking Objects and Linking Phenomena*, which I read in manuscript form, in connection with his having invited me to supply a foreword to it. But, so far as I know, without my having done any thorough review of the existing literature, most of what follows is original with me.

The inability to grieve is, for the borderline individual, one of the most difficult areas to mask, in his larger, over-all difficulty in participating fully in the emotionality which daily human living calls for. The death of a parent, for example, tends, as do few other daily-life events, to highlight, for all to see, how largely unable he is to have the feelings which other people have, and which they expect him, now, to manifest. It usually requires much work, on the part of both participants in the therapy, for the patient to become able to reveal openly his difficulties in the realm of genuine emotionality—to be able to say, as one man said after some years of analysis, "I don't feel sorrow. I've never felt sorrow."

The Patient's Amnesia

In my experience, one of the reliable criteria for the patient's being in a borderline condition is his manifesting, usually in the initial, history-giving interview, a striking loss of memory—amnesia—for the events of his childhood. Typically, there will be stretches of years, somewhere between the ages of, say, three and eighteen, for which he will have few, or even no, memories. I do not mean that he will have few or no memories for that whole 15-year span of time I mention by way of example; I mean, rather, that somewhere within that time span there will be one or more stretches of years (say, two or three or four or five years) for which he will have essentially no memory. This stands in striking contrast to the predominantly neurotic individual's memory, at the outset of treatment, for his childhood.

In the instance of one's work with the borderline individual, it is typical, by the same token, that even after years of one's working with him, one still has only a relatively fragmentary and clouded picture of the chronological events of the patient's childhood and adolescence, and of the personalities of the other family-members. The more powerfully-maintained is the patient's amnesia, the more powerfully, of course, is he unconsciously reliving his childhood in the transference-relationship with the analyst. But the analyst often feels greatly hampered, nonetheless, in attempting to identify the nature of the transference, and to locate it in its proper era in the patient's developmental history, for the reason that he, the analyst, still has so little of consciously-recalled history from the patient, to serve as a kind of framework upon which the transference-derived information can be based. Here, instead, the transference-derived information must serve to a large extent as the framework, or foundation, itself.

At the most difficult times in my work with borderline patients, I find that part of what is most stressful, for me, is that I feel unable, for weeks or possibly even months at a time, to locate what is happening between the patient and myself in either *his* developmental history or my *own*. As a beginning psychiatrist and still, a few years later, as a beginning psychoanalyst, I assumed (as did, I believe, my peers in training) that if one's work with one's patient reminded one very much of something from one's own childhood, it shouldn't; this was to be regarded as one's needing more of personal analysis. But in my work with difficult patients, now many years later, I find it very helpful if the stressful and confusing interaction with this disturbing patient, here, is reminiscent to me, at least, of scenes and events of my *own* childhood, even if not reminiscent to me of the patient's childhood as I have heard about it from his consciously-recalled memories of it, or from what we both have learned together of his childhood, thus far, from transference-manifestations earlier in our work together. It seems to me that, on the other hand, when psychoanalysis or psychotherapy is going well, the analyst (or therapist) can readily perceive what is happening both as part of a pattern of the patient's life on the one hand, and as part of the pattern of his own life on the other hand.

In the above-mentioned stressful instances in which one cannot sense wherein this disturbing interaction is rooted either in the patient's past or even in one's own past, I think it erroneous to assume that if only one were to gain more of personal analysis of one's past, all would become well. I believe, rather that the analyst's experience, here, is (as it proves to be so reliably, time after time) in the nature of valuable, and highly specific, information about the patient's past. My belief is that what the analyst is experiencing, here, had a counterpart in the experience of one or both parents of the patient.

That is, it seems to me to have been typical, in these so-amnesic borderline patients' childhoods, that the parents, in their rearing of this child, were trying largely to forget their own pasts, rather than to use these, in any well-integrated, freely remembered and reminisced-about, fashion as a guide or context for their relating to him. Typically, such parents have so much of unintegrated hatred and un-worked-through grief, disappointment, hurt, and so on, from their own childhoods, that they cannot consciously put their past largely in the past, but instead to a large extent relive, unconsciously, their past with the patient installed, often at a very tender age indeed, as the parent's transference-mother or -father.

So, to repeat now, I suggest that the analyst, at a time when he cannot see meaningful historical antecedents, either in his own past or in the patient's past, to the stressful interaction in which he and the patient are caught up, is provided, thus, with a glimpse into the inner life of the patient's mother or father, whose own childhood was rendered largely unavailable to her or him, in this rearing of their child, by the unconscious defenses of dissociation and splitting.

The patient's amnesia serves as an unconscious defense against, of course, all sorts of negatively-toned emotions—guilt, fear, sadness, grief, and so on. It serves as a defense against murderous feelings; these patients can be seen to have murdered, unconsciously, large areas of their own pasts, for the reason (among others) that the recall of what actually transpired during those areas brings with it the experiencing of murderousness (toward parents, siblings, and so on) of formidable intensity. In this sense, the patient's previously-maintained amnesia has served to protect the parent's (for example) life.

Similarly, the amnesia may be found to have served both as a defense against, and a symbolic form of, suicide. In the instance of one man, I had come to realize, after some years of working with him, that two of the areas of his remembered past belonged in chronological sequence, whereas these had been discrete and unrelated in his own memory of them. I pointed out to him this seemingly simple fact, and then for several days, afterward, I had reason to fear that he would suicide; his having kept these, unconsciously, as chronologically non-sequential had protected him, heretofore, from intense guilt, concerning the events of these areas of his past, of near-suicidal proportions. My technical error, here, probably had mainly to do with the fact that my interpretation was not primarily, if at all, a transference-interpretation, such that he had reason to feel abandoned, by me, to deal with areas of his past with which he had been unable, as a child, to cope, and with which he still could not cope. That experience served as still another reminder of how essential it is to make one's interpretations in the form of *transference*-interpretations, and, by the same token, of how essential it is, as regards the patient's amnesia for his own life-history, that this amnesia be explored in terms of his difficulties in remembering the developing history of the therapy itself.

In this connection, it is typical, in the transference-countertransference situation involved in one's work with such a patient, for either the patient or, oftentimes, oneself, to have striking difficulty in remembering, reasonably fully and in sequence, the events which have occurred over the months or years of the therapy thus far. In my work with any patient who tends not at all readily to see connections between the present session and earlier ones, I find it of interest to notice at what point, in this present session, something he says reminds me of the preceding session or, perhaps, of some much earlier part of our work. More often than not, within a few moments I find occasion to share this with the patient, and I find patients receptive enough, to this kind of therapeutic intervention, to encourage my doing so more and more freely. The patient, in this instance, tends to feel more appreciated (by this evidence that the therapist remembers) than narcissistically wounded and relegated to his own pre-treatment past, as in the example of the non-transference intervention cited earlier.

Another form of the patient's amnesia is this: he recalls most of the family-members relatively well, and is able thus to give the analyst a relatively good, three-dimensional image of what each of those family-members was like; but there is one family-member whom he scarcely ever mentions. I have learned that this is a reliable indication that the family-member in question was quite the opposite of having been relatively insignificant in the patient's upbringing. The fact of the matter, as I have found time and time again—always, nonetheless, to my considerable surprise at first—is that the patient is so fused with that family-member that the latter exists very little as any separate object in the patient's remembered past.

As one example of this, a woman referred not infrequently, for years in her therapy, to "my sister," whereas she had told me at the outset of the treatment that she had two sisters, both older than herself. "My sister" always referred to the eldest sister, an idealized mother-figure to the patient. Only after years of treatment did it start to become clear that the patient was much fused with the other sister. It became clear in retrospect, that during the frequent largely-silent sessions we had had, I had represented this intensely ambivalently-regarded sister in the transference. Similarly, this helped to explain why the patient, in speaking of her marriage, would usually say "I," rather than "we." In marrying her husband, she had married, unconsciously, her next older sister as well. Many of the difficulties which "I" had in the context of the marriage actually belonged to this transference-sister husband of hers. Thus, when she would speak of money-worries which, clearly, her husband as well as she was facing in their marriage, she would say only what "I" felt about them, and would often leave me wondering what her husband's feelings were about these matters. But it developed that she was as little individuated from him as she was from the next older sister, and from me in the treatment-situation.

Defensive Functions of the Patient's Vengefulness

Vengefulness is an important aspect of the borderline individual's personality-functioning, although hardly to be regarded as a specific criterion of the borderline state. His areas of amnesia serve, as I have already indicated, as an unconscious defense against murderous vindictiveness, among other emotions. He who has not yet become mature enough to forgive must forget, as a poor substitute for forgiving. In my paper in 1956 entitled, "The Psychodynamics of Vengefulness," I emphasized the defensive functions of vengefulness, particularly with regard to repressed grief and separation-anxiety. Many borderline patients show a tenacious, rageful determination to "go back and show 'em!"—to go back, that is, to some particular earlier place and time and prove to "them" (parental family-members, schoolmates, or whomever) that they had failed to appreciate, at all fully, the patient's good qualities—or, more adequately put—to make them see that the patient was not the person they thought he was, but rather the so-different person he is convinced that he is, and was, in essence, then.

The analyst can readily find evidence—though it may take long to interpret effectively to the patient—that the patient, in this vengeful determination, is defending himself against feelings of grief and separation-anxiety *vis-à-vis* those earlier persons and settings. But it is useful, in addition, for the analyst to see that the patient's vindictiveness represents an attempt to overcome an underlying sense of discontinuity in his personal identity. That is, the patient himself cannot at all fully accept his more recently-acquired personality-aspects and, in his burning determination to go back to that earlier time-and-place to which he is so emotionally-fixated, he is endeavoring to establish a stronger sense of continuity of identity. He would try coercively to make "them" accept those attributes of himself which, to a significant degree, he himself has not been able to integrate well into his over-all personality functioning. In order for him to become better integrated, and therefore no longer vengeance-oriented, he will have to accomplish more of working through of grief (and so forth) regarding those persons and places in his childhood and youth.

One can see here, too, relatively readily, the role of his projection upon "them" of his own tendency to depreciate the positive qualities of other persons. It is unlikely that they were actually as depreciatory of him, at that earlier time, as he, now, in his need to keep his grief (and other positively-based feelings) so largely dissociated, is depreciatory of them.

A man said, "I have no more resemblance to myself twenty years ago today than I have to you—just a completely different person—no sense of continuity—my present life began four years ago when I married Edith. A few little things remain [from his earlier life]; I rediscover a little thread—recently [for example] I found myself rocking, and realized that I had done that for years as a child."

A paper in 1980 by Horowitz, Wilner, Marmar, and Krupnick entitled, "Pathological Grief and the Activation of Latent Self-Images," is relevant here. These authors describe states of pathological grief in terms of the reemergence of self-images and role relationship models that had been held in check by the existence of the deceased person.

Now that the relationship with that person has been lost, the patient becomes immersed in a review of his repertoire of self-images and role relationship models. The authors describe that the review—in contrast with that found among relatively normal persons in states of bereavement—becomes unusually intense and interminable, or excessive controls prevent review of activated role relationship models so that mourning is never completed.

As the patient's amnesia begins to lift, it is striking that, on occasion, it will lift so fleetingly that he will remember, for a few seconds, a flood of previously-forgotten memories, only to find they are covered, once again, by the amnesia at the end of those few seconds, and he feels entirely helpless to recapture them and report them to the analyst. This kind of thing lends itself, of course, to his sadistic tantalizing of, and sexual teasing of, the analyst (an aspect of their interaction which I shall describe further in a few minutes), but at a level which may be genuinely unconscious, in the patient, for many months or even years.

The Patient's Difficulties in Realizing That a Dead Parent Is Not Merely "Dead" (Psychologically Unrelated) Once Again

It is impossible for a patient to grieve the loss, through death, of a parent who had been, throughout the patient's experience with him or her, in such a state that the patient never really did "have" the parent in any case—never was, more than fleetingly, in any full relatedness with him or her. It is relatively simple in those instances in which the parent was physically away nearly all the time; I am referring to those far more frequent, and much more difficult, instances in which the parent had been physically present relatively much, but psychologically largely absent, nonetheless.

These parents, collectively, were psychologically absent for a great variety of reasons. Some few of them were recurrently frankly psychotic. Many were chronically depressed. Many had, themselves, personalities of an "as-if" (H. Deutsch 1942), or other variety of borderline, nature. In ordinary rather than psychiatric parlance, one cannot go through an average-normal, healthy process of grieving the death of a parent who had been nearly always, throughout one's childhood and adolescence, emotionally remote, or preoccupied with one had no way of knowing what, essentially dead to the living events in which the others in the family were participating.

The parent whose own ego-functioning was poorly integrated (whether of a borderline or schizoid nature, for example) had so much of unintegrated-loss feelings from his or her own parental-family past, that he could only rarely emerge into relatively full relatedness in the marital family. This is entirely analogous with one's finding that the patient, himself, can only rarely enable one, for many months of the work, to feel, strongly and immediately, what the patient's childhood family-situation was like.

The analyst sees, in the patient's identifications with the parent in question, the kind of non-relatedness which had been relatively predominant in the parent himself or herself. I could see, for example, in one woman's reaction at the beginning of a session, a glimpse of how removed her mother had usually been. She reacted in an unusually startled way when I opened the door to the waiting room to indicate for her to come in; she seemed startled, fearfully, out of deep and anxious preoccupation. In the opening moments of the session itself, after she had assumed the couch, she was saying, ". . . Feel like my mind is somewhere else this evening—not sure where. . . ." She spoke in a tone here, as usual, that was enigmatic as regards any affective quality. I had much evidence, by now after years of her analysis, to know that her now-dead mother had been predominantly like this in life.

In a case discussed in the preceding chapter, I mentioned that

> . . . Another borderline woman, whom I interviewed before a group of psychiatric residents, replied, when I asked her something about her mother, that "The first thing about my mother is that she's dead," and, although this was literally now the case, several of the residents present had the sense, as did I, that the patient had perceived the mother so even while the latter had been alive. When I asked a borderline man, during one of his analytic sessions, whether he had ever confided in his much-elder sister anything of the area of concern which he was presently exploring, he reacted with a degree and kind of shock which helped me to realize that, for him during his childhood, his sister had been psychologically dead, and that many of our more moribund sessions had to do with his transference to me as being that "dead" sister.

Another man, whose father had died when the patient had been 15, said, in describing a recent telephone conversation in which he had spoken in a calming way to his anxious older brother, "I think that's what my *father* woulda done had he *lived*." This man continued, for years in his analysis, to idealize his dead father. But I knew, on the basis of abundant material, both from the patient's own conscious memories and from the unfolding of the transference, that the father had been highly sequestered from the emotional life of his marital family, and, apparently, much more immersed in the long-gone life of his own childhood family. When the patient made the brief statement I have quoted, although he said it without any discernible, conscious anger or contempt toward his father, he nonetheless said it in such a tone as to convey the unconscious meaning, "I think that's what my *father* woulda done had he ever *lived*." This patient was vulnerable to feelings of fearful unsureness, for years before and after the beginning of his analysis, as to whether he himself existed, and this symptom proved to be based largely upon his being assailed, unconsciously, by his identifications with a father who, in his own experience with him, never really and fully existed, in the interpersonal-relatedness meaning of that term.

The Patient Who Chronically Teases the Analyst

In this connection, the chronically-teasing variety of patient merits at least brief mention. An appreciable percentage of borderline patients behave, for year after year in their analyses, in a predominantly teasing fashion, as to whether they are ever going to become fully committed to the analysis, and thus enable the analyst to feel able fully to function as analyst to them, or not. I have had so many sessions, by now, with such patients as to have developed the conviction that one of the varieties of hell, for me, will be a realm wherein, all day long, day after endless day, I will be attempting to analyze patients who report dreams, and report abundant associations to those dreams, and all that kind of thing that "good" patients do in analysis—but do so in such a teasing fashion that I *almost*—but never quite—have acquired the necessary material for making an interpretation of the transference.

I have developed increasing compassion for these torturers insofar as I have discovered, with one or another of them, evidence that this sadistically-teasing behavior of his or hers is based largely upon identification with a (now dead, in most instances, but significantly ungrieved) mother or father who, throughout the patient's upbringing, had genuinely functioned as a parent in no more than a teasing degree. The father, for instance, had teasingly held out the hope, year after year, that one day he would *really become* a father to the patient. By the same token, in the transference-relatedness, the patient (who from the analyst's view is himself so teasing) finds a basis (and not only through projection of his own difficulties in this regard) for feeling tantalized analogously, year after year, with the hope that the analyst will one day, at long last, come forth and commit himself fully to *being* the analyst to him.

The Patient as the Parent's Transference-Mother or -Father

Typically, the borderline patient was unconsciously perceived, by the parent, as being the personification of the parent's own unintegrated past. Such a parent, who manifested this "transgenerational" transference to the child, is one who had been unable to work through the loss of (among other persons and places, and so on) the parent's own parent. Thus, a mother who has not been able to work through the loss of her own mother will tend to form a transference to her child as being that mother (the child's actual maternal grandmother). The more ill we find the adult borderline patient to be, the more justified we are in assuming, until proven otherwise, that this kind of thing happened strikingly early in his childhood. What I am describing here is even more strikingly true, and began at an even more shockingly early age, in the childhood of the person who later becomes not borderline but chronically psychotic.

Probably there is no more basic determinant of the borderline patient's vengeful desire to "go back and show 'em!" than his need to somehow make his parent realize and accept that he—the patient—has long been functioning as psychological parent, rather than child, to the biological parent—and to achieve this realization at an internal level within himself, in terms of introjects and identifications involved in his sense of personal identity.

The Patient Unconsciously Perceives the Analyst as Living Vicariously Through Him; Acting-Out

Such a parent as he or she whom I am describing as typical of those of borderline patients—the parent, that is, who has never achieved any full individuation from (= loss of) his (or her) own parent, but who forms a symbiotic transference with the child as a means of perpetuating the parent's child-hood-symbiosis with the parent's own mother or father—typically does much of vicarious living through the child (from whom the parent is so incompletely differentiated) as the child is growing up. Thus, the child is given to feel that it is not really his own life which he is living, but rather that of the parent.

When such a child becomes then, in due course, an adult borderline patient in psychotherapy, he typically coerces the analyst, naturally enough, into feeling that he, the analyst, bears the primary, basic, and essentially total responsibility for the way the patient's life now goes. The patient lays his career-failures, for example, at the door of the analyst in such a manner that it is difficult, indeed, for the analyst to extricate himself from the guilty conviction that the patient's failure to thrive is basically due to the analyst's own presumed malevolent orientation toward him. One cannot help, after all, genuinely hating such patients. By the same token, much of such a patient's "self"-injurious acting-out, of various forms, is based upon the patient's having introjected the hated parent-figure analyst whom the patient assumes (in light of the unconscious transference) to be unwilling and unable to let him, the patient, have his own individual life. Thus, it is this hated, internalized parent-figure analyst whom the patient is injuring in his "self"-injurious acting-out, whether in suicide-attempts or whatever.

Splitting

Splitting is, as has been described by Kernberg (1975), Giovacchini (1975), Masterson (1976) and other writers, one of the major defense mechanisms characteristic of borderline patients. I shall limit myself, here, to mentioning two points which, so far as I am aware, these previous writers have not dwelt upon.

To the extent that the patient is still invested in an infantile-omnipotent orientation, he tends to experience grief not as being a natural part of human living and dying, but rather as something which perceivedly omnipotent beings are attempting to inflict upon him. As one works year after year with a number of such patients, one learns to what a striking degree this was indeed true in their childhoods. One sees this through one's being on the receiving end of those split affects and transference-images which derive from the patient's childhood experience with a parent whose ego-functioning involved much of splitting.

Specifically, one finds that the patient will sadistically hold over one's head the threat, year after year, of his separating himself permanently from one—the threat of his leaving, one of these days, and never returning. His splitting is playing a major role in this for the reason that he is conscious of the liberating, and other positive, aspects of the prospective separation, but projects into the analyst his (the patient's) own feelings of reluctance, loss, and grief, which such a separation holds for him. For the child who grows up

at the hands of a parent who thus splits, any healthy grieving would be a genuinely inappropriate response to separations from, or threatened separations from, such a parent,
for, as one sees in one's work with the patient himself, any
revelation of anguish on one's own part feels to be serving no
purpose beyond giving gratification to the patient's sadism—rendering his sadism effective.

A woman was in analysis for a number of years, dwelling almost exclusively upon daily-life events, before she
started giving me glimpses of her extraordinarily shock-
ingly-deprived (in many regards) childhood, a childhood
which heretofore had been shrouded largely in amnesia.
These memories were so shocking to me, to hear, that I felt
at first that it had been primarily my own inner limitations
which had prevented her from conveying to me, much earlier, readily-available memories of her early years. But I
realized, as we went on, that these memories were available
to her, herself, only as frequently as I, and the relationship
between her and me, were strong enough to stand the emergence of these disturbing memories from their long dissociation. After her having remembered, during a session, and
reported to me some further details from her impoverished
daily life as a child, she said, "You didn't know it was so
terribly poor, did you? The more I think about it, I guess it
was. . . ." Another way of thinking of this is that her long-
maintained denial, of the extraordinarily deprived, and in
other regards traumatic, aspects of her daily life as a child,
was now being eroded through by our analytic work.

Still, for many months further in our work, the memories of her childhood emerged only infrequently, in shak-
ingly vivid fragments a few months apart. My belief is that
she, during her childhood, could not stand seeing the reality
of her life any more continuingly and fully than I was proving able, now many years later in my analyzing of her, to
stand seeing it.

To Grieve Effectively the Loss of a Relationship, One Must Have Been Involved Genuinely in the Relationship

The loss of such a childhood situation cannot be grieved if the situation was so bad, for the patient and probably for all the other family-"participants," that they collectively were not really fully in it. Instead, they—and certainly this must have been true for the patient herself as a child—were shrouded in a cocoon of denial such as prevailed in the patient during the early years of our work together.

The principle which I have stated here, namely, that in order to become able to grieve the loss of a situation, one must first have been really in that situation, is one which I had thought of several years ago, as regards the optimal timing of any patient's discharge from a psychiatric sanitarium. That is, it became apparent to me that, in order for a patient to become able to leave the sanitarium constructively, he or she must first have come to be in the sanitarium, psychologically as well as physically. The patient who keeps himself convinced, by various unconscious denial-mechanisms, that he has never really accepted his being here in the sanitarium will be minimally prepared to integrate the inevitable unconscious loss-feelings that his moving out of it will bring. His inability, then, after discharge, to mourn the loss of the sanitarium will tend powerfully to lead him to act out in ways which are designed, unconsciously, to restore him to the sanitarium which he has not failed, throughout, to hate, despise, and refuse to accept.

As regards the sporadic, fragmentary, and subjectively unpredictable nature of the amnesia-ridden patient's memories of disturbing events and situations in his earlier years, there is a counterpart in the analyst's own tendency—largely unconscious, of course—to maintain amnesia for particularly shocking revelations from the patient earlier in their work. For example, in one instance of father–daughter incest, and in another of a mother's having killed her infant daughter, the therapist whom I supervised in each of these instances was struck by his own managing to forget, for relatively long periods in the work with the patient, what the patient had suddenly remembered, and confided to him, earlier, of that shocking event. The therapist would be shocked anew, now, to hear of it as if for the first time and to hear, further, some additional details of it which had managed to escape from the patient's own unconscious denial that it had happened.

Incidentally, always to be kept in mind, in such instances, is the possible additional factor that both participants in the therapeutic interaction are displacing into the past a sense of shock which is stemming, at an unconscious level, predominantly from something they are doing to one another in the present session.

By way of discussing another manifestation of borderline patients' splitting, I want to mention that frequently in my work with a number of such persons, when the patient says, at the beginning of our first session following an interruption in our scheduled meetings, "I missed you," I get a fantasy of a disappointed sniper. The gentle reader might, of course, assume that this is merely further evidence of a paranoid stance on my part, in my relationships with my fellow human beings. Surely such a patient, who is struggling to prove to himself that he is a predominantly loving person, and struggling to maintain his more hostile attitudes in a state of dissociation, would have the analyst think himself basically paranoid for having such a fantasy.

But I have had a sufficient wealth of experience with feelings of indubitably genuine missing and being missed, in both professional and personal relationships, so that I can regard as reliable analytic data my fantasy of the patient as being a disappointed sniper. Sooner or later, I report this fantasy to the patient, and I find that my doing so, although inevitably somewhat jolting and wounding to him at first, enhances our collaborative work upon the matter over the course of time. The analyst cannot help the borderline individual to achieve genuine rather than "as-if" emotional relatedness unless he, the analyst, can deal with spurious emotionality as being such. One such woman, who for years in our work had been hampered, in her conscious efforts toward loving relatedness with people, by this split-off, disappointed-sniper area of her ego, came to say, "I was thinking yesterday, 'I miss you like crazy.' But then I also thought, 'I miss you like poison.'"

Grieving Regarded Unconsciously as Being Innately Murderous

I believe, but cannot prove, that there is an important factor, in the patient's dissociated disappointed-sniper self-image which I have postulated here, which goes beyond the fact that his loving impulses are still opposed by unintegrated murderous hostility toward the analyst. This factor, I believe, consists in his unconscious belief that grieving itself is innately murderous to the one whose absence one is grieving. That is, I surmise that the patient is dominated, at an unconscious level, by a primitiveness of thought which holds that one's grief is at least as much the cause, as the result, of a beloved person's death. I have little doubt that cultural anthropology would provide many examples of this kind of thinking among primitive peoples, and I have seen clear-cut evidence of it in my work with a chronically schizophrenic woman whose long psychosis began shortly after her mother's death—a death which, as with death generally, the patient cannot accept as a reality. Significantly, this woman, who still feels a loving-god-like responsibility for all her good objects, past and present (including, of course, her mother), has never been able openly to weep, and has long been troubled by that inability. She is convinced that if one really loves one's mother, she (the mother) will never die.

Sadism as a Defense Against Feelings of Loss

For some years in my work with a borderline man, to a striking degree, and to a perceptible degree in my experience with a number of similar patients, I have felt that it was in the moment of my signaling, punctually, the ending of the session, that I was earning my entire fee for the session. One aspect of my feeling, in indicating the end of the session, is that I have felt so irrelevant and useless, throughout the session, that the patient must wonder how I can bear to end the session and leave it at that for today. Not uncommonly, the patient will give one some glimpse that this is indeed how he feels at this moment; it is even worse when he leaves one entirely at the mercy of one's own thwarted self-expectations.

I have found it helpful to see the important role which the patient's sadism is playing in the events which now require me to end the session in this context. With other patients, I am conscious of their leaving the session in a manner which bespeaks a sadistically abrupt, and unnecessarily total, withdrawal of feeling before leaving the room. In many other instances, I have noticed that the patient's free associations, in the closing couple of minutes of the session, will contain a sadistic-depreciatory thrust toward the analyst. On the other hand, this last-mentioned phenomenon can be seen as an unconscious, sadistic defense against any genuine loss-feelings, at the ending of the session, on the part of both patient and analyst. That is, the patient may not only be minimizing, thus, his own loss, but also protecting the analyst from feeling more of loss than of relief at their imminent end-of-session separation.

The Relinquishment of the Patient's Illness Involves a Mutual Loss-Experience for Patient and Analyst

We analysts tend to feel guilty at finding any gratification in a patient's psychopathology, particularly if that psychopathology is very severe; we tend to fear that we are morbidly fascinated with illness, and that we secretly prefer it to health. But in my experience, both in my own work as an analyst and in my supervisory work, it is necessary that the analyst come sufficiently to share the patient's own gratifications in the latter's illness so that he, the analyst, can share the patient's heretofore unintegratable (largely because of his interpersonal isolation) feelings of loss in gradually giving up the illness. To put it in another way, the analyst must first help the patient to experience to the full the gratifications of the illness, through the analyst's own having dared, as it were, to permit himself to become aware of and accept such gratifications. Then the patient's grief-work, in the process of giving up the illness and all that it has represented to him for so many years, can be a genuinely shared experience, shared with the analyst. I do not see how any successful grief-work can have been otherwise than shared with someone, or ones. In the typical psychiatric and even psychoanalytic teaching of years ago—and it still is widespread, indeed—the therapist was trained to help the patient to "get over" the latter's illness without the patient's or anyone else's—least of all the therapist who was trying to help him to "conquer" the illness—becoming aware of the positive meanings which the illness held, unconsciously, for the patient, and the genuine grief which must be worked through, therefore, if the patient were to become really "free from" the illness.

One of the principles which I am suggesting again and again, in this chapter, is that for one to become able to grieve effectively the loss of something—whether a relationship with another person now dead, or one's life in a sanitarium or mental hospital, or a mental illness—one must have become able to know and accept, first, that one was really involved in it. Concerning the working through of the loss of one's illness, my paper, "Transitional Phenomena and Therapeutic Symbiosis" (Searles 1976) is relevant. There I suggest that in effective psychoanalytic therapy there is a phase in which "the patient's symptoms have become . . . transitional objects for both patient and analyst simultaneously." This gives some glimpse of how deeply mutual is, in my view, the shared grief-work in the patient's relinquishment of his illness.

A borderline man, able to finance no more than once-a-week therapy, described in one session, after about one-and-one-half years of our work, some aspects of his parental-family life which were so fascinating to me, so enthralling in their schizophrenogenic-family aspects, that later on in this session, or soon after it, I wondered how much in the way of anxiety-lest-the-patient-suicide, and anguish about the setting of limits, and so forth, does an analyst realistically have to accept in order to pay, as it were, for the tremendous gratification one derives from working with borderline patients. His so-enthralling description, to which I refer, occupied no longer than about two, and certainly not more than five, minutes in a session largely devoted, as were most of his sessions, to present-day, daily life events, far from his parental home of years ago.

Then in a session on the following day with a supervisee who was presenting to me, each week, his work with a severely borderline woman, I heard from him a detailed description of a beautifully ambivalently-symbiotic session which he had had with his patient in recent days, and the supervisee and I agreed as to the guilt-engendering (for the typical therapist) aspect of such tremendously symbiotic intimacy. Then I told him that I had wondered how much one must expect to have to pay (in terms of anxiety, and so forth) in working with borderline patients (and others comparably ill) for the gratifications which one derives from the work; I told him my impression of there being unconscious guilt for which one has to atone by so paying. He immediately felt the idea to be a valid one. He himself had had a very considerable number of years of experience in working, predominantly in a hospital setting, with severely borderline and schizophrenic patients.

My best impression is that such guilt as I have mentioned, here, functions mainly as an unconscious defense against the analyst's (or therapist's) feelings of loss as the patient improves and the more primitive, symbiotic mode of relatedness is largely relinquished. Such feelings of loss, for the analyst, are of a piece with the earliest feelings of loss in his own life. He must "pay," eventually, for the intense gratifications which he derived from (for example) his transference-and-countertransference-based participation in such a patient's parental-family symbiosis, by coming to experience, with the patient, the loss of that symbiosis—a loss inseparable from the loss of the symbiotic modes of relatedness in his own early parental family.

Premature Termination: The Stresses Which This Places upon the Analyst

One of the most stressful aspects of the analyst's work with borderline patients is that, when the treatment ends—as it very often does—prematurely, the analyst, in finding himself experiencing, then, little of the phenomena of healthy grieving—but experiencing, instead, only relief, admixed with unappeased hatred, and dread or paranoid fear of the patient's returning—tends to find this to be one more important piece of evidence, for the nth time now, that he, the analyst, is basically an unfeeling son-of-a-bitch. That is, for him as for such patients, the test of whether he is capable of grieving is felt to be the acid test of whether he can feel _anything_. An analyst can adapt to a rare treatment-outcome of this sort; but if a considerable percentage of his patients are borderline patients, he finds that such outcomes are not rare, and the accumulating effect of such outcomes tends progressively to undermine his confidence in his own ability to feel loving feelings, and to be capable of grieving. Keep in mind that I am referring, here, to those relatively frequent instances in which the borderline patient breaks off treatment in a setting of predominantly negative transference, convinced of the analyst's malevolence and showing, himself, no sign whatever of any felt loss of this analyst who in actuality has gone through a great deal with him in the preceding months or years.

What I am describing here links up with, although in reversed form, the experiences which patients have when their analyst, himself denying unconsciously any feelings of grief or loss, is about to go off on his vacation and is giving the patient to feel that this forthcoming separation is a kind of acid test of the patient's ability to grieve over separations, and more largely a test, therefore, of the patient's ability to feel any valued human emotion.

The Patient's and Analyst's Defenses Against Fusion with One Another

One of the fear-of-fusion characteristics of many—although by no means all—borderline patients consists in the patient's mocking, derisive, ironic, scornful typing, or classifying, of other persons in terms of one or another part-aspect of the other person, often a part-aspect of which the latter is largely unaware. The patient in whom this is a prominent defense possesses, typically, a devastating ability in thus writing off persons round about him, in daily life, with epigrammatic, satirical characterizations of those persons, leaving the latter fixed, as it were, like so many various flies in amber, or oddballs in a wax museum of freaks. Such patients have proved, one after another, so formidable to me, for many years, that I have been slow to realize that this is a major defense, for such a patient, against his own underlying tendency to confuse all persons, round about, with one another—to become, that is, helplessly unable to differentiate among them.

It is in such a patient's transference-perceptions and -responses of this nature that he is at his most formidable, of course, for the analyst. Again speaking of my own experience with such persons, I find time and again that he will react to some part-aspect of me—a facial expression, a gesture, an intonation, an article of clothing, or whatever—as comprising a complete personification of me, and of me at my most socially uncomfortable, schizoid, hopelessly inadequate self. Typically, such patients react to aspects of oneself which are at the fringe of one's conscious sense of identity— aspects of oneself which one struggles to disavow. If the patient were reacting to aspects of oneself which were even farther from one's awareness, presumably one could more readily dismiss the slings and arrows.

This attribute of the borderline patient is all the more difficult to meet, technically, for the reason that this defense is predominantly an unconscious one in the patient himself: at a conscious level he is largely unaware of emitting any rather steady barrage of roundabout needlings of the analyst, and is far from feeling that he has the analyst chronically at his mercy. In my work with one such female patient with whom I have met for more than two years, a typical session involves her making some dozens of skillfully derisive characterizations of my various oddities, but nearly always in terms of her speaking of these as being displaced onto various persons in her daily life, present and past, and my attempts to invite her collaboration, in exploring these tantalizingly disparate components of negative transference, and finding something more coherent and therefore meaningful in these, serve only to make her feel recurrently rejected and to feel, for the nth time, discouraged at my taking everything personally.

It goes much better, in my work with this woman, when I can hold my tongue, and perceive these many indirect barbs as being defensive, on her part, against her longings fully to identify with me, fuse with me (with me as the personification of her early mother, in this instance, for the most part). There have been times of especially helpful insight when I have realized that, in her being superficially most formidably mocking in her characterizations of her husband, for example (= myself in the transference), she is desperately grasping, at a deeper level of awareness, at these straws (these derisively-perceived part-aspects) to keep from drowning in undifferentiatedness from—fusion with—me. She manifests, it seems to me, essentially the same defense as that manifested by society collectively against their fear of oneness with the schizophrenic segment of the population: the part of the society labeled as sane tends powerfully to react to schizophrenic patients, collectively, as being essentially alien, nonhuman.

Such borderline patients project this motive upon the analyst, so that when the latter attempts to single out for interpretation some aspect—inevitably only a part-aspect—of the patient's functioning, the patient reacts as though the analyst's main attempt is to ridicule and distance him. My own impression, however, is that more often than not there is appreciable accuracy in such an impression on the patient's part—that is, that we analysts indeed do a great deal of premature interpreting as an unconscious defense against our underlying fear of our longings to fuse with the patient.

One of my patients, a woman who manifests many typically "as-if" features, has been in analysis for several years, and it has been only relatively recently that I have found it feasible to make interpretations with any reliable and consistent frequency. Heretofore, she subjected each of my interpretations—or other comments of any sort—to such savage and persistent mockery as essentially to destroy it. She reduced it to the same undifferentiatedness, essentially, as she basically did, throughout each of the sessions for years, with each of her "own" part-aspects, part-aspects which were based, in actuality, upon relatively superficial identifications with other persons, persons for the most part in her adult life.

On many occasions, in earlier years of our work, I felt an impulse to make transference interpretations, but nearly always restrained this urge, for either of two reasons: (1) the transference-data in her communications was so tantalizingly incoherent or superficial as not to warrant my interpreting it as yet; or (2) I shrank from committing myself to sharing the acid bath, as it were, in which she was keeping herself immersed—shrank from the degree of interpersonal exposure this would involve, for me in the act of interpreting, to her acidly destructive mockery with which I was by now only too familiar.

In retrospect, I was most useful in serving silently as a holding environment until her transference-hatred had changed (as it did, to the tune of remarkably infrequent comments of any sort from me) into a predominantly positive feeling tone between us during the sessions. My earlier-reported concepts concerning therapeutic symbiosis (Searles 1965, 1979) stood me in good stead during those years of my work with her. It is probable that she was correct, meanwhile, in sensing that my interpretations were deserving of her savagely destroying them, for I now believe that they were more unconsciously-defensive on my own part than acts of constructive interpersonal relatedness toward her; they were mainly obstacles to the development of the therapeutically necessary degree of non-verbal symbiosis between us.

Summary

The borderline patient's personality-organization renders ever-present, for him, the danger of separation and loss. He is continually faced with the threat of loss, either of his tenuously established individual identity, through fusion with the other person; or of his fragile interpersonal relatedness, through uncontrollable flight into autism of psychotic degree.

The analyst typically tends to repress or dissociate, and project into the patient, the primitive personality-components which the latter arouses in him. Much "self"-destructive behavior on the patient's part consists in his having introjected some of these most primitive, "sickest" components of the analyst's ego-functioning and, in the acting out, venting aggression upon this introject.

The patient has deep-seated feelings of primary (maternal) responsibility for curing the "Bad-Mother," primitively hateful components of the analyst. To a significant degree the latter, like everyone else, possesses such components; but in addition the patient here is projecting into the analyst the former's own powerful but unconscious identifications with comparable components in his mother and other mother-figures from his childhood.

The patient's inability (without therapy) to grieve effectively is but one facet of his inability to experience the full range of human emotions. This inability is defended against by fantasied omnipotence and omniscience.

Among the reliable criteria of the borderline state is the patient's striking loss of memory for large areas of his childhood. Some of the determinants of this amnesia are touched upon. It is best dealt with in the transference context, in terms of the developing history of the course of treatment itself. Typical countertransference difficulties in this connection are briefly discussed.

This amnesia is defensive against grief, separation-anxiety, and hostility of murderous or suicidal degree, and bespeaks a discontinuity in the patient's sense of identity—a poor integration of disparate fragments, from disparate developmental eras, in his sense of identity.

The interpersonal basis, present and past, in the etiology of the patient's difficulties with grieving are mentioned here. For example, a child cannot fully grieve the death of a parent who, even in life, was predominantly not psychologically *there*.

The parent's—the mother's, for example—having inadequately grieved the loss of her own parents, and her establishing a transference to her little child as being the reincarnation of one or another of those deceased grandparents, is another important etiologic factor in the borderline patient's typical personality-functioning, including his difficulties in grieving.

The role, in the patient's pathological grieving, of his defensive splitting is discussed, with particular emphasis upon the interconnections between grief and sadism.

The patient can relinquish his illness, eventually, only if the analyst has come to know and to cherish, to a significant degree, the gratifications of that illness, such that the loss-of-illness experience can become a mutual, shared loss-experience for the two participants. Along the way, the development of the necessary degree of therapeutic symbiosis is resisted by each of the two persons, in various typical behaviors which I briefly describe.

References

Deutsch, H. (1942). Some forms of emotional disturbance and their relationship to schizophrenia. *Psychoanalytic Quarterly* 11:301–321.

Giovacchini, P. L. (1975). *Psychoanalysis of Character Disorders.* New York: Jason Aronson.

Horowitz, M. J., Wilner, N., Marmar, C., and Krupnick, J. (1980). Pathological grief and the activation of latent self-images. *American Journal of Psychiatry* 137:1157–1162.

Kernberg, O. (1975). *Borderline Conditions and Pathological Narcissism.* New York: Jason Aronson.

Mahler, M. S. (1968). *On Human Symbiosis and the Vicissitudes of Individuation—Volume I—Infantile Psychosis.* New York: International Universities Press.

Masterson, J. (1976). *Psychotherapy of the Borderline Adult: A Developmental Approach.* New York: Brunner/Mazel.

Mitscherlich, A., and M. (1975). *The Inability to Mourn.* New York: Grove Press. Originally published in German as *Die Unfähigkeit zu Trauern, Grundlagen kollektiven Verhaltens.* Munich: R. Piper & Co. Verlag, 1967.

Searles, H. F. (1956). The psychodynamics of vengefulness. *Psychiatry* 19:31–39. Reprinted in Searles (1965), pp. 177–191.

—— (1965). *Collected Papers on Schizophrenia and Related Subjects.* London: The Hogarth Press. New York: International Universities Press.

—— (1972). The function of the patient's realistic perceptions of the analyst in delusional transference. *British Journal of Medical Psychology.* 45:1–18. Reprinted in Searles (1979), pp. 196–227.

—— (1976). Transitional phenomena and therapeutic symbiosis. *International Journal of Psychoanalytic Psychotherapy* 5: 145–204. Reprinted in Searles (1979), pp. 503–576.

—— (1979). *Countertransference and Related Subjects—Selected Papers.* New York: International Universities Press.

—— (1980). Psychoanalytic therapy with borderline patients— the development, in the patient, of an internalized image of the therapist. Presented as the Fifth O. Spurgeon English Honor Lecture at Temple University School of Medicine, Philadelphia, April 25, 1980. Reprinted as Chapter 9 in this volume.

Volkan, V. D. (1976). *Primitive Internalized Object Relations—A Clinical Study of Schizophrenic, Borderline, and Narcissistic Patients.* New York: International Universities Press.

—— (1981). *Linking Objects and Linking Phenomena.* New York: International Universities Press.

Chapter 11

Separation and Loss in Psychoanalytic Therapy with Borderline Patients: Further Remarks

The borderline patient's personality-organization renders ever-present, for him, the danger of separation and loss. He is continually faced with the threat of loss, either of his tenuously established individual identity, through fusion with the other person, or of his fragile interpersonal relatedness, through uncontrollable flight into autism of psychotic degree.

This chapter is a revised version of "Some Aspects of Separation and Loss in Psychoanalytic Therapy with Difficult Patients," presented as the 32nd Annual Karen Horney lecture, in New York City on March 31, 1984, and was published under the title shown here in *The American Journal of Psychoanalysis*, 45:9-27, 1985. It includes some passages from Chapter 10, "Some Aspects of Separation and Loss in Psychoanalytic Therapy with Borderline Patients", which was

The Patient's Unconscious, Fantasied Omnipotence

A basic theme in one's work with these individuals is that of unconscious, fantasied omnipotence, variously an aspect of the patient's unconscious self-image, or projected into the therapist. This theme appears much more subtly than one finds it in overtly psychotic patients and requires one, therefore, to be attentive to its presence.

Typically, the therapist is assumed to be omnipotent and not himself subject, therefore, to any uncontrollable losses. Thus, if the treatment is interrupted by some loss on the therapist's part, this is assumed by the patient to be something calculated by the therapist to tyrannize, or otherwise seriously discommode, him. He reacts analogously when he, himself, experiences significant loss. First of all, such an experience is usually long in coming, in the work, for the patient's own fantasied omnipotence, although a long-established unconscious defense against early losses (and other intolerable psychological experiences), has itself long since become that which he most fears to lose. To experience significant loss means the relinquishment of—the loss of—the fantasy that he himself is omnipotent. But then the experienced loss is immediately assumed to have been intendedly inflicted upon him by a malevolently omnipotent therapist.

Also typically, the patient's own chronic feelings of helplessness serve as an unconscious defense against a dissociated self-image as malevolently omnipotent—as being re-

originally presented at a conference on The Borderline Syndrome: Differential Diagnosis and Pychodynamic Treatment, at UCLA Extension Department of Human Development, Los Angeles, CA, March 14, 1981, and which was published on pp. 131–160 in *Technical Factors in the Treatment of the Severely Disturbed Patient*, edited by P. L. Giovacchini and L. B. Boyer; New York and London: Jason Aronson, 1982.

sponsible for all significant losses suffered by anyone in the world. The patient is so little differentiated from the surrounding actual world that his own "world," the only world of which he is aware, is one largely comprised of his projected introjects, which helps one to understand why his feelings, words and deeds have so pervasive an impact upon the "whole world."

Another highly usual aspect of the patient's basically omnipotent reactions to threatened loss is to experience all his own subjectively good aspects as having been self-created in his development; hence there is no conscious danger that he may ever lose perceivedly good persons upon whom he is dependent—for in his view there never were any of those. It is easy, and by no means rare, for the therapist to become drawn into this way of viewing the patient's development, and to assume that the therapist himself is the first good person, or potentially good person, whom the patient has ever encountered.

As for a few brief, illustrative clinical vignettes, there is the patient whose mother repeatedly held over the child's head the threat, as punishment for the child's misdeeds, that she, the mother, would die; there was no acknowledgment from the mother that she inevitably and innately would eventually die, in any case. Another patient makes plain how self-absorbed is his own world in saying to his therapist (a man whom I supervised for a time), "See, everything still revolves around *me*. . . . I don't care how *you* feel as long as you love *me*. . . ."

A woman concerned about her diabetes says, "I've lost control of eating," said in such a tone as to convey the unconsciously grandiose meaning, "I've lost control of all eating everywhere," and whenever she refers to the subject of "ending therapy," this too, has a similar unconscious ring of "ending all therapy everywhere." Another woman, who frequently acted out with alcohol, reports that "I went on another binge this weekend, which stopped yesterday," but said this with the subtly-grandiose, unconscious meaning that her binge had *made yesterday stop* for everyone everywhere.

Some of these vignettes serve to remind us that unconsciously-fantasied omnipotence carries with it not only the connotation of triumphantly limitless power, but also that of a limitlessly burdensome sense of total responsibility: the connotation that for whatever loss whomever in one's world suffers, one is somehow, malevolently, responsible.

The Patient's Unconscious Conflict as to Whether to Relate at All to Other People

Whereas the neurotic individual is filled with conflict as to how to relate to other persons, or as to which ones to relate to in what fashion, the borderline individual is filled with unconscious, potential conflict as to whether to relate to people at all. In sessions, he may switch unpredictably from strongly felt relatedness with, to emotional detachment from, the therapist. It may require years for him to become aware in daily life, for instance, of his proclivity for becoming immersed in lively playfulness with his little daughter at one moment, and then, the next moment, feeling thoroughly bored with and disinterested in her—reminiscent to him of his own early experiences with his father or mother.

For such a person, coming into sustained relatedness presents a variety of threats, including that of fusion with the other person, and loss of an omnipotently-controlling (though basically autistic) self-image, which has been based on early perceptions of the mother as being omnipotent and above human relatedness. Parenthetically, if the prospect of fusion with another person gives one to feel overwhelmingly anxious, this suggests that one unconsciously views the other as being an overwhelmingly anxious person—a simple point, but well to keep in mind in working with those patients who idealize the parents.

A woman had been in treatment for several years when, upon looking back at me, as usual, before lying down on the couch, she explained, without any comment from me, "I always have to look at you, to make sure it's really you, and not an impostor—or not someone who looks just like you and is dressed just like you, but isn't you. . . . I always have to make eye-contact. . . . If I just came in here and didn't even glance at you, I wouldn't have any way at all of knowing that you're you."

The Therapist Feels Tantalized, Mocked, Caricatured, and Irrelevant

In the instance of a man who could afford only once-a-week therapy, it was typical of him to spend the bulk of the session in detailing the daily-life events which had occurred since the previous session. He spoke in a critical, derisive, mocking manner, caricaturing the eccentricities of many persons, but dwelling upon the most recent illustrations of his wife's and his boss's insensitive behavior toward him. Typically, his verbal and non-verbal communications were sprinkled with dozens of unconscious transference-reactions to me. These were usually of a hostile-competitive, contemptuous nature, but occasionally having a predominantly sexual connotation; positive transference-manifestations were relatively feeble and slowly-developing during the first two years of our work. His transference-communications, taken altogether, were so fleeting and insusceptible to repeated attempts on my part at exploration and interpretation that I learned largely to desist from such attempts until these transference-manifestations would become more coherent and stably enduring. Meanwhile, I felt chronically irrelevant but endlessly tantalized with these fleeting, evanescent transference-manifestations which gave me a glimpse each time, for a few seconds, of how wonderfully relieving and fulfilling it would be for me to become able to function really as a therapist to this chronically frustrated, unhappy man.

His sadism toward me became evident to me relatively early and I thereafter suffered much less. But especially memorable to me were my gradual realizations that (a) he himself felt as irrelevant to his "own" daily living as I was given to feel during our sessions; and (b) his mocking, caricaturing orientation was an unconscious defense against confusing everyone, one with another, and against becoming locked into total identification with one or another part-aspect of the other person—including myself in the transference. He came to realize that "I don't like being like a chameleon. . . . After I've been with that Princeton alumni group [as had happened over the weekend], I'm so Princetonian I can't *stand* myself!" Helene Deutsch's (1942) and Greenson's (1958) writings on "as-if" personality are relevant here, as are Winnicott's (1954) and Khan's (1971) papers concerning the "false self."

The Role of Splitting

The splitting so characteristic of the borderline patient greatly increases his consequent fear of becoming trapped in just one of his identity-bearing introjects. One man says, "I don't wanta be trapped in any one kind of emotion," and to avoid becoming "trapped" in dating just one woman, would take pains to date more than one concomitantly. The following vignettes highlight how fractionated are these introjects resultant from the splitting. A man whose father had sired two children in a previous marriage before begetting four more with the patient's mother, phrased it that "My dad had six children and my mother had four children," but said it as though these totaled ten—as though the mother-derived aspects of the last four children were split off from their father-derived aspects. A woman whose husband has gotten a position in another city speaks of "the prospect of my leaving Washington, and hence you, or *you and me* [my italics]," this last suggesting that she will leave behind that part of her which is involved in the "you and me."

The Patient's Subjective Unaliveness and His Coming to Value in Part Positively, Therefore, Any Feelings

As the patient becomes aware of his lack of deeply-felt and well-integrated, authentic emotionality, he comes to react to *any* intense feeling, not matter how "negative" it is usually considered to be—no matter whether it be sadness, terror, depression, or whatever—as a sign of transitory, authentic aliveness. His conflicts about his identifications with other persons can be utilized, by the therapist, to confront him with the possibility that the original possessor of the personality-trait in question may likewise have been in conflict about it; this kind of exploration of his remembered experience can foster his becoming increasingly aware of the emotional multidimensionality of his parental figures.

Suspense

Typically, one's work with the patient becomes permeated with an atmosphere of not only tantalization but also suspense. The therapist finds reason to feel suspense as to whether the patient may suddenly quit treatment, become manifestly psychotic, or commit suicide; and the therapist may view his own immediate future as being far from comfortably predictable. Moreover, the suspense usually takes a much heavier toll in the patient's experience of the work. I have come to see that the *future*-orientedness of the feeling of suspense serves, for each participant, as an unconscious defense against his recognition of the nature of the *immediate, present* situation—namely, one of a significant degree of highly ambivalent symbiosis—loss of ego boundaries—between himself and the (only partially) "other" person in the relationship.

Parenthetically, meeting as infrequently as once a week makes it next to impossible for the transference to develop with this so-necessary ego-boundary-eroding intensity. It has been my growing impression, during nearly 30 years of doing psychoanalysis and psychoanalytic therapy as well as supervision of such treatment, that therapist and borderline patient tend to allow various "reality" reasons (financial or otherwise) to preclude their meeting with the frequency actually necessary to this work, and do so in a mutual but unconscious avoidance of this innate threat to their respective ego-boundaries.

The Patient's Lateness as an Unconscious Defense Against Awareness of Inability to Relate

A patient's recurrent lateness can serve as an unconscious defense against his becoming aware of his inability to relate at all fully with the therapist. Typically, he will speak, many minutes after his arrival, as though he not only had *arrived* late, but *were still* late—as though he still had not fully arrived in the session. One woman who (because of a serious physical handicap) met with me for only one two-hour session per week arrived 15 minutes late for a session, for the reason that her cab driver had arrived late at her home. It was striking to me that she said, while preparing to leave the session about one and one-half hours later, "Well, Dr. Searles, I'm sorry I'm late."

The Patient's Identifying with Unconscious Identity-Components in the Therapist

Typically, the patient's fear of fusion with the therapist is so intense that his early identifications with the latter not only occur unconsciously in the patient, but are, moreover, identifications with aspects of the therapist which are part of the latter's unconscious, rather than conscious, sense of identity. They are identifications, that is, with various introjects within the therapist which have never become well-integrated into the therapist's own ego-functioning and conscious sense of personal identity.

The acting-out which the patient does between sessions consists in his inflicting loss, deprivation, and other forms of injury upon these unconscious identifications with the therapist, as an expression of negative-transference feelings and attitudes. The actual introjects (unconscious by definition) in the therapist are subject, in the process of the patient's introjectively identifying with these, to a great deal of distortion and intensification by reason of transference factors referable to the patient's very early years. Another way of looking at this same process is to see it as involving the therapist's projectively identifying with the patient—projecting his own introjects into the patient and then (still unconsciously) vicariously identifying with the patient who is giving expression to these.

It is thus no coincidence that the patient, upon coming to the session, behaves in terms that his acting out is doing more damage to the therapist than to himself. One such individual, giving lip-service to distress that the therapy was taking so long, said, "Five years is a long time out of *your* [my italics; he clearly meant, consciously, his own] life."

The patient who absents himself time and again from sessions, or who is unreachably detached during much of the session when he is physically present, may be unconsciously identifying with the more detached components of the therapist's personality. A gross example of this occurred during a session in which I (behind the couch) had been semi-dozing for a few minutes, without the patient's appearing to realize this. She then stopped talking and said, after a few minutes of silence, "I don't know whether you're really here," to which I then responded in a manner connecting this with her early experiences with her emotionally-detached mother, in a fashion which made sense to her. But much more often with such patients, it is difficult to be emotionally available even though wide awake, and when at the end of the session I fairly routinely say, "I'll see you tomorrow," this has to my own ear an apologetic undertone, as though I were saying, "I realize that I failed to see you today; but I *will* see you tomorrow."

Some Defensive Functions of Subjective Omniscience and Omnipotence

My earlier paper (Searles 1981) discussed some aspects of the borderline individual's well-known inability, at the beginning of treatment, to experience a full range of human emotions, and described his investment in subjective omniscience as being among his defenses against the full recognition of this inability. An event of potentially intense and varied impact is reacted to, by him, essentially without any feelings other than a basically "I told you so" reaction—a smug regarding of this event as confirmation of what he had foreseen would happen. He tends to present himself, in the sessions, as being broad-mindedly above embroilment in emotional turmoil, either in this room or in his marital home. This aloofness is based, however, not upon any genuinely mature capacity for empathy with the feelings of two or more participants in turmoil, but upon his inability to experience much of any feelings, whatsoever, about the tangled and conflictual relationship—other than a narcissistic pleasure in his own subjective broad-mindedness.

Subjective omnipotence serves as an unconscious defense against—among other experiences—empathic relatedness with the other person—against, that is, both one's feeling an appreciation of the other's feelings, and one's experiencing the other person as having an empathic appreciation of one's own feelings. Such empathic relatedness might be assumed to be innately desirable; but for the person who for whatever historical reasons has an inordinate fear of interpersonal fusion, empathy tends to invoke the threat of total and irremediable union. Many a patient is immersed, oftentimes in her daily living, in a seething, paranoid fury at her husband for his having, as she perceives him, no empathy for her feelings (of hurt, disappointment, despair, or whatever); but she is at an unconscious level so invested in paranoid grandiosity, so threatened lest she lose her ego-boundaries, that she cannot accept such empathic relatedness as he is able to offer her.

To the extent that one is paranoid, one unconsciously fears not only oneness with the other person, but also loss of the identity-bearing introjects within oneself through their dissolving into one another as well as into the other person. Moreover, to the extent that one needs to project one's introjects into the other person, defensively, in an increasingly intimate relationship, it is realistic for one to feel unconsciously threatened lest one "lose" one's introjects. Such threatened loss presumably confronts one, unconsciously, with one's being left in the bleak, empty, isolated, autistic state wherein, in one's very early life, the introjects developed, to people one's inner world as a defense against experiencing the fullness of one's actual interpersonal isolation.

Such an adult then, in therapy, although on the one hand growingly shocked and concerned at his large-scale inability to experience many, sustained human emotions, is on the other hand threatened lest he lose his unfeelingness, his ruthlessness, for he reacts to this latter threat of loss as one which would leave him incapable of severing developing emotional fusions between himself and other persons and things, unable to effect separations and preserve his individuality. Such a man, who chronically walked a tightrope between autism and fusion, said concerning a recurrently dissatisfied, and unsatisfactory, secretary in his business office whom he had long endeavored to help and was coming close to firing, "For Edna it will be a bad thing if I can't divorce myself from my feelings about the situation and look at it in a professional [i. e., unfeeling] way."

Dedifferentiation to Fusion with Elements of the Nonhuman Environment

In a monograph (Searles 1960) I discussed the role of the nonhuman environment in normal development and in schizophrenia. I described that for any infant and young child, the struggle to become a genuinely human individual involves not only the development and maintenance of meaningful interpersonal relationship *per se*, but also, and more basically, his or her becoming differentiated from the far vaster nonhuman environment, becoming able to differentiate between human and nonhuman ingredients of one's environment, and achieving emotionally-meaningful re-latedness with both human and nonhuman realms of one's environment.

That topic is highly relevant to the subject of this paper. My monograph describes, for example, that among the determinants of the human being's desire to become nonhuman is his attempt to escape from his anxiety concerning his mortality—concerning the inevitability of his death (Searles 1960, p. 224). That book contains many examples of patients' manifesting regressive dedifferentiation to fusion with elements of the nonhuman environment, as an unconscious defense against (among other painful feeling-states) separation and loss. I have found much of similar clinical material in my work with borderline patients in subsequent years.

A woman, injured in a taxi accident, received so severe a leg-injury that she had to have an above-the-knee amputation. For years after this tragic accident, the incompleteness of her grieving the loss of nearly all this limb was evidenced in her speaking of the prosthesis, which she became able to wear after several months, as though it were the lost leg-portion itself—as though the prosthesis and the amputation stump were one, were fused. This was not a delusion; she did not consciously believe this. But the distortion appeared with the subtlety of her other long-familiar borderline defenses.

For example, she would say, "I didn't like the way it looked after I took it off." I knew that the former "it" referred to her amputation-stump, and the latter one, to the prosthesis; but she spoke exactly as though referring to the same "it" in each instance. There were many sessions in which she spoke, in a manner both confusing and latently confused, of "it . . . it . . . it, . . ." in this way revealing of such fusion at an unconscious level.

"I wasn't sure about putting on my prosthesis; it got kind of irritated." This was said entirely as though her prosthesis, rather than her amputation-stump, had gotten kind of irritated. "See, I can't tell, till I take this prosthesis off, whether it's irritated."

On another occasion she said, "After I washed it [referring to her stump] it looked better, so I thought I'd wear it [her prosthesis] here." But she said "it" entirely as though referring to the same "it" in each instance. Once she commented, "it gets blue and red but they say it's all right to wear it."

She gave a holiday dinner for a few of her relatives, and at the end of the dinner she was standing (using her prosthesis) near the table, receiving the compliments of her guests, both about the dinner and about how well she was doing with her prosthesis. Suddenly she fell to the floor, and was later found to have cracked her pelvis. In describing this to me, she said, "I couldn't hold myself. . . . With this thing [the prosthesis] on, I don't feel for real; I feel like a mannikin, not *me*. . . . We were talking away—about how well I was doing. . . . I felt quite proud of myself and . . . a few seconds later I couldn't hold myself. . . . " She added a bit later, in a distinctly jealous tone, "They like the prosthesis so well." It was my impression that among the unconscious precipitants of her falling were: (a) her bursting pride in herself was more than she (whose self-esteem had long been abysmally low) could contain ("I couldn't hold myself"); and (b) her jealousy of the prosthesis, with which she had to share her guests' admiration, was such that she was determined to prove (by her falling) that it wasn't so wonderful after all. In the earlier chapters concerning jealousy involving an internal object, I have described that often the internal object in question is a subjectively nonhuman one, and this becomes projected upon some ingredient of the outer, actually nonhuman, environment, such that truly nonhuman objects come to have the jealousy-engendering capacity of actual human rivals.

To return to the theme of separation and loss *per se*, I shall cite another woman's describing that, on the previous day, she had been following in her car, with delight, a man whose car had a license plate only one digit different from that of her own. She then added, "I did feel a sense of loss when he turned into a bowling alley." She said this entirely as though the man had metamorphosed into the bowling alley. I found it typical of her unconscious defenses against loss that she would identify unconsciously more with my relatively unchanging office, for example, and with the plants in it, than with my much less stable and therefore less reliable self.

This same woman, at a time when her daughter had graduated recently from high school and was showing many signs of loss-reaction to the separation from her closely-knit high-school group, contrasted this to her own high school experience. She said, "See, I went to five different high schools," and explained that since she never had come to participate in any of the social activities in high school, "I never lost anything" upon going, then, out into the adult world. But the notable thing is that when she said, "See, I went to five different high schools," this conveyed an unconscious meaning of her doing so *simultaneously*, rather than in succession. It was clear that when she had been consciously in the fifth high school, for example, she had been unconsciously in the earlier four (the loss of which she had been unable to integrate) at the same time. This is similar to an observation which I have made concerning the borderline patient who has had more than one marriage: he or she will speak of "my wives" or "my husbands" as though married currently to both the present spouse and the former one or ones.

A woman says, at the beginning of a session, "I'm in a much different place than I was yesterday," and goes on to detail how differently she is feeling from the way she felt in yesterday's session. I was reminded, immediately, of a vastly more ill woman, chronically schizophrenic, whom I have long treated—of, specifically, that latter woman's many-years'-long delusional conviction that my office is, in actuality, almost innumerable offices—her conviction that, while being to my way of thinking in my office, she is in actuality suddenly moved, time and again, to an actually "different place" (as the former woman had put it)—an actually different office, one which looks much like the others but which, from subtle signs, she knows to be a different one now. Here again, the schizophrenic patient experiences literally that which the borderline individual is able to express metaphorically.

Although the patient's unconscious defense, of dedifferentiation to oneness with various elements of the nonhuman environment, does indeed function as a formidable protection against his becoming aware of feelings of separation and loss in his relationships with other human beings, this defense inevitably worsens his plight, for it arouses in him anxiety lest he lose, or lest he have lost already, irretrievably, his own subjective humanness.

Such a patient, who has not become differentiated reliably from his nonhuman environment, chronically has to demonstrate (basically to himself) his own humanness, primarily by projection of his subjectively nonhuman identity-components into the therapist. This in turn impels him repeatedly to rescue the therapist from perceivedly irreversible dedifferentiation into the surrounding nonhuman environment, for he loves as well as hates the therapist (= mother, in this regard), and senses, moreover, that his own problems cannot be truly resolved by projection.

In the supervision of therapists who are working with such patients, I find that the therapist typically is highly resistant to realizing how deeply convinced is the patient that he, the patient, is the predominantly healthy one in the therapeutic dyad, and that the therapist is very ill—very primitive in his personality-functioning, not at all well-established as a mature human being. One such patient made clear, in the early months of his therapy, that he felt himself to be the only person in his daily experience (both during and outside the therapy-sessions) who had a *self*. On one occasion, in response to an exploratory comment from his therapist, he protested, "I can't be *totally* open—after all, you're not a *mannikin*, are you?", he said, in a tone as though he were not entirely sure.

A woman in a session with me commented, ". . . This reminds me of my feeling annoyed at Jim [her husband]— something I haven't made much of. . . ." It was clear that "something" referred consciously to her "feeling annoyed at Jim"; but I found much reason, by now, to hear it as referring unconsciously to Jim, her husband, as being "*something* [my italics] I haven't made much of."

Many borderline patients are painfully aware of their inability to mourn, to weep—to feel sad, even—as being a serious flaw in their emotional equipment for living as human beings among other human beings. Such a patient welcomes, as therapy progresses, his becoming being able to feel sad. Typically, he has no memories of finding that either parent was able to manifest, and speak of, feelings of sadness and related feelings. The parent of such a patient was, typically, heavily defended against potentially overwhelming feelings of loss, and one comes to understand that the patient's own more autistic areas of personality-functioning, so resistant to the kind of therapeutically-symbiotic processes of which I (Searles 1979a) have written several papers years ago, were developed as early barriers to the kind of mother–infant symbiosis in which the baby is normally ushered into human living, for the reason that, in his instance, symbiosis meant becoming at one with a mother who was struggling to keep dissociated her overwhelming feelings of loss. An adult patient who has had this kind of experience in infancy and early childhood inevitably manifests, in the course of the therapy, an inordinate fear of loss of ego-boundaries in any situation (including the transference-situation) of developing intimacy.

I confess that I have found ironically amusing, at times, various communications from patients who are very conscious of their inability to mourn, and who are trying to present pseudo-mourning as being the authentic response. The therapist must risk, after all, self-condemnations as being callous, if he is to have the courage to know, and act upon, the distinction between authentic emotion and pseudo-emotionality. In my earlier paper on this present subject, I reported that sometimes, when this or that patient says to me upon my return from a vacation, "I missed you," he or she sounds to me mainly like a disappointed sniper. Similarly, when a man says of his girlfriend who is about to move to another city, "I'm sure I'm going to miss Susan terribly," I heard this as meaning, unconsciously, "I'm sure I'm going to do a terrible job of missing Susan." Similarly a male supervisee, at the end of our final session after about two years of difficult work together, clearly endeavored to express feelings of appreciation of me and loss of our continued work together, but succeeded mainly in making me feel eulogized as a corpse. Before authentic feelings of love and loss can emerge, death-wishes must become integrated, and his toward me had not been. It is because I have become reliably familiar with true feelings of loss, both within myself and as manifested by others, that I am able, in such instances as these, to know pseudo-emotionality when I encounter it.

I have found in many instances that one or another of the borderline patient's parents was so involved chronically in pathological defenses against mourning—was living so largely in an unrelinquished past—that he or she would become completely inaccessible to the child, unpredictably and for very prolonged periods. During such periods the child unconsciously reacted to the parent as being literally dead, although the present-day adult who had been that child will require much therapy before gaining conscious access to such perceptions of the parent. For such a patient, much therapy is likely to be needed before he or she can become able to differentiate actual death and the kind of depressed-parent "death" which becomes undone, sooner or later (no matter how unpredictably) into resumed interpersonal relatedness between parent and child.

A widow, speaking of her husband who had died several years before, said, "When Joe was alive, . . ." in such a tone that I sensed an unconscious meaning that there were times *during Joe's life* when Joe was alive, and times when he was not. In this same session, she said of her father and mother that "When she died, his existence didn't continue on beyond that," explaining that her father, although still physically alive, never got out of mourning the death of the patient's mother. "Perhaps I repeated that with Joe's death," she said thoughtfully—which was essentially the same thought which had just occurred to me.

These patients project, to a striking degree, unconscious feelings into the surrounding nonhuman environment, reacting to various elements of that environment as being animate and essentially human. One man said, *"My mother-in-law's house is a very angry place* [my italics] these days: she's angry; my father-in-law is angry; and my wife's younger brothers and sisters, there, are angry." A housewife said, "The house makes a thousand demands on me," fully as though the house itself were an overwhelmingly demanding person. A man said, "Last night I came home and I was just *furious* at the house [said fully as though the house, empty of people until he walked in, were itself a person]. Mary had taken the kids to a movie, and they left the place a terrible mess." A woman reported a dream about an automobile in which "... *the car then decides* [my italics]—the driver then decides he'll stop in front of our house." She associated the car's driver with her father, who had died during the patient's childhood.

Another woman, speaking of the building where she was living, said, "There are a few apartments in the building who have used window shades; I guess they like them better than Venetian blinds." Later in the same session, referring to a newspaper article, she said, "They said that stores that are discount stores are thinking of opening up" in her neighborhood.

A man who for years was undecided about whether to remain in Washington or to move back to Chicago, the city of his birth, projected his conflict upon these two (predominantly inanimate, of course) cities, such that when he spoke of "the Chicago-Washington conflict," his tone conjured up a vast, interplanetary conflict between fully animate entities.

In the last example, we glimpse the unresolved, unconscious, fantasied omnipotence, the grandiosity, which I have mentioned repeatedly here. We see that element in the poignant next example, from my work with an elderly woman who had been chronically schizophrenic but who had been functioning, for many years now, at a predominantly borderline level of ego-functioning. "They used to have a song, 'It's a Big, Wide, Wonderful World.' Now the world is so small," she said, her words conveying an intense sense of loss, as though she felt, literally, the loss of the large, wonderful world of long ago and had now only a very much smaller one. "With flying, it takes so little time to go around the world," she said by way of illustration. Then, after a few moments of silence, "I just heard the voices say, 'The whole world did fall in with you a long time ago.'"

The Crucial Role of the Therapist's Working Through of His Own Losses

The final point I shall discuss here is this: effective therapy with these patients involves the therapist's own deeper working through of his own losses. In a paper in 1976 entitled, "Transitional Phenomena and Therapeutic Symbiosis," I suggested that the patient's symptoms become, with the development of the early phase of therapeutic symbiosis, transitional objects for both patient and analyst simultaneously. As with the patient's symptoms, so with his transference images of the analyst: I believe that in order for any effective transference analysis to occur with any patient, whether neurotic, borderline, or psychotic, the analyst must have come to accept at *least* a transitional-object degree—if not more deeply symbiotic degree—of relatedness with the particular transference image, or percept, which is holding sway presently in the analysis (Searles 1976, p. 576).

Closely related to those comments is my statement, in the summary of my previous chapter (Chapter 10) on the present topic, that the patient can relinquish his illness, eventually, only if the analyst has come to know and to cherish, to a significant degree, the gratifications of that illness, such that the loss-of-illness experience can become a mutual, shared loss-experience for the two participants.

As I indicated briefly near the beginning of this chapter, one of the ways in which the borderline individual's unconscious omnipotence is revealed is in his tendency to regard all his subjectively good, healthy aspects as having been created by himself, and all his psychopathology as being attributable to interactions with, and identifications with, the warped, hurtful, neglectful (and so forth) aspects of his parent-figures. This orientation, although shared by most therapists, bespeaks the patient's rigorous dissociation of the feelings of loving dependency which are bound up by his so-called bad introjects, and indicates how greatly he under-estimates the grief which will be involved, for him, in his relinquishing of those introjects in the process of increasing ego-integration.

As an example, a woman, after working through much hatred and fear of her tyrannical father, came to remember him as having been, as she put it in an intensely fond, admiring, nostalgic, grief-laden tone, "A real, true son-of-a-bitch!" A man, who with his several siblings had been subjected to appallingly harsh physical abuse from his father during his upbringing, and who on returning home a bit late from his first date as a teenager had reason to feel terror lest his father literally kill him in punishment for this, came later on in the therapy to experience his father's terrifying punitiveness as having been the father's intense way of *caring*, and the therapy evoked intense grief, as well as relief, at his own having grown away from his father. My work with each of these two patients involved, for me, a deeper working through of my loss-feelings with respect to the tyrants in each of my parents.

The awesome magnitude of the dissociated loss-feelings, relative to the strength of the ego to cope with these, sometimes reveals itself in a patient's seemingly casual comment. I shall give an example from my work, extending over many years, with the previously-mentioned woman who, chronically schizophrenic in the earlier years of our work, has functioned at a predominantly borderline level for a considerable number of years now.

This incident occurred during a session in which her transference to me was predominantly affectionate and comfortably dependent; the session felt to me to be as comfortable for both of us as any session we had ever had. She was saying, casually, about 15 minutes along in the session, "They promised rain. I hope it doesn't rain Dr. Searles. . . ."

The significant thing, to me (I did not attempt any

interpretation at this time), was that she did not pause at all after saying the word "rain"; had she paused, however briefly, I would have found her comment a quite unremarkable statement, "I hope it doesn't rain, Dr. Searles."

But I heard what she actually said as conveying, unconsciously, the idea that her loss of me, following such a session, tended to be so insupportable that she would experience me, instead, as covering her whole experienced world—with my being, literally, the prospective rain, falling everywhere upon everything. In her experience, then, it would be raining Dr. Searles.

I was reminded, immediately upon hearing this comma-less statement of hers, of one of the many children's stories my wife and I used to read to our children. This story (my favorite, of them all) is of a beloved Grandpa Bunny, who upon his death becomes a beautiful sunset. In my work with this woman, I had much reason to know, by now, that her feelings of loving dependency, and potential grief, concerning me were linked not only with her feelings toward a beloved father and older brother, but also with her feelings toward her mother who had appeared, in the earlier years of the therapy, to have been a classic example of the so-called bad, schizophrenogenic mothers.

In a paper in 1970 concerning therapeutic symbiosis, I described that the patient needed to come to experience the analyst as being equivalent to the early mother who comprises the whole world of which the infant is inextricably a part (Searles 1970; reprinted in Searles 1979a, pp. 162–163). Then, in a later paper (Searles 1973) on that subject, I reported that in my experience, for the resolution of the patient's autism to occur, the analyst must do more than function as a more reliable maternally protective shield for the patient than the latter's biological mother was during his infancy and early childhood, in the manner Khan (1963, 1964) has described. First the analyst must have become

increasingly free in his acceptance of the *patient's* functioning as *his*—the analyst's—maternally protective shield. In
my own way of conceptualizing it: to the extent that the
analyst can become able comfortably and freely to immerse
himself in the autistic patient as constituting his (the analyst's) world, the patient can then utilize him as a model for
identification as regards the acceptance of such very primitive dependency needs, and can come increasingly to exchange his erstwhile autistic world for the world consisting of,
and personified by, the analyst (Searles 1973, pp. 189–190).

Meanwhile, along the way, the therapist must come to
accept, to a significant degree, the patient's having a God
and the Creator's ability to determine, to mold, the therapist's own reality, in the microcosm of the therapeutic session. It is in this atmosphere that the patient's erstwhile
pathological grandiosity becomes channeled into deepened
human relatedness.

My 1973 paper on therapeutic symbiosis made plain
that I am not holding a brief, here, for shared psychosis. In
that paper I commented that in recent ones concerning autism (Searles 1970, 1971), I had described how the analyst is
thrown, in response to the autistic patient, back upon his
own autistic processes. A development which comes eventually to contribute to the resolution of this autistic mode of
relatedness is the analyst's surprised, recurrent, and deepening realization and acceptance of the fact that these two
seemingly so-separate worlds, his world and that of the
patient, are but separate outcroppings of the unconscious
ground joining the two of them (Searles 1973, p. 191).

Winnicott (1945) and Milner (1969, p. 404) have described that the healthy infant, or respectively the autistic
patient emerging into relatedness with external reality, at
first experiences this external reality as something created
by the infant (or patient) himself. My view is that for each of
us, at the most primitive level of our experience of an "outer

world," this whole outer world is mother, and to the extent that any one of us, as a patient in psychoanalytic therapy, has formidable areas of autism to integrate, then he needs to go through the experience of finding, at the level of treatment-fostered regression to a pre-individuation stage, that he has the ability to create, and then destroy, and then re-create, and then re-destroy this dawningly outer world comprised of the analyst–mother, in keeping with his (the patient's) own fluctuating needs, until he can adapt to a stably-enduring outer world which is not under his fantasiedly omnipotent control.

That is, to my mind, Winnicott's (1941) concept of the analyst's providing a good-enough holding environment implies that the analyst be not merely relatively stably there, for the patient, but also relatively destructible (psychologically) by the patient, time and again, as the patient's persisting needs for autistic (omnipotent) functioning still require. Hence the analyst needs intuitively to provide his own absence, perhaps as often as his own presence, to the patient at timely moments. Thus the analyst's guilt, upon finding that he has become emotionally detached from the patient once again, is not necessarily well founded, for he may have sensed, unconsciously, that the patient needed this absence on his part.

Spitz (1945) reported that "The [healthy] child . . . learns to distinguish animate objects from inanimate ones by the spectacle provided by his mother's face in situations fraught with emotional satisfaction." Mahler (1968) reports that "At the height of symbiosis—at around four or five months—the facial expression of most infants becomes much more subtly differentiated, mobile, and expressive" (p. 15).

It is my impression that the mother of the borderline patient, although relatively well able to help her infant to reach this stage of ego-development, is so dependent upon this achieved aliveness of his—so unsure that there is any aliveness innate to herself—that she is unable to adapt to his later becoming relatively fully individuated from her. Essentially, the parent and child roles are reversed, at this early stage in the child's development, with the mother looking unconsciously to the child hereafter to enable her to become more fully ego-differentiated and individuated. In the evolution of the adult borderline patient's mother-transference to the therapist, he comes to respond in terms that the therapist can be alive only vicariously, through the patient himself. To my mind—and I am unaware that any earlier writer has made this point—the dependency in the therapeutic relationship is indeed not all uni-directional, in this regard. It is customary for us to assume that the borderline patient reacts as though the therapist possesses the only enduring aliveness. What I am saying is that, although I believe that he does react so, the opposite is true also, and that it is more difficult for both participants to gain access to this latter side of the matter—the side having to do with the actual mother's, and the therapist's, startlingly primitive dependency upon the patient's "own" aliveness.

Relevant here is an earlier paper of mine (Searles 1979a, p. 310) which reported that in my work with an ambulatory schizophrenic woman who had moved from sitting in a chair to sitting on the couch, I found that the next analytic-developmental step, her becoming able to lie down on the couch, involved not merely *her* ability to adapt to the isolation attendant upon no longer being able to see my face. I came to realize after she had started lying down, but sitting up from time to time to get a look at my face, that my relief at these "interruptions" was fully comparable with her own. I had been myself repressing the feelings of deprivation attendant upon no longer being able to watch her fascinating, mobile facial expressions while she was lying on the couch.

I have stated, much more generally, that "the more ill a patient is, the more does his successful treatment require that he become, and be implicitly acknowledged as having become, a therapist to his officially designated therapist, the analyst" (Searles 1975; see p. 381 in Searles 1979a).

Although in the course of my training analysis I became familiar, indeed, with long-repressed grief, I find that the work with borderline patients, in whom very early losses were so fundamental to the causation of their illnesses, tends to open up, for me, comparably early (pre-oedipal, pre-individuation) losses which had not been at all fully explored in my analysis. I shall give two brief examples of this.

A man was remembering some of the feelings he had experienced as a teenager—feelings of adventurous anticipation, of beginning to enter a wonderful new world. As I listened to him, I remembered how often I had felt so during my undergraduate years in Cornell, and suddenly realized that I had never grieved my loss of Cornell. I realized in ensuing days that my leaving my alma mater and going to medical school had involved, for me, a loss of autonomy which had been developing relatively well. This change in schools unconsciously represented, to me, the too-early and loss-filled change, in my early childhood, from the orbit of my mother to the orbit of my possessive, and more than a little paranoid, father who had been determined, from my early childhood on, that I would become a doctor.

A woman who had been a middle child in a family which included three girls and two boys, and whose parents were now long dead, was saying, "I want to be alone with my mother and father. . . ." I felt a strong feeling of empathic sadness when I heard her say this, and sensed that she was expressing a long-unconscious yearning of my own. So simple a yearning had been opposed, in my history, not only by the presence of my older sister who strove to maintain the status of only child, and not only by the development of my oedipal strivings (negative as well as positive) which would preclude any full being with both parents together. The yearning was rendered seeming hopeless, further, by the fact that my parents seemed to dwell in two so separate worlds that it would be unthinkable to be alone with both of them simultaneously. But now at last, at age 64 and while listening to this borderline woman, I became aware of that long-buried yearning.

Summary

This chapter is a continuation of Chapter 10, and I will recapitulate only a few of the many areas touched upon here.

The borderline individual is faced continually with the threat of loss, either of his tenuously established individual identity, through fusion with the other person, or of his fragile interpersonal relatedness, through uncontrollable flight into autism of psychotic degree. A basic theme in one's work with these persons is that of unconscious, fantasied omnipotence, variously an aspect of the patient's unconscious self-image or projected into the therapist.

The acting-out which the patient does consists in his inflicting loss, deprivation, and other forms of injury upon his introjects of part-aspects of the therapist. The grief involved in the relinquishment of so-called bad introjects is discussed.

The patient early in therapy is aware of his inability to grieve, and endeavors to conceal this deficiency by spurious emotionality. I give examples of patients' manifesting regressive dedifferentiation to fusion with elements of the nonhuman environment, as an unconscious defense against feelings of separation and loss.

Effective therapy with these patients involves the therapist's deeper working through of his own losses. The significant losses occurred so early in these patients' lives that the therapeutic exploration of these areas may enable the therapist to gain access to comparably early losses on his own part—losses from a developmental era which many a training analysis may not have explored at all adequately.

References

Deutsch, H. (1942). Some forms of emotional disturbance and their relationship to schizophrenia. *Psychoanalytic Quarterly* 11:301–321.

Greenson, R. R. (1958). On screen defenses, screen hunger, and screen identity. In *Explorations in Psychoanalysis*, pp. 111–132. New York: International Universities Press, 1978.

Khan, M. M. R. (1963). The concept of cumulative trauma. In *The Privacy of the Self: Papers on Psychoanalytic Theory and Technique*, pp. 42–58. New York: International Universities Press, 1974.

—— (1964). Ego distortion, cumulative trauma, and the role of reconstruction in the analytic situation. In *The Privacy of the Self: Papers on Psychoanalytic Theory and Technique*, pp. 59–68.

—— (1971). Infantile neurosis as a false-self organization. In *The Privacy of the Self: Papers on Psychoanalytic Theory and Technique*, pp. 219–233.

Mahler, M. S. (1968). *On Human Symbiosis and the Vicissitudes of Individuation—Volume I—Infantile Psychosis*. New York: International Universities Press.

Milner, M. (1969). *The Hands of the Living God: An Account of a Psycho-Analytic Treatment*. New York: International Universities Press.

Searles, H. F. (1960). *The Nonhuman Environment in Normal Development and in Schizophrenia*. New York: International Universities Press.

—— (1970). Autism and the phase of transition to therapeutic symbiosis. *Contemporary Psychoanalysis* 7:1–20. Reprinted in Searles (1979a), pp. 149–171.

—— (1971). Pathologic symbiosis and autism. In *In the Name of Life—Essays in Honor of Erich Fromm*, ed. B. Landis and E. S. Tauber, pp. 69–83. New York: Holt, Rinehart and Winston. Reprinted in Searles (1979a), pp. 132–148.

—— (1973). Concerning therapeutic symbiosis: the patient as symbiotic therapist, the phase of ambivalent symbiosis, and the role of jealousy in the fragmented ego. *The Annual of Psychoanalysis*, Volume 1, pp. 247–262. New York: Quadrangle/The New York Times Book Co. Reprinted in Searles (1979a), pp. 172–191.

—— (1975). The patient as therapist to his analyst. In *Tactics and Techniques in Psychoanalytic Therapy, Volume II: Countertransference*, ed. P. L. Giovacchini, pp. 95–151. New York: Jason Aronson. Reprinted in Searles (1979a), pp. 380–459.

—— (1976). Transitional phenomena and therapeutic symbiosis. *International Journal of Psychoanalytic Psychotherapy* 5:145–204. Reprinted in Searles (1979a), pp. 503–576.

—— (1979a). *Countertransference and Related Subjects—Selected Papers*. New York: International Universities Press.

—— (1979b). Countertransference with the borderline patient. In *Advances in Psychotherapy of the Borderline Patient*, ed. J. LeBoit and A. Capponi, pp. 309–346. New York and London: Jason Aronson. Reprinted as Chapter 7 in this present volume.

—— (1979c). Jealousy involving an internal object. In *Advances in Psychotherapy of the Borderline Patient*, ed. J. LeBoit and A. Capponi, pp. 347–403. New York and London: Jason Aronson. Reprinted as Chapter 5 in this present volume.

—— (1979d). The analyst's experience with jealousy. In *Countertransference*, ed. L. Epstein and A. H. Feiner, pp. 305–327. New York and London: Jason Aronson.

—— (1981). Some aspects of separation and loss in psychoanalytic therapy with borderline patients. Presented at UCLA symposium entitled, "The Borderline Syndrome: Differential Diagnosis and Psychodynamic Treatment," Los Angeles, March 13, 1981. Published in *Technical Factors in the Treatment of the Severely Disturbed Patient*, ed. P. L. Giovacchini and L. B. Boyer, pp. 136–160. New York and London: Jason Aronson, 1982. Reprinted as Chapter 10 in this present volume.

Spitz, R. A. (1945). Hospitalism—an enquiry into the genesis of psychiatric conditions in early childhood. *Psychoanalytic Study of the Child* 1:53–74.

Winnicott, D. W. (1941). The observation of infants in a set situation. In Winnicott (1958), pp. 52–69.

—— (1945). Primitive emotional development. In Winnicott (1958), pp. 145–156. See especially pp. 152–154.

—— (1954). Metapsychological and clinical aspects of regression within the psycho-analytical set-up. In Winnicott (1958), pp. 278–294.

—— (1958). *Through Paediatrics to Psycho-Analysis.* New York: Basic Books.

Chapter 12

The Role of the Analyst's Facial Expressions in Psychoanalysis and Psychoanalytic Therapy

This chapter, while acknowledging implicitly the importance of transference-distortions in the patient's perceptions of the analyst's countenance, focuses primarily upon the real changes in the latter's facial expressions. The analyst's face has a central role in the phase of therapeutic symbiosis, as well as in subsequent individuation. It is in the realm of the analyst's facial expressions that

An abbreviated version of his chapter was presented as The Second Annual Harry Stack Sullivan Lecture at the Scientific Day Program, 19th Annual Meeting, The Sheppard and Enoch Pratt Hospital, Towson, MD, June 5,1982. This chapter previously appeared in the *International Journal of Psychoanalytic Psychotherapy*, 10:47–73, 1984, edited by R. Langs, New York: Jason Aronson.

The excerpts on pages 380–381 are taken from H. Kohut, *The Analysis of* the borderline patient, for example, can best find a bridge out of autism and into therapeutically symbiotic relatedness with the analyst. During this latter phase, then, each participant's facial expressions "belong" as much to the other as to oneself; that is, the expressions of each person are in the realm of transitional phenomena for both of them. The analyst's facial expressions are a highly, and often centrally, significant dimension of both psychoanalysis and psychoanalytic therapy. Illustrative clinical vignettes are presented from work with both patients who use the couch and those who do not.

Two of My Experiences with This Topic Early in My Career

She looked closely at my face and said, with conviction, "You *are* angry at me, aren't you?" She was standing just inside the doorway to my office and made no move toward her chair. She had arrived quite late, as so often before in the several months I had worked with her, and I felt, even more than usual, tense and uncomfortable with her.

In response to her question I protested, essentially, that I was not angry at her, and tried to persuade her to come in and sit down. But all this took only a few moments, and she turned around and walked out, never to return. Ever since then, her good judgment in so doing has been evident to me. I was in no condition at that time, now 35 years ago, to work effectively with this borderline young woman, who required one to have far better access to one's own feelings than I, either not yet into my personal analysis or barely into it (I don't recall that detail), had yet achieved. At that time it was

the Self. Reprinted by permission of International Universities Press, Inc. Copyright 1971 by International Universities Press, Inc.

not that I was consciously angry at this difficult and challenging patient, but unable to use my anger effectively in our work. Quite beyond that, my superego made such a feeling toward a patient unacceptable to my conscious sense of my identity. She saw on my face, I am sure, anger of which I was genuinely unaware; I felt only more tense, uncomfortable, and unconfident than usual in my previous sessions with her.

The main point of this paper is that the analyst's facial expressions are a highly, and often centrally, significant dimension of psychoanalysis and psychoanalytic therapy, a dimension that has been largely neglected, nonetheless, in the literature. This preceding clinical example might seem contrary to this point. One might infer from it that the analyst need only acquire enough of personal analysis to come into reasonably good contact with his own emotionality, and that his countenance will hover thereafter as neutrally and evenly as does, intendedly, his attention to the patient's productions, such that any significant expressions that the patient perceives on his face can be regarded, for all practical purposes, as purely projectional in nature. But please bear with me, for I believe that the cumulative effect of my clinical examples will serve, in due course, to convey my main point.

The second clinical example is from my work, about two years later, with a man who was one of my supervised cases in the Washington Psychoanalytic Institute. He had seen a senior female analyst in consultation, seeking analysis for transvestism, and she referred him to me and provided me with supervision throughout my subsequent years of predominantly successful work with him. The work had a shaky beginning, however. In my first supervisory session—prior, as I recall, to my seeing the patient himself—she said, looking dubiously at me, "I told him that you are experienced." Only in writing this did it occur to me to wonder what expression she saw on my countenance; I am sure, at any rate, that she perceived none that radiated any quiet, self-confident assurance. I had never attempted before to work with any patient who had been involved in transvestism, and had started with only one previous analytic patient of any variety. It was, however, my first session with the patient himself that provides the essence of this second clinical example.

He came in, an older man than I and seeming to me much more intelligent, worldly, and self-possessed than I myself was feeling. He sat down in the designated chair on the opposite side of the small desk behind which I took my seat. The first few minutes of his recounting of his history went well enough; but then he did something for which I was not at all prepared. He took out of his pocket several photographs and shoved them across the desk for me to examine. They clearly had been done by a professional photographer and were all of the patient himself, but wearing a long, blonde wig, lipstick, and scanty, sexy, female clothing, and lounging in various sexy poses.

I looked at these pictures, one after another, attempting to convey a calm, mildly interested manner, trying to assume and maintain the pose of one who was beginning his nth case of psychoanalysis and examining his nth set of such photographs. But I was actually experiencing my nth attack of acute anxiety, with palpitations, sweating, and all the rest. During these few moments, I felt alone with my severe anxiety and these weird pictures, and I felt my situation there to be intolerable. Then I glanced up briefly at the patient himself, and the thought came to me, with a rush of rage, "Why, the son of a bitch is watching me like a hawk!" My rage had dispelled instantly my anxiety, and I was now able to glance through the remaining pictures and proceed through the rest of the interview without any significant difficulty.

This chapter is not a tightly organized presentation of

theoretical points, illustrative clinical material, and relevant items from the literature. Rather, it touches upon diverse areas of a largely unexplored field, a field whose dimensions I have scarcely more than glimpsed, and about which I am not in a position to make comprehensive or definitive statements.

Some Reasons Why the Importance of This Topic Is Commonly Underestimated

We analysts probably find it difficult to become free from the tendency among people in general to think that the face is tantamount to superficiality, as is implied in many phrases in everyday usage, such as "of merely face value" or "putting a good face on things." Moreover, if nearly all our patients use the couch and see, therefore, little indeed of our face, we may tend to assume that our actual facial expressions (and I am much more interested in the real input from the analyst than in the patient's transference-distorted *perceptions* of the analyst's countenance) are of essentially no significance in the work. In addition, it is at least possible that one who chooses to spend, say, 95 percent of his adult working life in sitting behind the couch, his face being observed by no other person, has somewhat more than his share of unconscious conflicts, never thoroughly explored in his training analysis, concerning his face and the play of expressions, or relative lack thereof, upon it.

The Role of Facial Expressions in Therapeutic Symbiosis

My interest in what I have termed therapeutic symbiosis has deeply impressed me with the significance of the analyst's facial expressions. Many years ago (Searles 1959,

p. 308) I reported my experience that symbiotic relatedness constitutes a necessary phase in psychoanalysis or psychotherapy with either neurotic or psychotic patients. Later, I (Searles 1963, p. 645) reported that "a naturally occurring, and to a significant degree mutual, phase of symbiotic relatedness in the transference, holding sway not merely for moments but for months, is the core phase in the psychotherapy of schizophrenia," and emphasized that the therapist's face has a central role in this symbiotic interaction. I went on to discuss this particular topic for several pages, with references from the related literature, including Spitz's (1945) reporting that "The child . . . learns to distinguish animate objects from inanimate ones by the spectacle provided by his mother's face in situations fraught with emotional satisfaction" (p. 645). Spitz (1957) stated, "The inception of the functioning of the reality principle is evident at the three-months level, when the hungry infant becomes able to suspend the urge for the immediate gratification of his oral need. He does so for the time necessary to perceive the mother's face and to react to it. This is the developmental step in which the 'I' is differentiated from the 'non-I,' in which the infant becomes aware of the 'otherness' of the surround" (p. 645).

Freud's Views Concerning This Topic (Views Which Tended to Remove It from Our Attention)

Freud's (1913) oft-quoted, pioneering reference provides another useful point of departure:

> I hold to the plan of getting the patient to lie on a sofa while I sit behind him out of his sight. This arrangement . . . deserves to be maintained for many reasons.

The first is a personal motive, but one which others may share with me. I cannot put up with being stared at by other people for eight hours a day (or more). Since, while I am listening to the patient, I, too, give myself over to the current of my unconscious thoughts, I do not wish my expressions of face to give the patient material for interpretations or to influence him in what he tells me. . . . I insist on this procedure, . . . for its purpose and result are to prevent the transference from mingling with the patient's associations imperceptibly, to isolate the transference and to allow it to come forward in due course sharply defined as a resistance (pp. 133–134).

Jones (1955), in his biography of Freud, commented upon this aspect of Freud's technique:

He mentioned the historical source of the custom as dating from the days of hypnotism and also the personal point that he did not like being stared at for many hours of the day at close quarters. These, however, are extrinsic factors. More important is the necessity for the analyst to be in a position to give free rein to his thoughts without the patient detecting them from the play on his features, which would impair the purity of the transference phenomena (p. 236).

Typical Countertransference Experiences with Regard to My Facial Expressions in Face-to-Face Work with a Borderline Patient

A borderline man in his twenties, with whom I worked for three years at a frequency of one or two sessions per week, was similar in a number of regards to several patients, of various degrees of illness, whom I have treated. It never became feasible for me to recommend that he use the couch, for even though he improved very appreciably over this period of time, he gave me reason to feel that his ego integration was sufficiently precarious that it was better for him to remain sitting. This aspect of the work was quite stressful for me because of the extent to which he was attuned to my facial expressions. He seemed close to hallucinating during the first year of the work, seemed often to return to looking at my face as a refuge from myriad semihallucinatory figures off to the sides, and at many moments, while he was looking at me, I distinctly had the sense that what he was seeing was neither my face nor that of any other human being, but something very distorted, indeed (although he never would or could confirm this surmise). I came to realize, in time, that it was useful for me to note at what point there occurred this now progressively infrequent phenomenon in which his looking at my face in a basically realistic, separate-individual, interpersonally related fashion dissolved, once again, into his face's looking, once again, immersed in staring at God-only-knew-what, although *appearing* still to be looking toward my face.

I felt typically, in nearly all of nearly every session, in considerable conflict, and it was impossible for me, in my work with this man, to mask my facial expressions. My conflicts undoubtedly were introjected to a high degree from him, and he essentially looked to me to tell him what was going on in his own unconscious. Moreover, he was sufficiently verbal about his nearly schizophrenic parental-family life of years ago to give me rich material for interpretations. Also, our time together was so limited, and the moments for possible interpretation were so fleeting, that I felt a precious opportunity would be lost if I held my tongue.

On the other hand, my better judgment told me that, with rare exceptions, any interpretations would be premature. I did make relatively many, nonetheless, and found occasion to share with him, also, a rather large number of relevant vignettes from my own past, but with chronic self-censure for so doing. He would frequently ask me, "What are you thinking?"—invariably at a juncture when some new realization about him had just occurred to me. I eventually came to feel that a major, if not the major, reason why he predominantly throve in the years of our work together was that I found the courage to share with him as much as I did, despite the chronic intimidation from my superego.

Along the way, I came to realize that the aspect of premature interpretation had to be balanced against the potentially tantalizing and hostile withholding aspect of my (from his view) clearly having just had a significant thought that I now refused to impart to him. The work was inevitably chronically tantalizing for both of us; but he eventually came to convince me that he found great value in my revealing to him, as freely as I did, the fact of my being in various emotional conflicts during the sessions, and the natures of those conflicts as best I could articulate them. I believe that one of the great values of our work, for him, was that he was thus enabled to identify consciously, much more deeply than he had become able to do in his parental family, with one who is able consciously to experience, and to articulate, emotional conflicts.

In my work with him, as in that with a number of other patients of varying degrees of illness, I found evidence of his unconsciously identifying, in his facial expressions, with my own as he perceived (largely *unconsciously*) mine to be. That is, on occasion he would endeavor to quote or paraphrase something I had said in an earlier session, and his facial expressions (and other aspects of his demeanor), in his effort to do this, gave me to understand that he was unconsciously quoting or paraphrasing, as it were, not merely my words but my facial expressions (and other nonverbal aspects of my demeanor) in my making of those comments. For example, he said one time, "Do you remember what you said in last week's session? You said—" and then he fell silent for a few moments, looking very detached, and then he para- phrased, for perhaps a minute or two, some of the comments I had made in the previous week's session, reproducing these reasonably accurately, as I remember them; but the im- mensely interesting thing was the *way* in which he said them. After he had been silent for a few moments, near the beginning of this, I asked if that pause were part of what I had said, and he disclaimed that it was. Parenthetically, I have found patients typically highly resistive to seeing the unconscious identificational aspect of such behavior on their part.

He went on, paraphrasing what I had said, and mean- while floundering, speaking hesitantly, starting a line of thought and not finishing it, looking diffident and, far more than that, showing clear evidence of a marked thought dis- order. I found it privately hilarious and enormously reveal- ing of his unconscious perceptions of me, including my facial expressions. He immediately rejected my attempts, twice later in this few minutes of interaction, to suggest that this was the way I had looked and sounded to him while I had been saying the things he was quoting or paraphrasing. It was clear that he was attributing all his floundering for thoughts and words, all his vacant and lost-looking facial expressions, and so forth, simply to his own difficulty in remembering what I had said and in expressing it in a way that would do justice to what I had said. It is, of course, routine for patients to use such grounds to explain their difficulties in quoting something the analyst has said. As in the instances of other patients, his unconscious perception of me as the personification of person(s) from his past who had appreciable difficulties in ego integration, person(s) who were contributory sources of his own sickest introjects, was defended against by a tenacious overidealization of my men- tal functioning.

In my supervision, going on four years now, of a colleague's work with a severely borderline man, the therapist described that "He has said that he knows what he's feeling by the expression on my face; he's said that many, many times over the years. He said once that he knew he was angry because I had screamed at him." In this therapy it has been very striking to me, as well as to the therapist, how frequently the patient has become able to gain access to his own (dissociated and projected) emotions, first, *via* the expressions that he sees on the therapist's face.*

The Maturational Significance of the Deeply Ill Patient's Becoming Able to Focus His Attention upon the Analyst's Facial Expressions

In my experience, it represents deeply significant progress, in the development of improved ego integration and differentiation, for the patient to become able to focus his attention upon the analyst's facial expressions; but this development may be greatly slowed, or may never occur, if the analyst remains largely oblivious of the central importance of this dimension of the work.

I learned something about these matters during my one-and-a-half years of twice-a-week therapy with a 30-year-old man whose mother had become chronically psychotic during his early childhood. This man showed a borderline ego functioning, with features of psychotic depression. It was clear that he had narrowly avoided frank psychosis in recent years, and the issue remained in doubt for some time after our work began. He was an extremely intense, demanding individual, and the sessions were very stressful for me. At no time did he use the couch, nor did I recommend it. One of the helpful developments, for me, was when I came to realize, after more than six months, that part of the stressfulness of the sessions derived from his focusing upon my

*I am grateful to Patricia Fox, ACSW, for permission to include this material.

facial expressions as he talked (he did by far the greater part of the talking), while unvaryingly looking dissatisfied, giving me to feel that, whatever my changing expressions were (and I am sure they included a wide variety of positive as well as negative ones of various sorts), they were not satisfactory—they were not the ones he was needing. He made very important gains during our relatively brief work together and, although I did not realize it at the time, the fact that he had come to focus perceptibly much upon my facial expressions was one of the gains he had made; I simply assumed that I had not recognized, much earlier, the supposed fact of his doing this all along.

Despite his moving safely far from potential psychosis and getting considerably far into the realm of his oedipal conflicts, his predominant dissatisfaction with me, and my negative reactions to him, eventually prevailed, however. Approximately 16 months along in the work, I came to feel free to look at him with cold dislike, and this felt very liberating to me. This touches upon the matter of the degree to which any analyst in his work with any patient, at whatever stage of the work, may feel it necessary to mask his spontaneous facial expressions; surely it may bespeak much improved ego strength on the patient's part if the analyst need no longer endeavor at all to wear a neutral or benign mask on his face, so to speak, irrespective of what he is actually feeling.

Surely I had glanced, many times before, at various patients with an undisguised look of cold dislike on my face. But never before had I knowingly allowed such an expression to emerge as expressive of my basic attitude toward a patient with whom I consciously intended, despite the stress, to go on working. It really felt good to me; I felt that perhaps I could afford to be more myself, in my work with patients generally, than I had previously dared to think. Unfortunately (but surely not coincidentally), it was not many weeks later that the patient, saying he had been aware for a long time that I did not like him, told me that he had decided to go to another therapist.

The Question of Whether the Patient Feels Able to Influence the Analyst's Facial Expressions

I have learned in recent years that once it has become evident to both patient and analyst that the latter's facial expressions are of significant interest to the former, it then becomes of further significance to ascertain to what, if any, degree the patient feels able to influence the emotions that he sees on the analyst's face. The more well he becomes, the more readily he assumes, and knows, that what he says and does is intimately related to the responsive expressions on the analyst's face.

In the instance of the man I have just described, I did not sense that, in his focusing upon my face throughout session after session, with an intensely dissatisfied look on his own face, he was feeling any connection between what he was saying and doing, on the one hand, and the various facial expressions that he perceived on my face, on the other hand. That is, I did not have any sense that he was feeling any sense of self-dissatisfaction because of any felt failure on his part to bring to my face the expression(s) for which he hungrily looked.

Another patient who showed something like the same degree of relatedness and unrelatedness with my facial expressions was a 42-year-old woman with whom I worked, at a frequency usually of once a week, for a little more than one year. This woman, readily recognizable at the outset as borderline in her ego functioning, used words in a quite machine-gun fashion during the hours. I felt, from the beginning, subjected to a highly aggressive verbal barrage, although the patient herself seemed genuinely to dissociate the realm of her transference aggression toward me. In my brevity here, I do not mean to imply that I did, meanwhile, nothing. But I recall that it was only after several months, at least, that I was struck by how exactly the patient behaved as though she were watching television (as, I am sure, in her reclusive daily life she did literally for many hours per week): she would watch my face, while subjecting me to an unending, rapid-fire stream of borderline-psychotic verbal productions, but the look on her own face indicated that she felt no more the personal cause of the changes in my facial expression than any ordinary television-viewer feels; her look was of one who is passively watching a fascinating spectacle.

After several months I vented upon her the pent-up anger, about this, of which I had been increasingly conscious for some weeks. She was dismayed by my reaction, but far from crushed or crippled by it, and the work went better for the remaining months until, because of circumstances largely external to our work, she was unable to continue with me.

Mrs. Douglas (a pseudonym) is a chronically schizophrenic woman with whom I have worked for many years; I have written elsewhere (Langs and Searles 1980, Searles 1972) of some aspects of her tape-recorded treatment. Here I wish to report that the improvement in her ego integration and differentiation has been considerably accelerated, during the past approximately one year, in a setting of her focusing upon my facial expressions, or lack thereof, during the sessions. It has been fascinating to me, and of enormously constructive value for her, for us to become increasingly aware of the extent to which her verbal expressions of delusional experience are heretofore unconscious attempts to cause various expressions to appear on my face. It had been several years ago, already after many years of her treatment by me, when her own face had become more and more alive with long-dissociated emotions of myriad sorts; but she remained for some years, still, so out of touch with the emotions that one could see on her face that interpretations regarding these were not useful to her.

Only a few samples of the relevant data during one recent month are related here. Parenthetically, it had been very striking, and both exasperating and amusing, to me to see, about two months earlier, how unable she still then was to feel that she herself was in any degree responsible for various negative emotions she saw to come over my face. During one particular session in which I was feeling maddened and deeply conflicted under a noninterpretable assault of predominantly sadistic, delusional outpourings from her, she looked at my face and said, with sympathetic-sounding concern, "What are they doing to you?" The "they" clearly referred to the omnipotent persecutors who, in her experience, victimized not only herself but also me and everyone else. The disavowal of her own sadism toward me could not have been more complete.

Prior to the month in question she had spoken many times, for several months, of feeling the stress of having to think of things to say to make conversation during the sessions, and of dread, often, to come to the session, for this reason. I, for my part, had long been aware that I used compulsive talking as a defense during the sessions with her, and had been endeavoring for months to help both of us to become free from the need to keep conversation going.

In the first session of the month, she was speaking from the delusional conviction, which she had had for several months, that we were on the moon, and that she needed and longed to be driven to her (highly idealized, delusional) home down on earth. An imaginary friend, Ed, was to do the driving; but he was drunk in a motel near the halfway house where she actually lives, and "he has our station wagon, too.

We can't do anything until he sobers up." Then she paused for several seconds (which was not unusual); during this time she gave me a very direct look of the sort that meant, as I had learned long ago, that what she had just said applied, directly, to me—either that I was to rectify the situation she had just outlined or (often) that I was to reassure her that I personally would not do to her various terrible things that (oftentimes) she had just described as having been done, over and over, to her by the malevolent and omnipotent "them."

I commented, here, "You're giving me, again, that direct look. What am I to do—sober him up?—I'm supposed to—" She interrupted me, explaining, "That's—uh—Sibyl," which I knew, for months now, to be an introject who, as she put it, is in her right eye and often does most of the talking during the session.

I commented, to confirm, "Who looks at me like that." She replied, "Yeah. She looks at you like that, waiting for you to make the conversation." I commented, thoughtfully, "Oh." She went on, "I asked her [that is, Sibyl] if she was ready this morning. She said, 'Yes; but I want *him* [referring to me] to do the work.'" I asked, "Well, is *Sibyl* giving *me* the kind of look that *I* usually give *you*? Huh?" And she agreed emphatically, "Yeah." I commented, "I give you these direct looks?" Again, she confirmed this, "Uh huh."

I found this very illuminating—although, of course, dismaying also. In my several months of attempting to help her (as well as me) to become more free from a need of conversation, I had been quite unaware that I was still giving her (or, for that matter, had ever given her) the enormously pressuring, direct, putting-on-the-spot kind of looks to which, she convincingly showed me with her own look, I was still subjecting her.

This is an example of a patient's facial expression being an identification with that of the therapist as the patient has been perceiving the therapist's face to look. Further, I do not doubt that in this instance (typically for such examples) such an expression was in reality there on my face; but I had been unconscious of it heretofore.

In a session four days later, at one point I privately gained some deeper understanding of a long-held delusion that she was elaborating in a somewhat new way, and she said, glancing at my face, "You act as though you'd completed some great job." I replied, "Just now?" She said, "Yeah." I commented, "You haven't seen me look that way, before?" She confirmed this, saying, "No. That's the look you wanta have?" I replied, "Well, you can believe it is the look I *wanta* have—right?" She replied, "Yes."

I went on, "That would bring in the possibility that I am *in control of* my looks—huh?" She replied, "Well, it's *hard* to be in control of your looks; but, I mean, it might be what you're trying to *develop*." I commented, "*You* find it *hard* to be in control of *your* looks, for example?" She replied, "Yes. I *used* to be able to *do* it; but I can't *do* it any more; it's terrible." I commented, sympathetically, "Huh." And she went on, "I haven't gotten my head yet. [For many years she had been experiencing her head, and other body parts, as not being her own.] I'm supposed to get it on Monday, then we're supposed to go down to earth—home." I commented, in my usual semi-inquiring tone, "Well, having your own head would presumably include being able to have the kind of look you wanted to have on your face?" She said, "Yeah."

A few minutes later in the session, when she was vocalizing a long-familiar delusion, but doing so in a fashion that enabled me to see a clearer meaning in it, she said, watching my face, "There! Now you're getting the expression again!" "The expression" clearly meant, in light of our earlier dialogue, my expression as though I had completed some great job. Significantly, she said this in a tone of her own having accomplished, to her satisfaction, a difficult task, and her own facial expression was much like what she described to have reappeared on my face. I laughed loudly and said, ironically, "You're of course not trying to make me feel self-conscious, are you?" She protested, "No, I'm not; I just wanted you to keep that expression."

In a session five days later, about 20 minutes along in the session, at a point when I was feeling and showing exasperation (as often happens), she asked, looking at my face, "*Why* do they make Dr. Searleses [note the plural of my name; throughout our work she had perceived me, and other persons significant to her, as having many "doubles"] get so *mad* all the time? Is that—" I interrupted, "*This* one [i. e., this Dr. Searles] seems to be starting to get mad, too?" She agreed, saying, "Just starting today, yeah. *Some* of them they make *mad* all the time. The poor things have the most terrible time, controlling themselves." I replied, "Yeah."

She went on, "I guess that's what they do it for." I replied, "They apparently do it *so* that the Dr. Searleses will have a terrible time c—[I was starting to say, "controlling themselves," but then a different possible meaning occurred to me] well, ya think they're *trying to teach* them to be able to *control* themselves?" She immediately confirmed this: "Yeah." I replied, "Oh," indicating that I now understood how she meant this, and I went on, "Kind of an exercise in self control?" She agreed, "Yeah." I went on, "And you are left to simply *watch* the *spectacle*, right?" She replied, "*Yes*, and they just get *agonized*, and they *turn* all sorts of *colors*." I inquired, "There is a kind of *interesting* aspect to seeing it, is there not?" She conceded, "Well, it's sort of fascinating."

I responded, "Hm. You've *obviously* never had even a *momentary* sense of *contributing* in any *small way* to their exasperation, right?" She confirmed this by saying, "No," and added, while I was now chuckling in amusement, "Except that when we don't *talk*, they seem to get mad." I commented, "That's one of the *big* reasons, I guess, why you have—uh—*worried* about what to—have to *say* to them, huh?" She replied, "Yeah." I pressed her further here, "Is that it? They get mad if ya don't—have things to talk about?" She agreed, but added, "Well, *they* don't seem to have many ideas, themselves. Well, they spend all their time *controlling* themselves—and *changing color*." I commented, "So that they don't have much—energy to—devote to thinking, or—" She agreed, emphatically: "To *thinking*, no. Use up all their time."

After a momentary pause, she commented in a different tone, confronting and teasing, "Well, *you control* your self very well, though; you got it all—subdued." I commented, "But two or three minutes ago, though, you were starting to *wonder*?" She replied, "Yeah; it looked as though they started on *you*." She said this with a facial expression of grimly sadistic satisfaction (not rare among her expressions), and I inquired, casually, "D'ya ever find yourself— uh—kind of—*hoping* they *will*, or—?" She immediately replied, "No." I pressed her, "Huh?" And she said, "Uh uh" [meaning "No"]. I said, "No? You wouldn't *wish* that on me, I guess?" And she agreed that she would not.

This interchange was, for me, a striking example of how unable she was, still, to accept any responsibility for causing my facial expressions to be so exasperated, angry, or agonized—all of which they indeed are. Further, I was sobered by this additional evidence of how greatly pressured she still felt, by me, to have things to say during the sessions. I felt that all these perceptions of me, their transference origins notwithstanding, had much of immediate reality in them.

The Usefulness of the Supervisor's Attentiveness to This Topic

I am currently supervising a colleague's once-a-week psychotherapy with a borderline young woman who, during the first several months, talked in a nonstop and rapid-fire fashion, seeming aware only very rarely of him and his feelings, although looking often at his face in a covert way as she spoke.* Meanwhile, he said very little, and she seemed not to want more from him the greater part of the time.

In a session some six months along, she said, "I don't feel close to myself at all—I don't like looking at myself in mirrors—I'll look at my body, but not my face—it's kinda creepy. . . ." Later in the same session, after describing another of her myriad borderline experiences of herself and the world, she said of that particular (recurrent) experience, "I think it scares the shit out of me. . . . Don't you think it's kinda weird?" He remained silent, as usually seemed to work best in that era. I suggested to him my impression, based upon my work with a similar patient, that her question signalled her puzzlement at not seeing on his face an expression that indicated that he shared her sense that the experience she had just described had been, indeed, weird.

I did not mean to imply that his face should have worn such an expression, but rather that the role of his face, and her interest in it, had come to be of greater significance in the therapy than she had been able consciously to give him to realize. I surmise, in fact, that it is in the realm of the therapist's facial expressions that such a patient can best find a bridge to an interpersonal relatedness with him, increasingly, as the work goes on—a bridge out of her autism, one might say. This patient manifested, in the first several months of the work, much of the self-absorbed dynamics of narcissism, as well as more typically borderline features. There is every indication, currently, that the psychotherapy is proceeding well, and I assume that her estrangement from her own face will become resolved through her coming to terms with her projection-laden perceptions of the thera-

---

*I am grateful to Lawrence Tirnauer, Ph.D., for permission to include this material.

pist's face. This brings up the question as to whom—therapist or patient—do the therapist's facial expressions "belong" in the work with such a patient.

To Whom—Analyst or Patient—Do the Analyst's Facial Expressions "Belong"?

In an earlier paper (Searles 1976) in which I was writing of psychoanalysis and psychoanalytic therapy with patients generally (rather than that with any one variety of patient), I ended the paper with the hypothesis that the patient's symptoms become, with the development of the early phase of therapeutic symbiosis, transitional objects for both patient and analyst simultaneously. As with the patient's symptoms, so with his transference images of the analyst: I believe that in order for any effective transference analysis to occur with any patient, whether neurotic, borderline, or psychotic, the analyst must have come to accept at *least* a transitional-object degree—if not more deeply symbiotic degree—of relatedness with the particular transference image, or percept, which is holding sway presently in the analysis.

Here I wish to suggest that, as it is with the patient's symptoms and his transference images of the therapist as described in that paper, so it is with the therapist's and the patient's facial expressions. That is, in the therapeutically symbiotic, core phase of the work with any one patient, each of the two participants' facial expressions "belong," in a sense, as much to the other as to oneself. In the work with a very ill patient, the therapist may find himself grimacing and having agonized (or other) facial expressions of a kind and degree that feel considerably foreign to him, and that are largely a response to dissociated feelings on the patient's part. It has been my impression, time and again, that only insofar as both participants can accept partial responsibility for such phenomena—can come to regard the therapist's and the patient's facial expressions as being, to apply Winnicott's (1953) concept here, transitional phenomena semi-"belonging" to each of the two participants—can the patient's previously largely dissociated emotionality become more truly his own, and the therapist's face come to feel, once again, more fully his (the therapist's) own, after its having served so deeply, for so long, as a plastic screen for the patient's projected emotions.

Rethinking, in this light, my experience with the man who quit treatment not long after I had become free (so I felt) to look at him with cold dislike, it may be that my "own" dislike of him was predominantly not my own, but was based largely upon my identification with contents that he was projecting into me. It is possible—although I do not find this easy to believe—that if I had treated the expression of dislike that I found on my face more as sharable analytic data, exploring for, in particular, warded-off feelings of dislike on his own part, from his childhood and other areas of his life, he might still be in treatment. It was as though I had prematurely reclaimed my face as being my own.

Chapter 4 is relevant here; patients, whether borderline or not, are described as going through a phase in the evolution of the transference whereby the analyst becomes a symbiotic identity partner for the patient. Kohut's (1971) paper concerning what he calls mirror transference is also relevant. So far as I know, Kohut never read any of my writings, including those published 12 years earlier concerning therapeutic symbiosis (Searles 1959), a topic closely related to some of his own views. Kohut writes,

> In this narrower sense of the term the mirror transference is the therapeutic reinstatement of that normal phase of the development of the grandiose self in which the gleam in the mother's eye, which mirrors the child's

exhibitionistic display, and other forms of maternal participation in and response to the child's narcissistic-exhibitionistic enjoyment confirm the child's self-esteem and, by a gradually increasing selectivity of these responses, begin to channel it into realistic directions. As was the mother during that stage of development, so is now the analyst an object which is important only insofar as it is invited to participate in the child's narcissistic pleasure and thus to confirm it (p. 116).

[He favors using, in a larger sense] the term mirror transference for the whole group of transference phenomena that are the expression of the therapeutic mobilization of the grandiose self (p. 123).

For prolonged periods while the analysand begins to mobilize old narcissistic needs and, often struggling against strong inner resistances, begins to deploy his exhibitionism and grandiosity in the treatment situation, the patient assigns to the analyst the role of being the echo and mirror of his reluctantly disclosed infantile narcissism. Apart from his tactful acceptance of the patient's exhibitionistic grandiosity, the analyst's contributions to the establishment and unfolding of the mirror transference are restricted to two cautiously employed sets of activities: he interprets the patient's resistances against the revelation of his grandiosity; and he demonstrates to the patient not only that his grandiosity and exhibitionism once played a phase-appropriate role but that they must now be allowed access to consciousness. For a long period of the analysis, however, it is almost always deleterious for the analyst to emphasize the irrationality of the patient's grandiose fantasies or to stress that it is realistically necessary that he curb his exhibitionistic demands (p. 271-272).

Kohut's comments are of much value, although I do not believe he was aware of the startling degree to which very ill patients had been called upon, remarkably early in their lives, to function as just such a mirroring mother to their own mothers (Searles 1966–1967, 1975). I wish merely to emphasize, however, that whereas Kohut does quite full justice to the patient's need for responses in the realm of empathic tact, gentleness and, in essence, kindly acceptance on the part of the analyst, he dwells in his books (Kohut 1971, 1977) scarcely at all upon the patient's equally great need for well-timed responses of a very aggressive sort, indeed, from the analyst.

The Need for the Analyst to be Attuned as Much to His Own Aggressive Feelings as to His Loving Ones

The analyst's attunement to his own aggressive feelings, and skillful utilizing of these in his responses to the patient, play a role hardly less than that of his lovingly maternal responses. Although it may feed the analyst's narcissism to experience himself as being a lovingly empathic mother nearly all the time, the emergence of the patient's adult feeling capacities, including his assertive and aggressive capacities, requires that the analyst have much readier access to his own "Bad Mother" kinds of responses than one would believe from reading Kohut.

For example, the chronically schizophrenic patient with whom I have worked most successfully (such that she has shown no more than a borderline degree of impairment of ego-functioning for years now) was an initially very fragile-appearing little woman who, mute and motionless for years early in my work with her, seemed to hover for many months on the brink of death. I have always felt, in retrospect, that a major (and possibly the major) turning point in our work consisted in our gradually reaching, against great resistances on the parts of both of us, a kind of relatedness in which we were savagely excoriating one another. I particularly remember one face-to-face session in which she was shouting indictments of me, her face suffused with self-righteous venom, and I was simultaneously shouting at her—with, I do not doubt, very much that same expression of venomous self-righteousness on my own face. That kind of mirroring, to my mind so essential for the necessary depth of both therapeutic symbiosis and subsequent individuation, Kohut does not describe. I look for it, too, as between my supervisees and their patients; thus I count it a most welcome development when a supervisee, who for years had taken refuge in the role of the healthy, adult therapist who is endeavoring (inevitably patronizingly) to extend help to the sick patient, evidently has come at long last to relate to the patient as being essentially his emotional equal and a fellow adult. I concur with Sager's (1957) simple statement, "It is our belief that in therapy [and, I would add, in analysis] one should work toward a relationship in which the patient accepts his equality as a mature human being with the therapist" (p. 306).

The man who sought analysis for transvestism used the couch consistently after the initial interview, and the just-described woman has done so most of the time for years now. With those exceptions, my clinical vignettes thus far in this chapter have been from the treatment of patients who have not used the couch. Those patients described in the remainder of this chapter used the couch.

Additional Clinical Examples from Work with Patients Who Use the Couch— Who See the Analyst's Face Only at the Beginning and End of the Session

Occasionally one sees a patient who frankly tells one at the beginning of the session that one is appearing so preoccupied, or fatigued or whatever, that the patient assumes that this session, which has scarcely begun, cannot possibly prove to be of any use. He is quite able to feel and express his dismay, exasperation, futility (and so forth) about this. When a patient is as readily able as this to let the analyst know that the analyst's facial expression at the beginning of the session is greatly significant to him, there is no problem upon which I need dwell in this particular chapter.

However, I have seen patients who are not able, for many months or even some years, to let me know that, all along, they had been appraising my facial expression, during the brief moments available to them as they walked into my office, in order to determine my mood, or my capacity or incapacity for deeply significant collaborative work during that session, or whatever. In most instances, I believe, this appraising on the patient's part was long as unconscious to him as it was unapparent to me. But I surmise that a great many hours with many patients are spent largely in vain because the patient, having glanced at the analyst's face upon walking into the office, has already written off this session as being an inherently futile one. I am aware that it is not easy for the analyst to interpret such nonverbal interaction, for one does not wish to increase the patient's inhibiting self-consciousness; but if the analyst is aware of this phenomenon and its frequency, he can find constructive ways of utilizing his awareness that it is occurring.

The previously described phenomenon of the patient's seeing his unconscious emotions in the analyst's face occurs frequently in one's work with patients who use the couch, during those moments when the patient glances at one's face upon his leaving.

For example, a 41-year-old borderline man devoted a whole session to seeking advice from me as to what to do about his younger brother's angry demands upon their father. He was speaking, throughout the session, in an apparently consciously unangry, undemanding, polite, respectful, considerate manner, expressive of his awareness that the giving of advice regarding his life outside the sessions was not one of my functions. But at the end of the session he said, as he got up from the couch, "You still haven't told me what I should do!" In saying this he sounded, and looked, very angry and dissatisfied—such that, for the nth time, I wasn't sure whether he would continue in the analysis. I doubted that he was well aware of how much anger there was in his saying this. I myself felt jolted, in a very unpleasant way, by the abrupt, blunt anger and dissatisfaction in his statement.

He did return on the following day, however, and about five minutes along in the session, while I remained silent as he spoke, once again, of the same daily-life situation that had been troubling him the previous day, he said, "What I said at the end of the session yesterday, when I got up from the couch, I meant as a joke; except when I said it, my voice didn't sound as joking as I thought it would—and your face didn't look as if you thought it was a joke . . . and you looked surprised. . . ." I told him, "I remember feeling something in the realm of jolted, and doubtful that you were aware of how angrily that came out." He strongly confirmed both aspects of my statement.

A 40-year-old woman, the mother of one child, showed a typical "as-if" type of borderline personality-functioning (Deutsch 1942) upon entering analysis with me. I worked with her for approximately six years, at a frequency of four hours per week throughout. She began using the couch after the first two interviews, and did so consistently thereafter. But for a number of years, I found that the work went best if I were very sparing with my interpretations; during those years, any interpretation I ventured was all too likely to be utilized by this very glib woman in the service of her resistance. (She used words primarily for unconscious defensive purposes, to keep her affects largely dissociated and to pro-

tect herself from any strongly felt emotional bond with me.)
Meanwhile, during those years, I found that her attunement
to my face proved to be a far more emotionally significant
avenue for the development and unfolding of the transference, than did the realm of words on the part of either of us.

During the first two years of the work, and possibly
somewhat longer, each time I would indicate that the end of
the session had come, she would get up from the couch and
then, before walking to the door, would turn and look at me
for a moment in a strange fashion that gave me to feel that
she was mentally photographing me. I did not experience
any interpersonal bond during this procedure (in keeping
with the large-scale absence of implicit acknowledgment
on her part, during the bulk of the session itself, of my
individual self). I felt much as though she were photographing a being from a planet alien to her own. I came to understand this as being part of her struggle to establish an
internalized image of me, an image that, by her thus photographing me each time at the end of the session, she could
maintain until our next session.

As our work together proceeded and became genuinely
work together, I found much evidence, from a variety of
sources, evidence of the kind reported in Chapter 4, that her
transference to me had developed in the form of my representing her symbiotic identity partner. That is, in terms of
her unconscious experience, I came to personify herself, and
she came to personify myself—or, in each instance, parts of
that self. It became evident, in retrospect, that at the beginning of treatment her own self had been as alien to, as
distant from, her as she had given me to feel during, for
example, her momentary "photographing" of me (as I am
calling it here).

As the symbiotic identity transference flowered in the
ensuing years, the full spectrum of her emotional life
emerged, bit by bit, from its long dissociation, and became,
gradually, richly differentiated. Her "photographing" of me

continued in the ritualized manner, but I found that it had come imperceptibly to have, now, a much more highly differentiated and emotionally significant meaning than it had possessed before. I now felt that she was a person "photographing" not merely another person, but "photographing" my particular facial expression (if any) at the end of a session that she had filled with, variously from one session to the next, material of a particularly repellent, or infuriating, or discouraging, or provocative, or nostalgic, or grief-laden (or what-not) variety.

In a detailed way, the nature of the looks we exchanged, as she turned to looked at me before she left, could sometimes be seen as having a highly significant role in episodes of acting out, both sexual and aggressive, on her part. For example, following our looking at one another in an unprecedentedly warm and friendly manner at the end of a session—but a manner with relatively little, from my point of view, of any erotic meaning—she went to a bar where she found herself exchanging lustful looks with various of the men there, and had an undisguisedly sexual dream (rare for her) that night.

Still later, now after years of our work together, I felt that when she turned toward me before leaving, she was not doing so in order to appraise my facial expressions, in however much detail; instead, now, I felt she was showing me her own face, filled with anguish, hurt, grief, and various other intense emotions. I no longer felt photographed, nor did I feel that she was presenting her face to be photographed. Meanwhile, during all the development traced briefly here, verbal interpretations had been playing an extremely small role in the analysis, and I had not seen fit to make any verbal interpretations concerning these developments.

A 45-year-old mother of two children, a person with a narcissistic personality disorder with manic-depressive features, began in analysis with me at a frequency of five sessions per week. Nearly three years later, I made the following note after one of my sessions with her:

> Although I feel chronically frustrated in my work with this woman, for the reason that she keeps the work in her own hands to such a very high degree and makes me feel chronically useless, nonfunctional, noncontributory, I almost invariably greet her in a friendly, firm way at the beginning of each session. And, far more important for the point here, at the end of the typical session in which I am given to feel that there is a great deal of turbulence going on in her with which I am unable to help her in any *verbalized* way (especially typical of my work with her is my being *silent*, session after session, month after month), I nonetheless say, as she looks carefully and searchingly (though briefly) at me before she opens the door to leave, "See you tomorrow," or "See you on Wednesday" [for example], in a firm, friendly, *confirming*, confident tone—in a tone that I feel conveys basically the confirming assurance that this has been a good session and that I know our work to be going well.
>
> Typically, when she comes in at the beginning of the session, she appears preoccupied, scarcely looks at me—often doesn't, and when she does, does not seem really to see me—and there is nothing like the degree of solid relatedness I feel in our exhange of looks at the end of each session.
>
> Now, I came to realize last evening, some time after her session, that there is a significant question involved in all this: to what extent is my look to her [and my accompanying comment to her] at the end of the hour (a) contributing to a chronic *undoing* of the development and emergence of negative transference and countertransference (as I have believed, all along, that it does, to an appreciable extent) and (b) [a thought new

to me in my work with her] to what extent is it contributing to a *holding environment* that is still necessary in
the treatment of this woman whose transference reactions to me are seldom identifiable and, when they are,
are typically of a preindividuation variety?

One other point about the way the typical session
goes: after our significant exchange of glances at the
end of the sessions and I've said, "I'll see tomorrow" [for
example], she says, "Yes." Another bit of description: in
our mutual exchange of looks, she begins by looking,
not uncommonly, very grim, and I often sense a great
deal of underlying rage in her, as well as, very frequently, bleak despair. But my way of looking (and
speaking) seems to dispel, partially and momentarily,
those negative feelings.

I must explain, regarding the above note, that I had
come, long before, to feel that our exchange of looks at the
end of the sessions was the most significant thing happening
between us. By contrast to her emotionally walled-off behavior throughout each session until that point in her departure, her face was then filled with feelings of a variety of
sorts on different occasions, feelings ranging from violent
anger to loneliness, to despair, to fond comradeship, to
small-child dependency, and so on. My steadily consistent
response, seemingly largely irrespective of her particular
emotional demeanor, was not something predominantly
planned or contrived by me, but rather something I found
myself doing each time.

Two months later I made this note about something
that had occurred a week previously:

The session had been spent, as nearly always, with
her narcissistic defenses very much in evidence, and I
found the session as dull and uninspiring, and myself as
useless and irrelevant, as usual.

At the end of the session, we looked at each other as usual—she, as she was starting out into the waiting room, and I, as I was starting into my storeroom [where I go, to have a cup of coffee or to work a bit in my files, after nearly every session with each of my patients]. She looked at me in such a way as to persist momentarily until she had succeeded in bringing what she evidently saw to be a twinkle in my eye. I felt, in fact, that in response to pressure from her—pressure conveyed in the way that she looked at me—I did look at her with a reassuring, fond twinkle in my eye. My feeling, when this happened, was that I was confirming thus, from her point of view, the validity of her highly favorable estimation of herself—or, from my point of view, the validity of her narcissistic character-armor.

In the ensuing moments, I did not feel infuriated that this had happened. Possibly I felt somewhat chagrined, or exasperated, or defeated—but relatively little so, if at all. Mostly, I felt this to be an interesting phenomenon, and I think this is a very helpful analytic attitude for me to have reached toward my own, as well as her, facial expressions.

It is probably no coincidence that, only two or at most three sessions later, she gave me a very important glimpse of the remarkably traumatic aspects of her childhood, as regards serious problems of drug addiction among several siblings both older and younger than herself, and perhaps on the parts of each of her parents as well—a kind of material that gave me to feel a genuine sympathy and respect for her.

My response to the way she was looking at me, with a twinkle in my eye, supplying her with the facial expression which, as I was coming now to accept, she genuinely needed from me, is one bit of the kind of analytical material from my work with various patients that had led me to suggest that, during the phase of therapeutic symbiosis, each participant's facial expressions "belong" as much to the other as to oneself and are, thus, in the realm of transitional phenomena for both of them.

A session that had occurred two months prior to the first of my notes quoted above had helped me to develop a deepening realization of her need for me to function, in Winnicott's (1941, 1950–1955) phrase, as a "good-enough holding environment," and of the therapeutic validity of the nonverbal interaction between us:

> For the previous two sessions she had arrived late— once, by some 15 minutes—and had been making plain that she was very busy with other matters, and had been behaving in additional ways disregardfully, depreciatorily, toward me and the analysis. When she left a message, then, that she would be late once again, I felt considerable rage develop in me toward her, and I thought that, if she proved to arrive very late and to be behaving in a busily self-important way as often before, I would begin the session by telling her that if it is getting so that she is having great difficulty in fitting the analysis into her busy schedule, it is fine with me if she quits.
>
> She actually arrived only about six mintues late, and her manner was sufficiently far from her so-frequent officiousness that I said nothing, other than my usual greeting, upon her arrival.
>
> Another important background item: I have continued, practically since the beginning, to say almost nothing to her during the sessions—only greeting her at the beginning and calling time at the end.
>
> I sensed during this session that her so-typical reaction when I did offer a couple of brief comments— largely finding these, as usual, not to "click"—is that *any* words from me are too *limited*, too *limiting*, to

allow for the uprush of grief (and, no doubt, rage—but, especially today, grief) for which she still needs me to function as a holding environment. This was a new experience to me; I've never seen it as clearly with any previous patient.

During this session she went on to express both deeply felt gratitude to me for being here, so reliably, over the course of our work and equally intensely felt grief concerning a number of losses in her very early childhood, including the loss of a younger sister with whom she had formed a predominantly lovingly symbiotic bond, a bond like that which clearly had developed, beneath her wall of words, in her transference to me. It was becoming evident that her symbiotic bond with her younger sister had been patterned upon their mother's symbiotic relationship with the patient herself, and that the latter, while still a very young child, had largely lost, already, that relationship with her mother. I felt near to tears—an infrequent experience for me in my work with any of my patients—during a considerable part of the session.

Until such time as the phase of ambivalent symbiosis has given way to the predominantly positive phase of pre-ambivalent symbiosis, the patient's gazing as a symbiotic identity partner at the analyst's countenance can be severely stressful for the analyst, which is one of the major reasons why we analysts tend to disregard the significance of this realm of our work. For a forceful example of this point I turn far from the work with patients who use the couch, to my experience many years ago with a chronically schizophrenic woman, of whom I wrote in my monograph on the nonhuman environment (Searles 1960):

This woman, for many months after my beginning psychotherapy with her, often glanced at me with an expression on her face of mingled fear, shock, and awe, as if I were a weird monster at which she scarcely dared to gaze for an instant. My discomfort at being so regarded amounted, at times, to a formidable level of anxiety. This anxiety was heightened by the circumstance that I felt toward her, much of the time during that period of the therapy, an intensity of hatred and loathing which, my superego repeatedly admonished me, no human being should feel toward another person—and which a physician, in particular, should never experience toward his patient. I shall not go into the reasons for my feeling so negatively toward her at that time. My point here is that my conception of myself as a human being was under assault from two directions: the patient was reacting to me as being a kind of monster, and my superego was condemning me as being monstrous, inhuman, in terms of the way I was feeling toward this woman. The fact that her own appearance and behavior, throughout this time, were extraordinarily freakish, in the opinions of personnel members generally (indicating that her reacting to me in this fashion, as being a weird monster, involved much projection on her part), was only partially reassuring to me, and her becoming able to confide in me, "I know I look weird sometimes, but I'm all right," was a later development, when this difficult though necessary period, of her projecting upon me these weird self-conceptions, was drawing to a close (pp. 365–366).

Review of Relevant Literature

Greenacre (1966), in a paper concerning problems of over-idealization of the analyst and of analysis, notes that, "Under most conditions, the mother is the infant's constant

companion and very much the center of his universe.
. . . There is a play of emotional responses—observable in
her facial expressions . . ." (p. 747). In an earlier paper
(Greenacre 1958), she had described that

> The body areas which are . . . most significant in com-
> paring and contrasting and establishing individual rec-
> ognition of the body self, and that of others, are the *face*
> and the *genitals.* . . . It would appear that even at a
> mature age the individual is in need of at least one other
> person, similar to himself, to look at and speak to, in
> order to feel safe in his own identity, i.e., that there is a
> continual reinforcement of the sense of the own self by
> the "taking in" of a similar person without which an
> isolated individual feels first an intensification and
> then a diminution of the sense of self and identity
> (p. 614).

Lichtenstein (1961) conceives of the "imprinting" of an
identity upon the child by the mother in normal early development.

Elkisch (1957) describes three patients who "tried to
retrieve, as it were, in their mirrored images what they felt
they had lost or might lose: their ego, their self, their boundaries" (p. 236).

Youngerman (1979) describes an adolescent boy who
had been mute for over a decade who "was hospitalized and
initially treated with a non-verbal therapy within the context of a psychoanalytic developmental theory. . . . His non-
verbal expressions and gestures were mirrored and expanded into pantomime and absurd theatre" (p. 286).

Khan (1982) writes of his work with a borderline young
woman: "I waited, with my face in my hands, as is my style,
when listening facing a patient. First, I don't like watching
a patient with a pretend-blankness of neutrality, nor being

stared at myself. Second, I can peep through the chinks of my fingers when I *need* to *look* at the patient" (p. 466).

Winnicott (1959) reports that

> It is amazing how even small children learn to gauge the parents' mood. They do this when each day starts, and sometimes they learn to keep an eye on the mother's or the father's face almost all the time. . . . As an example I give a boy of four years, a very sensitive boy, much like his father in temperament. He was in my consulting-room, playing on the floor with a train, while the mother and I talked about him. He suddenly said, without looking up: "Dr. Winnicott, are you tired?" I asked him what made him think so, and he said, "Your face"; so he had evidently taken a good look at my face when he came into the room. Actually, I was very tired, but I had hoped to have hidden it (pp. 75–76 in this 1965b volume).

Winnicott's writings (e.g., 1956, 1960, 1965a, 1965b) concerning the relationship between mother and infant (or young child) were the richest source of relevant material as a background for this chapter.

Conclusions

The analyst's facial expressions are a highly, and often centrally, significant dimension of psychoanalysis and psychoanalytic therapy, but one that has been largely neglected, nonetheless, in the literature. While acknowledging implicitly the obvious importance of transference-distortions in the patient's perceptions of the analyst's countenance, I have focused here upon the real changes in the latter's facial expressions.

The analyst's face has a central role in the phase of therapeutic symbiosis, as well as in later individuation. It is significant to what, if any, degree the patient has come to feel able to affect the emotions that he sees on the analyst's face. It is in the realm of the analyst's facial expressions that the borderline patient can best find a bridge out of autism and into therapeutically symbiotic relatedness with the analyst. During this latter phase, then, each participant's facial expressions "belong" as much to the other as to oneself; that is, the expressions of each person are in the realm of transitional phenomena for both of them.

The analyst's empathic attunement to his own aggressive feelings and skillful utilizing of these in his responses to the patient play a role hardly less than that of his empathic utilization of his lovingly maternal emotions.

References

Deutsch, H. (1942). Some forms of emotional disturbance and their relationship to schizophrenia. *Psychoanalytic Quarterly* 11:301–321.

Elkisch, P. (1957). The psychological significance of the mirror. *Journal of the American Psychoanalytic Association* 5:235–244.

Freud, S. (1913). On beginning the treatment. *Standard Edition* 12:121–144. London: Hogarth Press, 1958.

Greenacre, P. (1958). Early physical determinants in the development of the sense of identity. *Journal of the American Psychoanalytic Association* 6:612–627.

——— (1966). Problems of overidealization of the analyst and of analysis: their manifestations in the transference and countertransference relationship. In *Emotional Growth—Psychoanalytic Studies of the Gifted and a Great Variety of Other Individuals—Vol. II*, pp. 743–761. New York: International Universities Press, 1971.

Jones, E. (1955). *The Life and Work of Sigmund Freud—Volume 2.* New York: Basic Books.

Khan, M. M. R. (1982-1983). Speech, the psychoanalytic method and madness—a "case history." *International Journal of Psychoanalytic Psychotherapy* 9:447-474.

Kohut, H. (1971). *The Analysis of the Self—A Systematic Approach to the Psychoanalytic Treatment of Narcissistic Personality Disorders.* New York: International Universities Press.

—— (1977). *The Restoration of the Self.* New York: International Universities Press.

Langs, R., and Searles, H. F. (1980). *Intrapsychic and Interpersonal Dimensions of Treatment—A Clinical Dialogue.* New York: Jason Aronson.

Lichtenstein, H. (1961). Identity and sexuality. *Journal of the American Psychoanalytic Association* 9:179-260. Reprinted in Lichtenstein's *The Dilemma of Human Identity*, pp. 49-122. New York: Jason Aronson.

Sager, C. J. (1957). The psychotherapist's continuous evaluation of his work. *Psychoanalytic Review* 44:306-320.

Searles, H. F. (1959). Integration and differentiation in schizophrenia. *Journal of Nervous and Mental Disorders* 19:542-550. Reprinted in Searles (1965), pp. 304-316.

—— (1960). *The Nonhuman Environment in Normal Development and in Schizophrenia.* New York: International Universities Press.

—— (1961). Phases of patient-therapist interaction in the psychotherapy of chronic schizophrenia. In Searles (1965), pp. 531-559.

—— (1963). The place of neutral therapist-responses in psychotherapy with the schizophrenic patient. *International Journal of Psycho-Analysis* 44:42-56. Reprinted in Searles (1965), pp. 636-653.

—— (1965). *Collected Papers on Schizophrenia and Related Subjects.* London: The Hogarth Press. New York: International Universities Press.

—— (1966-1967). Concerning the development of an identity. *Psychoanalytic Review* 53:507-530. Reprinted in Searles (1979), pp. 45-70.

—— (1972). The function of the patient's realistic perceptions of the analyst in delusional transference. In Searles (1979), pp. 196–227.

—— (1975). The patient as therapist to his analyst. In *Tactics and Techniques in Psychoanalytic Psychotherapy, Volume II: Countertransference*, ed. P. L. Giovacchini, pp. 95–151. New York: Jason Aronson. Reprinted in Searles (1979), pp. 380–459.

—— (1976). Transitional phenomena and therapeutic symbiosis. *International Journal of Psychoanalytic Psychotherapy* 5: 145–204. Reprinted in Searles (1979), pp. 503–576.

—— (1977). Dual—and multiple—identity processes in borderline ego functioning. In *Borderline Personality Disorders: The Concept, the Patient, the Syndrome*, ed. P. Hartocollis, pp. 441–455. New York: International Universities Press. Reprinted in Searles (1979), pp. 460–478. Reprinted as Chapter 4 in this volume.

—— (1979). *Countertransference and Related Subjects—Selected Papers*. New York: International Universities Press.

Spitz, R. A. (1945). Hospitalism—an enquiry into the genesis of psychiatric conditions in early childhood. *Psychoanalytic Study of the Child* 1:53–74.

—— (1957). *No and Yes: On the Genesis of Human Communication*. New York: International Universities Press.

Winnicott, D. W. (1941). The observation of infants in a set situation. *International Journal of Psycho-Analysis* 22. Reprinted in Winnicott (1958), pp. 52–69.

—— (1950–1955). Aggression in relation to emotional development. In Winnicott (1958), pp. 204–218.

—— (1953). Transitional objects and transitional phenomena—a study of the first *not-me* possession. *International Journal of Psycho-Analysis* 34:89–97. Reprinted in Winnicott (1958), pp. 229–242.

—— (1958). *Through Paediatrics to Psycho-Analysis*. New York: Basic Books.

—— (1959). The effect of psychotic parents on the emotional development of the child. Lecture to the British Association of Psychiatric Social Workers, November 1959. Published in *British Journal of Psychiatric Social Work* Vol. 6, No. 1, 1961.

—— (1960). The theory of parent-infant relationship. *International Journal of Psycho-Analysis* 41:585–595.

—— (1965a). *Maturational Processes and the Facilitating Environment*. New York: International Universities Press.

—— (1965b). *The Family and Individual Development*. London: Tavistock Publications.

Youngerman, J. K. (1979). The syntax of silence: electively mute therapy. *International Review of Psycho-Analysis* 6:285–295.

Index